PASTORAL WORK

Pastoral Work

Engagements with the Vision
of Eugene Peterson

Jason Byassee *and*
L. Roger Owens

CASCADE *Books* · Eugene, Oregon

Cascade Books
An Imprint of Wipf and Stock Publishers
199 W. 8th Ave., Suite 3
Eugene, OR 97401

www.wipfandstock.com

ISBN 13: 978-1-62564-022-2

Cataloging-in-Publication data:

Pastoral work : engagements with the vision of Eugene Peterson / edited by Jason Byassee and L. Roger Owens.

xvi + 206 p.; 23 cm—Includes bibliographical references.

ISBN 13: 978-1-62564-022-2

1. Peterson, Eugene H., 1932–. 2. Pastoral theology. 3. Clergy—Office. I. Byassee, Jason. II. Owens, L. Roger. III. Title.

BV4011 P347 2014

Manufactured in the USA.

Table of Contents

PART THREE: PEOPLE

PART FOUR: LIFE

Introduction

AMID MASSIVE CONFUSION ABOUT the vocation of pastoral ministry in the last fifty years, Eugene Peterson has offered a clear and compelling vision of the life and work of a pastor. Perhaps more than any single author, his vision has shaped the understanding of the pastoral vocation across denominational and theological lines. It's easy to find Peterson's own books and others expressing appreciation for his clear vision. It's easy to find testimonials about how his vision of the pastor as a spiritual guide has saved pastors heading toward burnout. And it's easy to find people who invoke Peterson in their arguments with other visions of the pastoral vocation, especially those visions influenced by business leadership. But this book offers what's nearly impossible to find—appreciative, critical, and constructive engagements with Peterson's own vision of the pastoral vocation.

First, these essays are *appreciative* engagements with Peterson's vision of the pastoral vocation. Each of the authors has been shaped in positive ways by Peterson's vision of the pastoral life. For some of the authors, Peterson's vision has been a determining influence in how we imagine our work. A reader of this book, if interested in learning about what Eugene Peterson says about pastoral vocation, will find here appreciative discussions of his vision.

But they don't stop there. When it comes to Peterson, hagiography is not hard to find. But each of these essays resists hagiography, knowing that there are conflicting accounts of what constitutes good pastoral ministry. So these essays engage Peterson *critically* as well, asking what, if any, are the gaps in his work. Where is his vision too narrow? Where is it insufficient to account for the growing complexities of ministry in a new century? These essays show that Peterson is most useful not when his vision is blindly adhered to, but when it's engaged, questioned, and wrestled with.

Finally, these essays are *constructive*. Each pastor must live this vocation for him or herself. As powerful and influential as Peterson's vision is, each pastor must, in some sense, struggle with God, Scripture, the community of faith and wise teachers like Peterson to—paraphrasing Paul—"work out their own pastoral identity with fear and trembling." So, these essays also offer constructive engagements with Peterson's vision, giving each of these respected authors—wise teachers themselves—the opportunity to show how engaging Peterson has helped them to work out their own understanding of the pastoral vocation in their various contexts.

This book is needed for three reasons.

First, this kind of sustained engagement with Peterson hasn't happened yet. It is long overdue. With the recent publication of Peterson's memoir, *The Pastor*, the time is right for this kind of engagement with his vision to happen. If Peterson's vision is going to remain helpful to generations to come, it needs to be engaged, critiqued, and built upon now. That's what this book does.

Second, this book is significant because of its contributors. The essays in this book are written by some of the most important voices writing about and practicing pastoral ministry today. A diverse group of authors in denomination, race, theology, and gender, this book hopes to generate the most wide-ranging and diverse engagement with Peterson possible.

Finally, this book is significant not just because it's about one of the most important writers on pastoral ministry in the last generation, but because it is about the pastoral vocation itself. The pastoral vocation is still in crisis, and the conversation about what constitutes faithful pastoral ministry is ongoing. This book hopes to be a significant addition to that conversation because it is an engagement with one of the most important voices in the conversation by several other significant voices in the conversation.

The book is divided into four parts—"Words," "Institutions," "People," and "Life." In his *Working the Angles*, Peterson compares the shape of pastoral ministry to a triangle, suggesting the work of ministry has three lines—preaching, teaching, administration—and three angles—prayer, Scripture, and spiritual direction. Our structure takes this as a starting point, but broadens it into these four sections.

Words

"Words" includes those aspects of ministry that deal with words and the Word, including preaching and teaching, but also praying, storytelling, and reading. For Peterson, attentiveness to words and the Word is at the heart of his vision of the pastoral vocation, because such attentiveness trains us to attend to God. The essays in this section engage Peterson's vision of the pastoral vocation from the angle of the pastor as one working with words and the Word.

Stephanie Paulsell's essay shows, right out of the gate, that this collection means to be more than hagiography. She praises him fully, especially for his influential portrayal of the role of the imagination in interpreting the Scriptures. She appreciates Peterson's confession of how often he does not know what he is doing as a pastor. Yet she has some hard questions for him. Are not the characters in his memoir stock characters? And worse, how can he justify, in 2011, his portrayal of an incident of sexual abuse of a minor in a church in which he was an associate? At the time his bewilderment is understandable and he does the right thing. But why does he not now question the obviously dated advice that professional gives to the abused child? One can hear the wisdom born of Paulsell's years of teaching ministers at Harvard Divinity as well as a holy impatience with any kind of equivocation on this issue.

Mark Ralls's essay could serve as an introduction to the way of reading the Bible either in Peterson or in his great mentor Karl Barth. He engages mostly with *Eat This Book*, one of Peterson's hefty collections of essays from across the years, this one focused on the practices of reading Scripture. And he suggests Peterson is a worthy heir, a sufficiently attentive reader to Barth, to be an attentive reader of the living message of Scripture. This is interesting—most of Barth's self-styled heirs either become systematic theologians in the academy or argue over Barth minutiae. Peterson read Barth over and over as a parish pastor and presented his way of reading, with God's action having priority over ours, throughout his preaching and writing career. This way of reading is not "personally immense," it is "immensely personal." It is enough to make one envious of Ralls's parishioners in Winston-Salem, North Carolina, to hear sermons styled after Peterson's Barthian way of reading.

Tony Robinson reflects on his own book, *Transforming Congregational Culture*, ten years after its publication. And he notes the ironic reception of the book by mainline leaders as just the next hot program to fix membership decline (leaders in the Emerging Church movement also found they were being turned into a fix-it program, with "Emerging Pastors" and "Services" sprouting up. We mainliners are nothing if not determined to stick to technical solutions . . .). Robinson credits Peterson with helping him see the issue is God, not our programming. Then he tweaks Peterson for having nothing good to say about "leadership," before using Ron Heifetz to show the term's potential for thinking more theologically about the church. Robinson's essay is particularly confessional in its description of his failed initial effort to turn around a dying congregation. His goal was to right the ship by his own energy and effort, not to wait for the Lord. Ignatian retreats and praying Scripture taught him that the leader's first move is second. We wait first, God works, then we respond.

Institutions

The section on "Institutions" includes the work of administration, but we broaden that to understand more broadly ministry as leadership of an institution—the church. The very choice of the word "Institution" suggests it's in this area we think Peterson's vision can be critiqued. One emerges from reading Peterson with a deep appreciation of community. But community without institutional backbone can collapse to the floor in a puddle, running the risk of being romanticized or fetishized. The essays in this section engage Peterson's vision of pastor as leader (broadly conceived) and his criticism of certain understandings of institutional leadership that have also influenced conceptions of pastoral leadership.

Tee Gatewood's essay praises Peterson's push to have ministry be done locally, attentively, and with love for the particular. He suggests reading the trilogy of *Five Smooth Stones*, *Working the Angles*, and *Under the Unpredictable Plant* backwards from the order of their publication. We don't know why it works. We do know that it does—starting forward we got stuck as readers; going Gatewood's backward way, the books almost read themselves. Then Gatewood pivots and launches the sort of attack his intellectual model, theologian Robert Jenson, might have launched. Why, with all the anti-gnostic rhetoric, does Peterson disdain the institutional structure of the Presbyterian Church in which he and Gatewood have both made ordination vows and of the wider ecclesia, the church catholic, often manifest in other denominations now? As with all of the critiques in this book, Peterson or his defenders might have material with which to respond.

That said, the critique is fair and deserves a hearing. One can also hear Gatewood's own struggles as a relative traditionalist in the PC-USA, many of whose peers have fled that denomination seeking "safer" waters in one of several shards of Reformed breakoffs in the USA. Gatewood has stayed, influenced by Peterson, and wants Peterson to make a similarly declarative, uncomfortable public commitment to a flawed and particular people like the Presbyterians.

Will Willimon's essay both praises and criticizes Peterson perhaps more highly than any other essay. Like all our writers, he deeply appreciates Peterson's critique of an Americanized church. That critique, of course, echoes those also long launched by Willimon and his companion in arms, Stanley Hauerwas, both of whose work has influenced Peterson. Yet Willimon worries that Peterson's shrill criticism of the specific institutions of the church, from his own Pentecostal background to his Presbyterian Church of ordination and long service, cause him to wind back up unwittingly in Americanized, interiorized, individualized Christianity despite himself. Perhaps it is the church, institutionalized and compromised though she may be, that is the only way God has of saving us from our Americanized selves.

Kristen Deede Johnson attends to the work of her mentor, James Davison Hunter. Hunter is tired of hackneyed and sentimental claims that individuals can change the world. The view overlooks the role of institutions, networks, and even elites. She argues that Hunter needs a bit of Peterson for his model to work, especially since the church plays a significant role in Hunter's prescription for influencing culture. And she suggests Peterson requires a bit of Hunter as well. When his attention is not on institutions he can speak of them lovingly; when he turns to them the language can be brutal. Perhaps institutions can be influenced by Peterson's vision—and who among us, whose lives depend so deeply on institutions, would not want that?

Jason Byassee's essay attends to the hyphen in Peterson. Eugene Peterson is the model of a scholar-pastor. How would our institutions that pass on theological wisdom look if remodeled on the gifts of a saint like Eugene? He may be the most important theological voice alive just now. But neither the church nor the academy tend to see Peterson as such—they are so little aware of one another's life. Yet they depend on one another. Peterson continues a long tradition of genuinely great theologians without a terminal degree; of genuinely great pastoral writers ignored by the academy as currently organized. Couldn't we reacquaint these two with one another, perhaps via Eugene's work?

People

The section "People" focuses on the centrality of relationships for Peterson's vision of the pastoral vocation. Peterson has said that he would never pastor a church with more members than names he can remember. The promise shows how important knowing one's flock is to his vision of pastoral ministry. He has also critiqued the way that psycho-therapeutic understandings of pastoral care have usurped the pastor's traditional role as a spiritual director within the community. The essays in this section will engage Peterson's vision of the pastoral vocation from the perspective of the pastor's working with people.

Carol Howard Merritt's essay engages questions of human culture in a variety of settings, from Uganda to Peterson's *Message*. She asks Peterson about his rhetorical denunciation of reading the Bible in ways that are affected by human culture. Is this not what he has done, and so brilliantly, with his own translation of the Bible? We are never free from "culture" as we do anything, not least interpret Scripture. How do we make that intersection between cultures life-giving?

Kyle Childress's essay gives a lovely portrait of Wilson, an old-timer at his first rural Baptist parish in Texas. The young preacher Childress, stirring up matters of race that the community would have preferred unstirred, was given the gift of friendship by this patient man. Wilson taught him to visit, to get to know, to steep in the life of the people of his church. Kyle did, and found himself in pastoral conversations after years that could have never happened in months. Kyle is inclined to criticize Peterson for not raising a voice during those turbulent decades when they were both in ministry, yet he owes more to Peterson than such a criticism would suggest. We defy you to read Kyle's conclusion, about a return to that first parish years later, without crying or at least saying "thanks" to God. Just for good measure Kyle throws in passing glances at *The Canterbury Tales*, Wendell Berry, and the leading lights of the civil rights movement, for a full intellectual feast.

Lillian Daniel's essay leaves us asking: my goodness, does anyone know a funnier writer than Lillian?! She lovingly details the way Peterson's great *Under the Unpredictable Plant* kept her in the ministry, alongside other pastor-writers with realistic views of ministry and a passionate hunger for

God. The life she satirizes is surely recognizable, as is her shock at a writer like Eugene who will sear us with descriptions like "Prostitute pastor." "Who writes like this?" she asks, and indeed, no one but Peterson. Except he learned it from somewhere: the pages of the Bible, which speak with no less a searing eye and a lacerating pen. Whatever his other virtues or faults as a writer and pastor, Peterson speaks biblically, caustically, beautifully, as this singular writer bears witness to his affect on her.

Trygve Johnson's essay tackles a question that many of ours' dances around: *can't* we live out Peterson's vision in a congregation of more than 150 people? Trygve's "yes" draws on some of the most obscure portions of the Peterson corpus. He argues that Jesus's priestly prayer, his constant intercession of us by name, allows us to pastor those whom we do not know. And he recounts his daily self-questioning of whether he has loved his people, his place, and the Word. By loving those three he can pastor personally, whether on a first-name basis or not.

Roger Owens's essay attends to some of the spiritual writers who have tried to "democratize" contemplation, to make it accessible to every Christian, not just "experts." And he asks what pastoral ministry would look like with the pastor as a leader of contemplation. He attends to others who have made a similar move to Peterson in this. Who else's portrait belongs on the wall besides Peterson's than John Henry Newman's, Alexander Whyte's, and Baron von Hügel's? How about yours and ours?

Life

The fourth section, "Life," acknowledges that the pastoral vocation is isolated activities—working with words, institutions, and people—but these activities find their coherence in pastoral life. That it is a life itself attentive to God and discerning of God's presence; and a life that delights in Sabbath rest. One of the beauties of Peterson's memoir *The Pastor* is how it displays his growing understanding of the pastoral life as one greater than the sum of pastoral tasks. The essays in this section will engage broadly Peterson's understanding of pastoral ministry finding its integrity in the unity of the pastoral life.

Tim Conder's essay is a rollicking homage of praise to Peterson for his influence on Tim's quarter century of ministry. Tim studied with evangelicals and worked in megachurches before "downsizing" to a smaller university Bible church and then planting an Emerging-style neighborhood missional community, Emmaus Way in Durham, North Carolina. Peterson has been a constant amidst all this change, and Tim praises him appropriately. He challenges Eugene by the end to add a fourth angle to his important three in *Working the Angles*: missional activism, with the line of this polygon as the human body. Conder's sympathetic addition echoes Kyle Childress's, though put less strongly: where is the activism, the community engagement, in Peterson?

Martin Copenhaver's essay has a very different tone. Though a long-term pastor in one place himself, he takes on Peterson's relentless advocacy for staying in one place. Surely the determination to stay can itself be a form of disobedience? While Martin cherishes knowing "the back stories of the back stories" at Wellesley Congregational, he worries he may stay too long, and so jokes about a poison pill entrusted to a confidant. Martin reminds us of two UCC pastors we met at a church in Maine, the senior who has been there twenty-three years, his associate twenty-five. She, the associate, told us, "I think they're starting to trust us." On the other hand, a Methodist points out (perhaps overly defensively, given that tribe's penchant for moving entirely too often), that there is *one* good reason to leave a pastorate or to do anything else: the call of God. How do we get that right? We would love to hear Copenhaver and Kyle Childress argue this one out.

James Howell's essay asks whether his 5000-member megachurch can embody some of the virtues that Peterson so passionately extols. He thinks so, but has more to say here about the formation of his own soul as a pastor. He recommends most highly two slightly under-read Peterson volumes: *Reversed Thunder*, on the Apocalypse of John, and *Take and Read*, a list of salutary reading that could keep one busy for decades, as Howell points out. Howell is a master reader himself, and we found most interesting listening in on how Howell reads Peterson, what passages he returns to, how he imagines his own image in comparison to Eugene's visage. We all need models to emulate, disagree with, improve upon, and Howell does here what all this book's authors are trying to do.

Jenny Williams's essay critiques her own (United Methodist) tradition's default assumption that the pastor will do all the pastoral care. She wants congregations instead to be instigated to be in their neighborhood in mission. The future of the church depends on concentrating on the latter. But a pastor cannot both be in the hospital for every hangnail and empower and invite others in mission and ministry. She quotes a parishioner on the difference. A pastor doing all the visiting is like heroin! It feels good, but it will kill the congregation eventually.

Prince Rivers's essay answers some of the questions James leaves off: how can we appropriate Peterson in a larger church context, such as Prince's own United Metropolitan Missionary Baptist Church in Winston-Salem? For Rivers, the African-American church has historically embodied the attention to the local and the particular that Peterson so beautifully praises (though Prince worries that the influence of the prosperity gospel can threaten this heritage). Too, pastors must attend to the cure of souls above all else—not local boards, not institutional upkeep, not even budgets and maintenance, but prayer. He asks, hauntingly, why he is never asked about the state of his prayers, but always about the state of the institution's budget or maintenance. And he tells of his own efforts one Lent to concentrate his efforts on being a pastor, not an institutional administrator. Many writers in this volume are in similar ecclesial settings, and as lovers of Peterson, hope we can adapt him to our callings as Rivers has done here.

We hope these essays will contribute to greater reading of Eugene Peterson both in the church and the academy. We have tried to pay him the ultimate academic compliment of critique. And we have tried to pay him the ultimate ecclesial compliment of saying we want our lives to look more like his. This book is for others who want also to read him critically, with appreciation, and with thanks to God.

PART ONE

WORDS

The Pastor and the Art of Arts

Stephanie Paulsell

IN HIS GREAT SIXTH-CENTURY treatise on the work of pastoral ministry, Gregory the Great described that work as "the art of arts," a phrase he borrowed from the fourth-century theologian, Gregory of Nazianzus. Because human beings are "diverse and manifold [in] character," as Gregory of Nazianzus put it, and full of hidden wounds, as Gregory the Great put it, the pastor must be able to marshal all possible resources to minister to them.[1] The kind of pastoral care offered to one person will not reach another; one size does not fit all. In order to respond to the complex diversity of human experience, pastors need, not a blueprint to follow in each pastoral situation, but a stance towards life that is prayerful, improvisational, steeped in Scripture, and psychologically astute.

In his many books on pastoral ministry, Eugene Peterson has reiterated the wisdom of the two Gregories, although it is the theologian Baron Friedrich von Hügel whom he credits with teaching him, during his early days as a pastor, that "every soul is unique and cannot be understood or encouraged or directed by general advice or through a superficial diagnosis using psychological categories."[2] Von Hügel confirmed what Peterson was learning as the pastor of a congregation: that clichés cannot draw us into life with God and others; that language possesses "sacred qualities"[3] that reflect its source in the Word; that pastoral ministry requires prayerful attention

1. Gregory the Great, *Pastoral Care*, 21.

2. Peterson, *The Pastor*, 226.

3. Ibid., 239.

3

to the local, the particular, the invisible. In his recent memoir, *The Pastor*, Peterson tells a story about what ministry can look like when these lessons have not been learned. He describes enduring a few minutes of condolence from a pastor in the form of "preacher clichés" after the death of his mother. "Oh Karen," he says to his daughter after the man leaves, "I hope I have never done that to anyone."[4]

"The art of arts" seems an apt description of Eugene Peterson's approach to pastoral ministry, not only because he shares the vision of the complexity of pastoral work offered by the two Gregories, but also because Peterson's vision of ministry has been profoundly and thoroughgoingly shaped both by his long love affair with words and stories and by the theory and practice of art. In the brief, six-page introduction to *The Pastor*, Peterson grounds his understanding of pastoral ministry in the words of one poet and two novelists. In Denise Levertov's account of her poetic vocation in the phrase "every step an arrival," Peterson recognizes the incremental unfolding of his own vocation. In the title of Anne Tyler's novel, *Saint Maybe*, he finds a truthful gesture towards the "unavoidable ambiguity" of pastoral work. He sums up the introduction with William Faulkner's description of how to write a book: "It's like building a chicken coop in a high wind. You grab any board or shingle flying by or loose on the ground and nail it down fast." Peterson adds: "Like becoming a pastor."[5]

As these references suggest, literary artists provide a crucial source for Peterson's vocational understanding. His own vocation is "pastor and writer, a single coherent identity,"[6] and it is writers to whom he most often turns when he needs words to describe the pastoral vocation: Keats, Shakespeare, Kant, Dickens, Tolstoy, Thoreau, Muir, Dickinson, Melville, Hawthorne, Nietzsche. The way Peterson writes—"to explore and discover what I didn't know"[7]—is also a way of praying, preaching, worshiping, pastoring. It is a stance towards life and ministry that refuses to foreclose on the possibility of transformation, no matter how unexpected or unlooked for.

Writers are not the only artists from whom Peterson draws insight into the pastoral vocation. Cultivating friendships with artists of all kinds during his seminary years in New York City, he learns how to live creatively within a culture that does not recognize or value one's work by watching

4. Ibid., 294.

5. Ibid., 6.

6. Ibid., 238.

7. Ibid., 239.

these artists, unheralded by the world around them, persist in theirs. From jazz musicians, he comes to think of his weekday ministry as "salvation melodies and creation riffs" on "the larger rhythms set down in Lord's Day worship."[8] He looks to the vocational reflections of "writers and musicians and painters, weavers and potters and sculptors"[9] to support his own spiritual formation. It is no surprise, then, that some of the most beautiful writing and profound theological reflection in *The Pastor* appears in his account of his collaboration with an artist, the architect who helped Peterson's congregation decide on a plan for a new church building. Peterson calls the architect "Bezalel" after the craftsman who designed and created the tent of meeting and the ark of the covenant in Exodus, the artist who found a shape for the freedom into which Moses led God's people. Peterson is plainly fascinated by the way the architect is able to create a space for the congregation to be present to the invisible presence of God. "Artists do that," he marvels, "use material and sound, color and form to see the invisible, listen to the silence, touch the interior."[10] Artists use their art to help a congregation practice *their* art: the art of worship.

The intellectual and spiritual excitement that Peterson experiences through his deep engagement with the artist who would design a sanctuary for the church Peterson had planted and grown from nothing is contagious, both for us as readers and for the members of the congregation of Christ Our King Prebysterian Church. At the end of the chapter on Bezalel, Peterson describes coming upon three college students on the first Easter Sunday in the new sanctuary. They are deep into a conversation about the possible meanings held in the new space. "Pastor," a young woman named Wanda says, "we think we might be on to something. That empty tomb—could *yes!* that be an echo of the empty mercy seat of the ark?"[11] Having had their biblical imaginations nurtured through their pastor's preaching, teaching, and pastoral care, these students could move among Exodus, the Gospels, the architecture of their church, and the story of their lives together to generate more and more meaning, more and more ways to see their own story among the layers of biblical stories. Working with Bezalel was clearly a high point in Peterson's ministry, for him and for those in his care. It is a

8. Ibid., 296.
9. Ibid., 240.
10. Ibid., 186.
11. Ibid., 187.

high point in his book as well, full of the evocative and theologically rich language and insight that Peterson's readers cherish in his work.

Art is such a fruitful source for Peterson because, at its core, his pastoral work is language-work: "my artistic medium," he writes, "was words, written and prayed and preached." *The Pastor* is, in large part, about his search for language that can honor the irreducible complexity and ambiguity of human beings and the holiness of being alive. It is not enough for him, though, that language describe these things accurately. There is very specific work that he wants his language to do: to draw those with whom he ministers into God's narrative, to help them see their story within God's story. "True language has to do with communion," he insists, "establishing a relationship that makes for life."[12] True language for Peterson is participatory, the means by which we knit ourselves into relationship with others, the means by which we become a community.

How does language fulfill the high hopes Peterson has for it? Through story. As a teenager, Peterson hoped to become a novelist, and it was his early experiments with plot, he believes, that nurtured in him "a pastoral imagination adequate for entering into the complexities of good and evil, sin and salvation."[13] Peterson knows that the best stories unfold in unpredictable ways and leave room for many possible developments. Congregational life that is rooted in the language of story, then, opens space for change and growth and for a deepening of our relationship with God and one another that cannot be known in advance.

> Story is a way of language in which everything and everyone is organically related. Story is a way of language that insists that persons cannot be known by reducing them to what they do, how they perform, the way they look. Story uses a language in which listening has joint billing with speaking. Story is language put to the use of discovering patterns and meanings—beauty and truth and goodness: Father, Son and Holy Spirit.[14]

This vision of story as a way of shaping our life together as Christians will be familiar to anyone who has read any of Peterson's books. Looking back on beloved volumes like *Five Smooth Stones for Pastoral Work*, *A Long Obedience in the Same Direction*, *Under the Unpredictable Plant*, and *The Contemplative Pastor*, however, it is interesting to note how few stories from

12. Ibid., 243.
13. Ibid., 59.
14. Ibid., 309.

his pastoral ministry appear in them. He does tell some stories from his years as pastor of Christ Our King Presbyterian Church, but they are always briefly told, wholly embedded in the stories of scripture, and often held up to the light of literature, from Dostoyesvsky's *Crime and Punishment* to Melville's *Moby Dick* to Annie Dillard's *A Pilgrim at Tinker Creek*. From such diverse threads, Peterson has woven his distinctive vision of ministry and the voice in which he speaks of it, a voice that has led countless readers into the stories of the Bible to find there the freshest possible news about their own lives.

Peterson notes in the acknowledgments for *The Pastor* that, the memoir not being his natural form, he needed some encouragement to write one. "I have always written from a text," he reminds us, "mostly a biblical text. To have my vocation as the text felt awkward."[15] And indeed the stories that best illustrate his convictions about the work language and story can do in a Christian community are often ones that explore his pastoral vocation at a slant—not from the perspective of a settled pastor but from the perspective of his childhood. One such story is Peterson's extended meditation on working in his father's butcher shop as a boy, a story about the growth of the biblical imagination for which Peterson is so well known. Beginning when he was five years old, Peterson donned a butcher's apron, identical to his father's, sewn by his mother from flour sacks, and accompanied his father to work. In the butcher shop, young Eugene practiced growing into adulthood, learning to respect both his knife and the slabs of meat on which he used it, learning to treat all customers with dignity as his father did, learning to work steadily and hard. He also grew into his biblical imagination, viewing his work at the butcher shop through the lens of the biblical stories of Samuel, who also wore an ephod made by his mother and learned the vocation of priest from Eli at the Shiloh temple.

Carving and grinding meat, Peterson learned "a kind of submission of will to the conditions at hand, a cultivation of what I would later call humility."[16] He came to associate this with Keats's "negative capability," the capacity to hold what cannot be known "without any irritable reaching after fact and reason"—a literary capacity, but also, for Peterson, a pastoral one, in which each person is viewed not as a problem to be solved but as a mystery to be honored.[17]

15. Ibid., 319.

16. Ibid., 37.

17. For a rich theological discussion of the distinction between "mystery" and

In the butcher shop, Peterson became deeply familiar with the materiality and messiness of sacrifice: "blood sloshing on the floor, gutting the creatures and gathering up the entrails in buckets, skinning the animals, salting down the hides."[18] When, as a child, he hears passages about sacrifice read aloud from Leviticus in church, he recognizes what is going on, feels the reality of it in his bones. And when he grows up to be a pastor, he does not expect "the world of worship to be tidy and sedate"[19] but rather as messy as anything else human beings attempt to do together.

Looking back, Peterson sees his time in the butcher shop as crucial preparation for his life in a congregation. The priests in their ephods—Peterson and his father—greeted each person by name, knew their stories, cared about their lives. But there were things he learned in the butcher shop that, as a pastor, he would have to unlearn. First and foremost: the salvific power of work. Remembering one Holy Saturday, during which he and his father "worked a long and lucrative day," Peterson recalls selling four scrawny ham hocks to a Native American woman for her family's Easter dinner. He knew her as the wife of one of a group of men who spent the day drinking in a nearby alley. The despair he glimpsed in that alley as a child scared him; it was a sign of something gone terribly wrong. As a pastor looking back, however, he sees that acknowledgment of despair as a truer way of observing Holy Saturday than the successful day of working and making money in which he and his father engaged.[20]

Stories like the ones that Peterson tells about his father's butcher shop put flesh on Peterson's theoretical articulations about the complexity and unknowableness of human beings and the work of the pastor in relation to such mystery. While the world around him urges one interpretation of the men in the alley with their bottles of Thunderbird, the rhythms of his faith teach him that there is more to those men's lives than he can see or understand. He learns to see his life as connected to theirs, and he finds they have something important to teach him.

There are other stories in *The Pastor*, however, that undermine the spacious understanding of human beings that Peterson articulates in the narratives of his childhood and his engagements with Scripture and literature, stories that remind us how difficult it is to keep the hidden mystery of

---

"problem," see Marty, *The Mystery of the Child.*

18. Peterson, *The Pastor*, 38.

19. Ibid.

20. Ibid., 41–44.

each other in mind. The book is burdened by straw characters who appear in Peterson's stories not because they are full of mysteries but because they represent something Peterson wants to critique: capitulation to American culture, for example, or denominational myopia. Whenever they appear, these flat characters provide a foil for Peterson, and he becomes, in many cases, the hero of the story, the only one with eyes to see.

One familiar straw character who crops up regularly is the seminary professor who has little to contribute to the education of future ministers because he or she has never been a pastor. "My seminary professors had no idea what pastors were or did,"[21] Peterson insists. Closely related to this familiar character is the arrogant pastoral theologian who writes a whole book on ministry and never mentions prayer. Peterson dumps his books in a landfill. "Nobody in my neighborhood was going to read these books if I had any say in it,"[22] Peterson writes.

Other straw characters populate the pages of Peterson's memoir: the pastor who has sold out to the secularized, commodified American version of ministry; the dismissive architectural consultant recommended by the denominational office; the dishonest denominational executives who claim to have been reading Peterson's lengthy reports on his new church while remaining ignorant of the fact that he has been salting them with false tales of alcoholism and adultery; the elementary school teachers who do not know enough to let their students leap with joy in the sanctuary of a new church. At one point the entire congregation of Christ Our King seems to function as a straw character in the story of Peterson's vocation: "They were reducing me to their level—flat and complacently self-satisfied in the wake of our achievement."[23] Peterson shares in the achievement. The complacency in its wake, however, he assigns to his congregation alone.

The novelist Charles Johnson, who was mentored as a young man by John Gardner, the author of *On Moral Fiction*, once described in an interview what it was like to have Gardner read drafts of his work. "Shame on you," Gardner would write in the margins when he encountered a straw character in Johnson's writing. "What am I supposed to do with this character, dislike him?" Johnson came to believe that the "ideal novel would be one in which there are no minor characters, where there are no flat

21. Ibid., 162.
22. Ibid., 151.
23. Ibid., 210.

characters." A novel which shows every character evolving and changing would be, for Johnson, "the ultimate moral fiction."[24]

As an artist, Johnson wants to develop ways of telling stories that make visible each character's interior life, to allow for the possibility that each character, no matter how "minor" or even represensible, might change. As a pastor, Peterson seeks something similar: language that can do justice to the mystery of each human being, pastoral practices that open the possibility for transformation. The work of both shows just how difficult this is to do. John Gardner was asking a lot of Charles Johnson when he asked him to rid his fiction entirely of undeveloped characters. And we would be asking a lot from Eugene Peterson if we were to insist that he find a way to gesture towards the possibility for transformation of the characters in his stories who embody the ignorance, inattention, and cultural captivity that Peterson believes undermines Christian community and the practice of ministry.

Still, the contrast between Peterson's theological understanding of people as mysteries and his practice in his memoir of having particular people function as illustrations of particular failings is arresting. When he writes of the pastoral theologian whose books he deems worthy of the city dump or the architectural consultant who arrogantly assumes he needs to teach Peterson and his congregation a thing or two about church architecture, we seem a long way from the butcher shop, where Peterson learned to receive everyone—from tradespeople to awkward pastors to the women who worked in the brothel down the road—in a way that preserved their dignity as human beings made in the image of God. The straw characters who appear in Peterson's stories about his pastoral ministry seem out of the reach, somehow, of the dignity conferred by pastoral attention: they seem wholly figured out, impervious to transformation, caught in the role Peterson has asked them to play, flat. Because Peterson is a writer-pastor who relies heavily on reflection on the practice of writing to understand his life in ministry, the frequent appearance of characters with no other work to do than to provide a foil for Peterson's deeper insights and better practices is jarring. Reading is a formative practice, as Peterson has taught us through his own engagements with literature. When he clearly disdains a character in one of his stories, he asks us to feel disdain as well. When he withholds empathy from a character, he asks us to read without empathy.

24. Little, "An Interview with Charles Johnson," 111–12.

The most jarring story in *The Pastor*, however, is not a story about a straw character but rather a story he tells from his early ministry as an associate pastor in White Plains, New York. He describes being left alone with the ministry while the senior pastor took a summer vacation. While he was in charge, a janitor at the church was, in Peterson's words, "apprehended molesting a nine-year-old boy in the men's restroom."[25] The parents, Peterson remembers, were "irate" and wanted to know what the young pastor was going to do about the situation.

"I panicked," Peterson writes. "I was into something way over my head."[26] Wisely, he understands that he will need help and turns to a prominent psychiatrist in the congregation for assistance. The psychiatrist is immediately responsive and asks Peterson to bring the boy to his office.

> He asked Dennis what had taken place. Dennis was matter-of-fact. Dr. Wall said, "Dennis, you remember very well. You have a good memory. Do you ever forget things?" Dennis nodded.
>
> "This is something I want you to forget. Use your forgetter on this one."
>
> And that was it.
>
> That evening Dr. Wall stopped by the home of Dennis's parents and talked it over with them. I wasn't there. He let me know that he would check in with the parents monthly for the next year to see how things were going. And that was the end of the matter.[27]

Eugene Peterson is beloved and widely read by pastors across Christian denominations in part because of the clarity of his vision. When it comes to the vocation of the pastor, he is plainspoken and full of common sense. Ministry, Peterson teaches us, is not about church growth or fancy programs. Ministry is about leading people into a deeper relationship with God, each other, and the world around them. It is about worship. It is about helping others see their story within God's story.

Peterson's vision of ministry is compelling in its unromanticized, common sense simplicity, and it has helped countless pastors focus their energies on the very heart of Christian life. The story of Dennis and Dr. Wall, however, exposes the limits of moving too quickly to common sense simplicity. This is not to cast blame on the young associate pastor who was, no doubt, correct in his assessment that he was out of his depth in this

25. Peterson, *The Pastor*, 133.

26. Ibid.

27. Ibid.

situation. But it does seem important, in an essay about Peterson's use of words and stories, to raise some questions about the way Peterson tells this story many years later. The young associate surely wanted to find as quick a solution as he could to a problem he did not himself know how to address. But the experienced pastor telling the story in retrospect seems not to have thought any further about it. In the telling of the story, he seems as eager as the young associate he once was to bring the situation to a definite close. He punctuates the story with marks of closure: "And that was it." "And that was the end of the matter." Dr. Wall told the child to use his forgetter. That's it. The end.

In the years since Peterson was an associate pastor in White Plains, we have learned a lot about how churches have responded to the sexual abuse of children. One of the things we have learned is that children have often been told to forget what happened to them. Archbishop Daniel Pilarczyk, the first American prelate to be subpoenaed by a grand jury in the struggle to obtain church records relating to the sexual abuse of children,[28] explained to the *Cincinnati Enquirer* that "the common wisdom" among church officials had been "to get the offender out of the child's life and tell the child to forget about it." In 2002, he admitted that this was a mistake. "Would we do it that way now? Certainly not, because we know more and we have more experience."[29]

Peterson's account of the story of Dennis and Dr. Wall is very compressed. There is much he does not tell us: whether or not the police were called; what happened to the janitor; how the parents helped their child deal with the experience; how Dr. Wall helped the parents. No doubt Peterson has changed names and details in order to protect the privacy of those involved, which further limits what we can know.

What seems to be at stake for Peterson in this story is what he learned about the limits of what the pastor can offer in such a situation. When we are out of our depth, he tells us, we need experts to help us; that can certainly be true enough. Peterson does not portray himself as the hero of this story; that role is played by Dr. Wall who is described as a Good Samaritan who handled the situation with "intuitive dispatch."[30] What Peterson expresses in his telling of the story is relief and clarity—relief that he had access to such an accomplished professional when faced with the sexual abuse

28. The Investigative Staff of the *Boston Globe*, *Betrayal*, 113.

29. Francis X. Clines, "Scandals in the Church," *New York Times*, April 19, 2002.

30. Peterson, *The Pastor*, 137.

of a child in his church and clarity about the division between the work of the pastor and the work of the psychiatrist. Peterson sums up the episode like this: "For me it was the beginning of a discernment and clarification of relationship between pastor and psychiatrist, what we have in common and what we do that's different."[31]

Eugene Peterson is known and cherished for getting to the heart of the matter in his discussions of ministry and congregational life. If he is going to tell a story about the sexual abuse of a child, we need him to speak to the heart of this matter as well. For anyone who has heard or read even a little about the stories of survivors of childhood sexual abuse in churches, schools, families, and sports programs, the story Peterson tells raises questions. These questions might not have occurred to him when he was a panicked new associate pastor, but they ought to occur to him now. Can a child be told to forget an experience and at the same time have confidence that the adults who care for him believe him? If he knows the adults in his life want him to forget the experience, will he ever feel that he can speak of it again? Does the desire to mark such a definite end to the story—"and that was the end of the matter"—leave room for the child to do everything he needs to do to heal? In this situation, is there truly nothing for the pastor to do other than provide a ride to the psychiatrist's office? At no point in his discussion of Dennis and Dr. Wall does Peterson ask these kinds of questions. At no point does he pull back and wonder if Dr. Wall's instructions to Dennis were the panacea he believed they were at the time. At no point does he pause to reflect, not upon what the pastor cannot do in this situation, but what the pastor has to offer to Dennis and to his family. Without this deeper reflection, readers are left with the sense that Peterson feels some human experiences are out of the reach of the care of the pastor. And without this deeper reflection, the instruction to the child to forget the experience seems to stand as pastoral advice.

Peterson's common sense approach to ministry is so often liberating. He cuts, with "intuitive dispatch," through our anxieties about church growth and church programs and how to appeal to a consumer culture in order to reveal the essential contours of Christian life in community. But not everything can or should be done with dispatch, as Peterson himself acknowledges throughout his body of work. Indeed what he loves about being a pastor is the slow unfolding of transformation: "a slow recognition

31. Ibid., 133.

of life, God's life, taking form in a person and context, in words or action that takes me off-guard."[32]

His memoir ends with a letter to a young pastor in which Peterson makes movingly clear his love for the ambiguity at the heart of pastoral work. "It amazes me still how much of the time I simply don't know what I am doing, don't know what to say, don't know what the next move is."[33] What a consolation to hear Eugene Peterson, decades into his ministry, acknowledge this. Who among us can claim that we always know what the next move is? Nothing human is alien to the pastor; all of life is the pastor's business. No one can be perfectly prepared for everything that happens in pastoral ministry in the sense of possessing the right "administrative or therapeutic or scholarly or programmatic competences"[34] for every situation. What we can do, as Eugene Peterson has done, is to immerse ourselves in relationships, in Scripture, in art, in worship, in the complexities of human life, and in the invisible presence of God and be led by the resonances we find among them. Pastoral ministry is the art of arts, as the Gregories remind us, and Eugene Peterson stands in their lineage, knee deep in the stories of Scripture and the words of the writers he loves, throwing out lifeline after lifeline of words and stories, hoping they will make a difference to all of us who, like him, struggle to find our way as pastors.

32. Ibid., 283.
33. Ibid., 315.
34. Ibid.

Wanderers Between Two Worlds

KARL BARTH, EUGENE PETERSON, AND THE "LIVED QUALITY" OF HOLY SCRIPTURE

Mark Ralls

TWO YEARS AFTER THE end of World War I, a Swiss Reformed pastor, wrote a nostalgic letter to his friend Karl Barth. He recalled brisk walks and breathless conversations from years earlier. "How good were those years," he wrote, "when our ideas disclosed themselves in our hurried walking back and forth . . . and [all who saw us] could only shake their heads at the sight of two strange *wanderers between two worlds*." This mutual fervor had little to do with the conflagration of the Great War that had ignited a few hundred miles from their neighboring congregations. It was not a by-product of the spirit of crisis soon to engulf all of European culture. What had kindled the odd intensity of their afternoon reveries was the discovery of a world beyond canton, country, and continent. As sojourners to the strange, new world of the Bible, they had been transformed by their expeditions. A residue of contrasting feelings remained. Both imperiled and secure. Disoriented yet edified. At once lost and found.

Eugene Peterson and Karl Barth are also "wanderers between two worlds." I hope to make this common stance evident in relation to a best-selling, post-war memoir in Germany with this title. Read together, Peterson and Barth teach us to attend to the "lived quality" of the Bible. This allows it to be for us what it already is in itself—a world both strange and new, and yet, in the deepest sense, familiar.

15

Eugene Peterson has never been shy about his indebtedness to Karl Barth. In his recent memoir, *The Pastor,* he extols Barth as the one who placed before him the charge that has shaped his theological vocation: To read the Bible as Holy Script, as God's living message to us. This charge is more spiritual quest than line of inquiry. It is about neither "explaining" nor "defending" the Bible. "Barth," notes Peterson, "didn't have much interest in that." He was instead "calling attention to the *lived* quality of scripture."[1] He showed us how "to *read* the book receptively in its original transformative character."[2]

But how? Once again, Peterson appeals to Barth:

> In 1916 a young Swiss pastor, Karl Barth gave an address in the village of Leutwil where his friend Eduard Thurneysen was pastor. . . . A few miles away the rest of Europe was on fire with war. . . . [Yet] just across the German and French borders in neutral Switzerland this young pastor had discovered the Bible as if for the first time, discovered it as a book absolutely unique, unprecedented. . . . Barth, in his small out-of-the-way village, was [coming to grips with] the extraordinary truth-releasing, God-witnessing, culture-changing realities in this book, the Bible.[3]

What captured Peterson's imagination was the unexpected attention Barth paid to ancient texts amid the immediate distractions of World War I. For Peterson, it is this perilous choice that marks recognition of "the *lived* quality of scripture."

As a pastor myself, this is also my goal. I am charged with leading my congregation beyond its present state as a collection of individual inquirers, encountering the Bible merely as informative text. I am to cultivate an intentional community sharing a quest to engage a living message that forms our life together. With this goal in mind, I will read Eugene Peterson and Karl Barth alongside one another. Together, they respond to two crucial questions so intimately connected they merge into one.

---

1. Peterson, *The Pastor,* 2.
2. Peterson, *Eat This Book,* 5–6.
3. Ibid., 5.

What is the lived quality of Holy Scripture, and how do we learn to pay attention to it?

The First Question: Karl Barth

What is the lived quality of Holy Scripture? For more than fifty years, from 1916 to his death in 1968, Barth pursued a faithful response to this question. He did so with the intensity—and requisite humility—of an artist attempting to portray a bird in flight without rendering it lifeless. Like the great artists of nature (think John J. Audubon), Barth sought to capture a "lived quality" without making it captive to canvas or page.

Four years into this quest and only fifteen months after the armistice that ended the Great War, Karl Barth was invited to speak at a prestigious conference in Aarau, Switzerland. The invitation must have come as a surprise. In 1920, Barth was a thirty-four-year-old pastor of a small congregation of struggling factory workers in an obscure Swiss canton. Only a handful of those who attended the conference would have recognized his name in the program. And, no one would have expected very much based on the pedestrian title he gave to his address: "Biblical Problems, Perceptions and Perspectives."[4]

The fledgling pastor was slated to follow an address by Adolf Harnack, a venerable professor of the University of Berlin. In recognition of his masterwork, *The Essence of Christianity,* and his service as a chief advisor to Kaiser Wilhelm II, the old professor had recently been knighted *von* Harnack.[5] The august scholar used his time at the podium as one might expect from someone in his lofty position. He reassured his audience that neither the cruelty of war nor the ignominy of defeat could derail human history from its appointed end. The "single—albeit not unbroken—line of progress," Harnack intoned, will continue. And, Germany will somehow retain its unique role as the vanguard of both reason and culture. As von Harnack returned to his seat, the steady, subdued applause indicated that he had accomplished neither less nor more than what was expected of him.

---

4. Barth, "Biblische Fragen, Einsichten und Ausblicke."

5. Adolf von Harnack had been Barth's mentor at the University of Berlin. It was a deep disappointment for Barth to see Harnack's signature on the "Manifesto of the 93," and his deep involvement in leading Germany to the First World War. Harnack helped draft the Kaiser's address calling the German people to war. See Wilson, *Introduction to Modern Theology,* 135.

It was then Karl Barth's turn. Standing at the podium, he began with a question that was simple and direct. Following the lofty pronouncements of von Harnack, Barth's opening line must have sounded abrupt and off-key: "In light of [recent] world events, what does the Bible really mean to us?"[6] Perhaps those in attendance expected Barth merely to extend the reassuring tones of his predecessor at the podium. Instead, Barth followed his innocuous prelude with a jarring rejoinder: "To ask, 'What does the Bible mean to us?' demands our answer to another question that must be acknowledged as ominous: What *is* Holy Scripture?"[7]

Why ominous? Perhaps Barth has in mind the World War I memoir of Walter Flex and the emotional response it ignited across Germany. Published in 1916, *Der Wanderer zwischen beiden Welten: Ein Kriegserlebnis* (*The Wanderer between Two Worlds: An Experience of War*), was a sensation. In just two years, Flex's memoir sailed through an astonishing thirty-nine editions. The extraordinary success of *Wanderer* was due in part to its unexpected form. It was both a soldier's personal memoir and a melodramatic eulogy of a devout Christian named Ernst Wurche. His inspiring life and sacrificial death brought solace to a grieving nation.

When Flex first met his comrade, it was clear what the Bible meant to him.

Wurche "sat quietly in a corner" of the barracks "reading *his* New Testament." Deeply engaged, "his eyes shone with the brightness of the sun." As he read, observed Flex, the young soldier embodied a "Christianity [that] was *all power and vitality*."[8] Before the war, Ernst Wurche excelled as a student of theology. After his conscription, the words of Scripture inspired him to merge religious devotion with patriotic zeal. Wurche never failed to carry his New Testament into combat, and he approached every battle as a religious crusade. Flex recalls how his friend marched not just resolutely to the front lines of battle but with a joyful anticipation akin to eschatological hope. "His eyes," wrote Flex, were "bright and full of longing." He did not march as a soldier. He journeyed as "a pilgrim."[9]

The staggering popularity of *A Wanderer Between Two Worlds* lies in part with the timing of its release. Published just before the failed Ludendorff Offensive, *Der Wanderer* provided a way to secure spiritual meaning

6. Barth, "Biblische Fragen, Einsichten und Ausblicke," 70–71.

7. Ibid.

8. Flex, *Der Wanderer zwischen beiden Welten*, 17.

9. Ibid., 36.

amid military defeat. Though he was killed in battle before war's end, young Wurche envisioned the loss of the war with the equanimity of a monk: "The egoism of the I" will be surrendered in defeat and every patriotic German will discover the "true meaning" of their lives in "the machinery of the whole."[10]

Der Wanderer sparked lively debate in the German Protestant Church. Theologians parried opposing jabs about the proper way to bring the message of the Bible to bear on recent world events. A Heidelberg historian advocated the example of Ernst Wurche without reserve: The Protestant Church, he insisted, must become "a school of . . . reverence and love of the Fatherland."[11] A Göttingen theologian countered, "How could we undertake to solve the terrible problems of the present without the severest criticism of our dearest hopes and our most precious memories!"[12] Perhaps Barth recognized that beneath the rhetoric both sides of the theological debate shared the same assumption. What difference does it make whether we turn to Scripture to undergird our vision for society or to break that vision apart? Does it matter if we use Scripture to console the disillusioned or to cajole the zealous? Either way, the Bible is no more than a means to our own end, a megaphone in our hands amplifying no other voice than our own.

Barth sets forth a kind of categorical imperative. If the Bible is Holy Scripture, if it is the vehicle of God's living Word, then it is no means to some greater end. It is an end itself. It is not a tool we can place in our own hands. We cannot "grasp its message." We can only "be grasped by it." Whenever we attempt the former, we take "something mysterious, something ultimate," and render it "familiar." We take something "immense," that ought to "embrace us," and we try to "domesticate" it. We do all of this with the seemingly harmless goal of making the Bible "relevant . . . to our present crisis."[13]

The Bible is more than we imagine it to be. It is not the world in miniature—a diorama in our hands. It is immense. It is not the known world, malleable enough to be made familiar. It is ultimate. If the Bible is all these things, then it is always different in kind from whatever it may mean to us. It is no tool we can hold in our hands and apply to some preordained

10. Ibid., 30–31.

11. Cited in Scholder, *The Churches and the Third Reich*, 39.

12. Ibid.

13. Ibid., 72–74, 75, 77.

purpose. It is Holy Scripture, and its message—that *"God chooses to be in relationship with us"*—cuts "a distinct path from the murky beginnings of human history . . . to the haze of our present crisis." It is not "one path among others." It is not even the path itself. It is "the reason for the path."[14]

As such it defies any mode of knowing that assumes objective inquiry. The message of Holy Scripture is too vital for that. No lifeless cadaver, it resists autopsy. No known world, it may be explored but never charted. Our experience of it can only be expressed in paradox: "A glimpse of the invisible. A hearing of the inaudible. A grasp of the unattainable."

A year after his address, Karl Barth alluded specifically to Walter Flex's best-seller to sharpen his point: "Homeless in this world, yet not at home in the next, we human beings are wanderers between two worlds." In Barth's hands, the metaphor turns bleak. The Bible is not simply another world that we may wander in and out of, collecting what we deem useful for our "present crisis." It is God's World both enveloping and standing over against our own. As wanderers, we are "neither here nor there." All we can do is to acknowledge ourselves lost and incapable of securing our own rescue.[15]

Ours is a nomadic existence. To be human is to be a wanderer. We wander the frontier between the world God created to be and the world as we allow it to be. Yet because the living message is not primarily our story but God's, Barth can establish alternative ground for hope. "Precisely as wanderers, we are also children of God in Christ. The mystery of life is *God's* mystery." Our inability to reach God need not prevent God from coming to us. Our present identity as those who are lost does not keep us from being found. To acknowledge the mystery of our lives as "God's mystery" is an act of submission. A bird in flight may be portrayed but never captured, on occasion glimpsed but not ever grasped.

In the face of two unacceptable options—the pessimism of negative theology and the unbridled optimism of liberal theology—Barth offers an alternative. As wanderers between two worlds, we approach the unapproachable. We attend to the lived quality of Holy Scripture.

How? To respond to this question, Karl Barth needs Peterson.

---

14. Ibid., 72–74, 75, 77.

15 Barth, *Konfirmandenunterricht,* cited in McCormack, *Karl Barth's Critically Realistic Dialectical Theology,* frontispiece.

The Second Question: Eugene Peterson

In his recent memoir, Eugene Peterson discloses his personal strategy for writer's block. "When I don't know what to do, I read a murder mystery. Murder mysteries are the cleanest, least ambiguous moral writing that we have." [16] For nearly fifty years, Peterson has written spiritual theology that can be favorably compared to the best writing of that genre. Think P. D. James and Laura Lippmann. With almost as many titles to his credit, Peterson—like James and Lippmann—has achieved a rare feat. He has attained the prolific without sacrificing the poignant. He makes spiritual mysteries accessible without rendering them conventional.

In *Eat This Book,* Eugene Peterson takes Barth's Aarau address as his point of departure. In his closing remarks, Barth offered this cryptic metaphor: "We exist as if we are peering from a high window. And, what we see below is a person standing on the ground peering urgently toward the sky above, straining as if to see some unseen object high above the roof tops." [17] From our perch above, we cannot observe what the person sees. Yet, we can see the person below as vital and still as a coiled spring, bearing witness to something "perpetually beyond our own life of sight." [18]

Peterson expands the metaphor. He imagines a group of children who have lived their entire lives in a warehouse. To them, the warehouse is immense. Following the adults who raised them, the children simply cannot imagine another—more expansive—world beyond the warehouse walls. No one has ever bothered to clean the windows of the warehouse. They remain "thick with dust." The facility is not only their home. It has become their world. [19]

One day, a child performs a simple yet unprecedented act. He "drags a stepstool under one of the windows, scrapes off the grime, and looks out." Before him is the unknown outside world. He calls to his friends and together they stare in rapt attention at "people walking on the streets." Then the boy sees something peculiar and alluring. "A person out in the street is looking up and talking excitedly." Others from the outside world gather round this person. They too begin to crane their necks, shield their eyes and look up. What could this be? When the warehouse children look up all

16. Peterson, *The Pastor*, 250.

17. Ibid., 77.

18. Ibid.

19. Peterson, *Eat This book*, 7.

they see is gray ceiling. They can't imagine blue sky. And yet they kneel in rapt attention at the strange people on the other side of the glass, bearing witness to some forgotten horizon "stretching endlessly above and beyond," which they can no longer imagine. No answers are given; only this single clue. So, the children grow bored. They turn their attention to concerns that are comforting in their familiarity. They settle once again into their warehouse world and allow its windows to grow thick with dust and grime.[20]

Peterson asks tantalizing questions: What might happen to these children if they could remain at their window peering toward the transcendent? Would their imaginations grow as they begin to pine for this other world? Would they come to cherish their warehouse less for its ceiling and walls and more for its windows and doors, portals to another world? How do they, and we, begin? How do we attend to the message of Holy Scripture if its lived quality exceeds the horizon of our imaginations?

The children are unable to recognize what they see for what it is. At first drawn to this larger world, they eventually shrink from it. They question the validity of what lies plainly before them. They begin to practice a "hermeneutics of suspicion." Resigned to cool objectivity that masquerades as hard truth, the children refuse to take what lies before them at face value. They "narrow their eyes," suspicious of the validity of what lies before them in plain sight. In other words, they stop acting as children and begin to mimic the adults of the warehouse, who taught a pinched view of the world, walled and gray. "As we narrow our eyes in suspicion, the world is correspondingly narrowed down," and most of us—perhaps all at times— transfer this habit of seeing the world into a pinched practice of reading Scripture.[21]

Peterson beckons us to regain our "childlike wonder, to look at the world . . . ready to be startled into surprised delight by the profuse abundance of truth and beauty and goodness that is spilling out of the skies at every moment." He then beckons us to read the Bible with a posture of adoration. We replace a "hermeneutics of suspicion" with a "hermeneutics of adoration" so that through the windowpane of Scripture we "see how large, how splendid, how magnificent life is."[22] So, a short answer to the question *how do we attend to the lived quality of Holy Scripture?* is this: We

---

20. Ibid., 6–7.
21. Ibid., 68.
22. Ibid., 68–69.

learn a hermeneutic of adoration. We open the warehouse door and take the first step in a larger world, on a redemptive path.

Two Ways

Immensely Personal

Consider this scenario. A well-intentioned friend becomes aware of your daily devotions and becomes curious. She asks, "Why do you read the Bible—and not some other book?" Struggling for a disarming, engaging response you say, "Because this book inspires me like no other. It provides solace when I am grieving, encouragement to face the challenges of each day and most of all guidance as I try to cultivate a life of meaning and purpose. I guess my reasons are personal." For Peterson, such a response would be imprudent. Your friend may indeed be stirred to "take up and read," but she is likely to do so for the wrong reasons. Misunderstanding why she reads, she may never learn how. She will suppose that Christians read the Bible for immensely personal reasons and this will direct her away from the heart of the matter.

For Peterson, the Bible is God's invitation into a world of creation and salvation that is larger than we can ever imagine; a world that will render us disoriented, confused, at times even undone. It is in this undoing that we will discover the promise of becoming—through grace, imagination, and faith—a new person in Christ. One of Peterson's greatest insights is deceptively simple: *why* we read shapes *how* we read. And, we do *not* read for personal reasons. We read in order to participate in a world so immense—so infinitely bigger than our concerns—that we are both lost and found.

Returning to the curious friend, a more promising response would be, "In this book alone, all creatures are personally addressed by God. I read not because it compares favorably to every other book. I read it not because I choose to but because I must. It breaks me apart and then begins to put me together again as the person I am to become for eternity." Such a response may be off-putting. It may even dissuade from Scripture. Yet if she "takes up and reads" for this purpose, she will take a crucial step in the right direction. She will enter the immense world of God.

The first response starts from a preconceived notion of the *immensely personal*. Prioritizing immanence, it begins with self-reflection: "What is my purpose in reading God's Word?" The second response pursues the possibility of something that is *personally immense.* Prioritizing transcendence, it begins with testimony: "What is God's purpose in God's Word?" The first response may be winsome, but it will lead in exactly the wrong direction. The second response may be off-putting. But it is akin to those strangers on the other side of the warehouse window who gape in wonder as they point toward the sky.

Personally Immense

To read this book rightly, we must allow ourselves to be confronted by purposes that are not our own. The Divine Author remains sovereign in the heart of the human reader without ever ceasing to be "emphatically personal."[23] This discloses our true purpose. "We read," says Eugene Peterson, "in order to get in on the revelation of God." We do not read for "information." We read to receive a revelation that can never be possessed. Yet if we learn how to read with "imagination and faith," it may lead to our "formation." All other books inform. This one forms. "We receive these words so that we can be formed now and for eternity to the glory of God."[24] Offering his own testimony, Peterson says this: This book alone "forms my core identity."[25]

God's purposes demand a particular kind of reading that is "personal, relational, participatory." For him, "this may be the single most important thing to know as we come to read . . . these Holy Scriptures."[26] We seek to read not acquisitively, but receptively. "Christian reading is participatory reading, receiving the words in such a way that they become interior to our lives, the rhythms and images becoming practices of prayer, acts of obedience, ways of love."[27] This kind of reading is personally immense. It leads us out from under the low, gray ceiling of our own purposes to a place where we might see the infinitely broad horizons of the purposes of God.

The hero of Flex's best-selling memoir, Ernst Wurche, read the Bible for immensely personal reasons. This shaped how he read and what he appropriated. The Heidelberg historian who saw great promise for Germany's future in Flex's work advocated reading the Bible for "spiritual uplift." The

---

23. Ibid., 30.

24. Ibid., 31.

25. Ibid., 27.

26. Ibid.

27. Ibid., 27–28.

Göttingen theologian who detected the dangers of patriotism viewed the story as a cautionary tale. He countered that the Bible must be read for "moral guidance."

Eugene Peterson might suggest that these two German scholars approached the Bible in the same way. One suggested that we read the Bible to inspire hope for our self-assessed dreams of the future. The other that we read the Bible to correct the self-assessed failures in our past. "Choose either of these options," writes Peterson, "and you will be *using* the Bible for *your* purpose." Both sides give primacy to the human reader over the Divine Author. They read the Bible through the lens of their "sincere and devout but still self-sovereign purposes." If you read the Bible for "the moral guidance it offers or for the spiritual uplift it provides," you miss the heart of the matter. You evade a genuine encounter with the "personally revealing God who has personal designs on you."[28]

When we bring our own purposes to bear on Holy Scripture, we not only misconstrue its living message. We actually read in a way that deforms our core identity. We replace "the three-personal Father, Son, and Holy Spirit" with a "divine self" asserting the "very individualized personal Trinity of my Holy Wants, my Holy Needs, and my Holy Feelings."[29] We replace the sovereign, personal God with a sovereign, "de-personalized" self. Our core identities—attained by following the secure threads of the purposes of God—begin to unravel. We lose ourselves in our meager pursuits of the personal.[30]

Invited to bring our "imagination and faith" to bear not *upon* but *within* the purposes of God, we approach the Bible in a decidedly different way. We take "our place under the broad skies of God's purposes."[31] This is Eugene Peterson's most important point in *Eat This Book*. "[U]sing Scripture as text," he says, "does not present us with a moral code and tell us 'Live up to this'; nor does it set out a system of doctrine and say, 'Think like this.'" The biblical way is to tell a story and in the telling invite: "Live *into* this—this is what it looks like to be human in this God-made and God-ruled world."[32]

---

28. Ibid., 29–30.
29. Ibid., 31.
30. Ibid., 31–32.
31. Ibid., 40–41.
32. Ibid., 43–44.

In *The Pastor,* Eugene Peterson illustrates this point recalling as a child how his mother invited him into the larger story of Samuel's anointing of David. "[I]n my mother's telling of it Samuel was an old man with his beard down to his knees. He was a thick, stocky man, built like a fire hydrant, who from a distance looked like a fountain, white hair pouring from his head."[33] Her story concluded with grand celebration where Samuel selected a "runt" named David as heir apparent to Israel's throne. Peterson fondly remembers how his mother told this utterly strange story with "a delicate combination of creative flair and selective reticence" such that the foreign festal rite became as familiar as a county fair. She accomplished this not by introducing "carnival rides and kewpie dolls, cotton candy and the aroma of hot dogs into Iron Age Bethlehem," but simply by sharing the ancient account in way that allowed "me [to become] fully at home in" the story.[34] From this experience, Peterson learned how to read Holy Scripture. We read ourselves into the story trusting that as we become personally involved in the immense world of the Bible, God will form us anew. "I became David," muses Peterson. "I was always David. I'm *still* David."[35]

Yet in the process of his imagination "being revamped to take in this large, immense world of God's revelation," he also became Eugene.[36] "One of the many welcome consequences in learning to 'read' our lives in the lives of Abraham and Sarah, Moses and Miriam, Hannah and Samuel, Ruth and David, Isaiah and Esther, Mary and Martha, Peter and Paul is a sense of affirmation and freedom: we don't have to fit into prefabricated moral and mental or religious boxes before we are admitted into the company of God; we are taken seriously just as we are and given a place in his story."[37]

Extolling Barth, Peterson insists that we attend to the living message of Scripture only by acknowledging that the Bible is qualitatively different from any other text. It is an invitation into "a strange new world." Our admission, Peterson explains, requires the humble acknowledgement that "[e]very expectation that we bring to this book is inadequate or mistaken." It calls for the daring imagination to accept that this text "reveals the sovereign God in being and action."[38]

33. Peterson, *The Pastor,* 29.

34. Ibid., 30.

35. Ibid., 32.

36. Peterson, *Eat This Book,* 67.

37. Ibid., 43.

38. Ibid., 67.

How do we to read the Bible as Holy Scripture? We begin by choosing to submit. We "accept the strangeness of this world," admitting that "it does not fit our preconceptions or tastes." We then acknowledge "the staggering largeness of it."[39] Returning our attention again and again to the purposes of God, we gradually stop "treating" our biblical text anecdotally as 'inspiration' or argumentatively as polemic."[40] We learn how not only to read the Bible but to allow its living message to read us, to disarm, dismantle, and finally to form us.

As we do this, we begin to hone our awareness, to detect minute tremors, slight disturbances, and inaudible sounds. As a student of Barth, Peterson carefully distinguishes between awareness and inner ability. We can no more possess the capacity for attention than a seismograph can possess the power of a quake. And, yet, by the grace and imagination and faith, we can attend to the lived quality of Holy Scripture.

Wanderers between two worlds. Lifting their heads. Pointing toward the sky. Karl Barth and Eugene Peterson need one another. Dogmatics find its completion in spiritual theology. Together, they point us to the presence of the transcendent—a gift at once impossibly immense and intimately personal: the living message of Holy Scripture. One describes what we are to look for. The other suggests how might begin to see.

39. Ibid., 67.
40. Ibid., 46.

It's About God, Stupid

LEADERSHIP AS A THEOLOGICAL PRACTICE

Anthony B. Robinson

"He also said, 'The kingdom of God is as if someone would scatter seed on the ground, and would sleep and rise night and day; and the seed would sprout and grow, he does not know how. The earth produces of itself, first the stalk, then the head, then the full grain in the head. But when the grain is ripe, at once he goes in with his sickle, because the harvest has come.'"

—MARK 4:26–29

BY WHATEVER STANDARD, AN odd story, this parable of Jesus. As agricultural method it seems hardly sufficient. The farmer, if that is the right term, is largely indifferent, often sleeping. As moral counsel it is baffling. What would this suggest one does about anything? Do I wait? Or do I act? And as theology it seems, well, thin. After the initial mention of "the kingdom of God," there is no further mention of God at all. So, it's a pretty typical parable of Jesus. Odd, baffling, hard to categorize, impossible to package as advice. How wonderful!

It is also a parable that catches the paradox, and the difficulty, of leadership as a theological practice. Who's in charge here? Who's on first? Well, not us: "the seed would sprout and grow, he does not know how. The earth produces of itself, first the stalk, then the head, then the full grain in the head." The human role is a limited one, reduced to scattering the seeds. No soil preparation. No fertilizing. No hoeing, weeding, watering, or tending. Still, something is happening. But it is happening without our agency, our activity, our plans, our labor. Whatever is happening is a mystery "he does not know how." Human doing here is, in large measure, not doing. It's what we don't do. But wait, when the grain is ripe, when the harvest has come, now is the time to act. "At once, he goes in with his sickle, because the harvest has come."

As theological practice, as "kingdom of God," leadership is not an either/or. It is not either God doing it all, with no role for human beings, whether as leaders or followers. Nor is it all up to us, our action, our decisiveness, our plans, our resolve. It is a both/and. But there is a sequence. The human being casts—"scatters"—seed. After that, God is active. God is up to something, at work, even if beyond our human understanding or full knowing. "The earth produces of itself." But then the time comes for human response, for human action. And action—our action—is urgent. The harvest cannot wait or be deferred. "At once he goes with his sickle . . ."

Leadership as a theological practice is both. It is waiting and watching, attending to what God is doing and helping others to also attend to what God is doing. It is trusting that God is doing something even when nothing is quite visible or manifest, even when nothing seems to be happening. It is knowing that we are involved with an Other. But the incursion of God, the advent of God, requires a response. There is a place, a crucial one, for human action. Initially, there is casting the seed. Leaders put possibilities in play. They ask worthy questions. Then they wait. But the time comes to move quickly, with a sickle, to harvest. Such is the paradox of leadership as a theological practice. We are not in charge. But we have a role, a quite crucial one. Likewise, leaders, at least those who lead from a theological center or framework, are both attentive and decisive. In an odd way they both do not and do "make it happen." They are both humble and passionate. Leadership is not an easy dance—knowing when to wait and when to move into action.

In 2003 my most popular book, *Transforming Congregational Culture*, came out. It proved a surprise best-seller for its publisher. The book was a "report from the field," on my own efforts and that of congregations I served to turn in a different direction, to do church in ways that while not discontinuous with our past, were nonetheless different enough to rouse both excitement and resistance. I suggested that instead of "assuming the goods" (faith, Christian practice, knowledge of God), we churches and those who lead them need, with the agency of the Holy Spirit, to "deliver the goods" (experience of God, faith practices). In place of "Christian education" and its often formal and didactic connotations, we needed a more full-orbed "Christian formation." Instead of being confident "givers and doers" we need to also be "receivers . . . who give." Other shifts too were part of my report and proposal: "from Board Culture to Ministry Culture," "from Democracy to Discernment," and so on.

Invited to speak here and there, I began after a while to encounter denominations, judicatories, and churches that welcomed me by saying, with some pride and enthusiasm, that they now had a "transformation program" in place. Or they had "twenty churches doing transformation." I wasn't quite sure how to respond. They wanted me, of course, to be positive. I probably was. But I was also, somehow, disquieted, uncomfortable, even alarmed. "Transformation" had been turned into a program, a plan, a method, a project. How could I have expected otherwise? And what was my problem? Could not this be counted success?

Not exactly. These earnest programs and projects of "transformation" forced me to ask what the word itself really meant. I found that what I meant was at odds with what was becoming the next or newest program. The bottom line challenge facing the mainline is not, as many construe it, declining numbers of members. It is that we have somehow contrived to do church without God, or with God reduced to verbal convention or liturgical ornament, not the living God whose word is a sharp, two-edged sword, whose breath is the breath of life. We had perfected "civic faith," which is mostly about our doing, our thinking, our feelings, and our projects. Civic faith wasn't a bad thing. But it wasn't a God thing. Where the parable with which we began clearly indicates that human beings "don't know," we in our modernistic and civic faith mode believed we did "know." In civic faith mode one could do church quite effectively, certainly in a very busy fashion, without God at all. In fact, God might be a hindrance. God, taken halfway seriously, might disturb or disrupt things, or at least slow them down.

While "congregational transformation" as I meant it did certainly have some themes, directions, and implications for the program and organization of congregations, it was largely about getting over the idea that we were in control and letting God be God. It wasn't just about us working harder. It was about us taking ourselves a little less seriously and taking God a whole lot more seriously. That meant taking Scripture, worship, prayer, theology, and church itself more seriously. Transformation did not mean tweaking. It meant something more like death and resurrection.

But somewhere along the way these became odd and difficult, even radical, notions. So thoroughly had churches, particularly but not exclusively of the mainline variety, drunk at the wells of modernity that we thought we were in charge. We imagined transformation was not so much being formed over or anew by the gospel, by grace, and by God as it was the name for a new denominational program or church project. "Good news," said my admirers, "we're doing transformation." "Bad news," I thought, "for transformation is more done to us than by us."

When we announce, "We're doing transformation," note the subject of the verb. It's us—again. What I was after, really, was letting God be the subject of the verb. By the mercies and grace of God we are being (often painfully, often in ways we would not have asked or imagined) transformed. In Paul's most famous use of the term, transformation is not something we do but something done to and for us. "Do not be conformed to this world," he wrote to the church in Rome, "but be transformed by the renewing of your minds, so that you discern what is the will of God—what is good and acceptable and perfect" (Rom 12:2).

This drove me back to Eugene Peterson, who certainly would not have been surprised about the way a good biblical word like "transformation" had become the latest casualty in our relentlessly atheistic way of doing church. Christendom, it turns out, is a hard habit to break. And a good deal of the Christendom outlook or orientation was that we knew what needed to happen. We just needed to get organized and do it. Driven back to Peterson I read again from *Under the Unpredictable Plant,*

> We have climbed to the abandoned places, the bereft lives, the "gaps" that Ezekiel wrote of (22:30), and have spoken Christ's Word and witnessed Christ's Mercy. That is our work, and it is enough. And anything else, no matter how applauded or honored, is not enough. We are there in our congregation to say *God* in a grammar of direct address. We are there for one reason and one reason only: to preach and to pray (the two primary modes of our address). We are there to focus the overflowing, cascading energies of joy, sorrow, delight, or appreciation, if only for a moment but for as long as we are able, on God. We are there to say "God" personally, to say his name clearly, distinctly, unapologetically, in proclamation and in prayers. We are there to say it without hemming and hawing,

without throat clearing and without shuffling, without propagan-
dizing, proselytizing, or manipulating. We have no other task. We
are not needed to add to what is there. We are required only to say
the name: Father, Son, Holy Ghost.[1]

During the Clinton dispensation, when the pithy wisdom was, "It's the
economy, stupid!" Richard Hays would begin his Introduction to the New
Testament classes at Duke Divinity School by writing on the board, "It's
about God, stupid!" If there is any single or core theme that continually
resonates in Peterson's work and his reflections on the vocation of the pastor, this surely is it: "It's about God, stupid!" We have to do with God. But as
Peterson later wrote, "In the secularizing times in which I am living, God is
not taken seriously. God is peripheral. God is nice (or maybe not so nice)
but not at the center."[2] It is the pastor's call to attend to God, to place God at
the center, to place ourselves at the center that is God. "Be transformed . . .
so that you discern the will of God."

One implication of this abiding orientation in Peterson's work has
been particularly helpful to me. It has to do with prayer, the first "angle"
of the three basic angles of pastoral integrity that Peterson explored in his
1987 book, *Working the Angles*. Peterson noted the way in which pastors
"routinely, by virtue of our work and what others think of as our work, are
called upon to pray in ceremonial and decorative ways."[3] I was far enough
into pastoral ministry by then to know whereof he spoke. "Would you start
us with a little prayer, Reverend?" Prayer was, whether we paid it much
heed or not, often the first word. The word to open a meeting, a celebration, to dedicate a home, or inaugurate a President. It was a word to start
things off. This resulted in a lot of what Peterson termed "cut-flower words
[prayers], arranged in little vases for table decorations."[4]

I was helped and reoriented by Peterson's claim that, "The appearances
mislead: prayer is never the first word, it is always the second word. God has
the first word. Prayer is answering speech; it is not primarily 'address' but
'response.' Essential to the practice of prayer is to fully realize this secondary quality."[5] This changed things for me. When praying with parishioners,
in meetings, or in worship, my prayers would begin by not beginning. They

1. Peterson, *Under the Unpredictable Plant*, 86–87.
2. Peterson, *The Pastor*, 142.
3. Peterson, *Working the Angles*, 31.
4. Ibid.
5. Ibid., 32.

began with silence, with waiting. With my attempt to attend to what God had already said or was saying, how God was already present, what God had already done or was doing. My prayers were no longer the beginning or first word. They were words prayed in response. As a consequence they were both more prayerful and more real.

You will notice perhaps how this takes us back to the parable with which I began, from Mark's Gospel and to what I have called the paradox of leadership as a theological practice. It is a matter of paying attention to God, to what God is doing, even when we so little understand how exactly it happens: "the seed would sprout and grow, he knows not how." But it's also a matter of casting seed out there, in faith. And it's a matter of acting decisively when the time is right, heading out to harvest, wielding the sickle. This has been my struggle and challenge as a leader, as one who seeks to practice leadership theologically. First, you gather seeds and scatter them. Then you pay attention to God, to trust that God is at work. You listen in silence and wait in wonder. Then in time you act, you move, even boldly and decisively, when the time is right.

This, I might add, is not just an intellectual struggle. It is a practical one. Long before I was encountering judicatories and churches with their "transformation program" in place, I had to face my own bent toward turning ministry into a program and church into a plan.

It happened this way. I was five years into ministry. Five years is apparently a predictably messy time in the life of many clergy, a point at which a fair number decide, "This isn't for me." I came close. I was one year into my second call. I had enjoyed sufficient "success" at my first post-seminary call that judicatory heads and churches came looking for me. I didn't have to look for them. So I left my first call too soon, after four years, four good and growing years. I went to a troubled church, confident that I was the one to return it to its former greatness and glory (and larger size). After all, the Conference Minister (our bishop equivalent) had told me precisely that. "You are what they need. This is a great church. It will bounce back in no time under your leadership."

But this church wasn't like a slightly deflated ball that only needed a little pumping up. It was in far worse shape. It was more like a crushed can at the side of the road. Soon after arriving, I discovered the congregation was split along multiple fault lines of class, ideology, theology, and mutual antagonism. I learned that my predecessor's ministry had ended when she took her own life, a fact neither known in nor processed by the

congregation. I found the facility was in bad disrepair, largely rented out
to make ends meet. And I found that one significant faction was unified
largely by its "avant-garde, anti-church, anti-Christian ethos." There were
about two dozen homeless people, all with some form of mental illness,
living on the grounds of the church.

At age thirty-one, with four years of ministry under my belt, it was too
much for me. After one year I was under water. Oh, to the onlookers I was
at least treading water, if not swimming bravely. But I knew I was under
the waves. Drowning. The medical diagnosis was "clinical depression." The
theological one was "a dark night of the soul." It was a strange, perplexing
and hard time. For a long time, I had no idea what was going on and why
I felt dead inside. Step by slow step I found some companions, some help.
Some of the help was more helpful than others. None offered instant relief
or a quick cure.

One step that proved more helpful than some was when I began
making occasional retreats at a "Spiritual Life Center," run on the Ignatian
model. I learned to pray Scripture, which was new to me. I was used to
studying it, exegeting it, turning it into sermons, but not praying it. On the
first day of my first retreat, Sister Katherine gave me Isaiah 43:1–3. As I
staggered off to my room, she called out, "Where it says 'Jacob' and 'Israel,'
you might insert you own name." I did. I prayed, "But now thus says the
Lord, he who created you, O Tony, he who formed you, O Robinson: Do
not fear, for I have redeemed you; I have called you by name, you are mine.
When you pass through the waters, I will be with you; and through the rivers, they shall not overwhelm you." I prayed it over and over. It was a balm
for my sin-sick soul.

On Day Two, Sister Katherine assigned a different passage, John
15:1–8, "Vine and branches." Honestly, I had never much liked this one.
Seemed a little too sweet, too much like a Hallmark Card. "I am the Vine,
you are the branches, tra-la, tra-la." Imagine my surprise, when as I prayed
the passage I heard a voice, a blunt, abrasive voice say, "I AM THE VINE,
YOU ARE A BRANCH, WHAT PART OF THIS DON'T YOU GET?"

"Is that you, Jesus?" I prayed. "What happened to meek and mild?
You're sounding kind of mean and a little wild." "I AM THE VINE,
YOU ARE THE BRANCHES. THOSE WHO ABIDE IN ME AND I IN
THEM BEAR MUCH FRUIT . . . WHOEVER DOES NOT ABIDE IN
ME IS THROWN AWAY LIKE A BRANCH AND WITHERS . . . SUCH

BRANCHES ARE GATHERED AND THROWN INTO THE FIRE, AND BURNED."

Withered was how I felt, without a doubt. Fit for the fire. So much for a Hallmark moment; it was more like a John the Baptist encounter. But this unanticipated encounter with a text I didn't much like was, though no instant cure, the beginning. It was a time when I began to get not theoretically, but quite existentially, that ministry wasn't all about me, my agenda, my strengths, my gifts, my skills, and my resolve. There was a place for all that. But not a lead place. Not a primary place. I needed to be a branch, to let Jesus be the vine in my current tough, confusing, and burned-over vineyard. In fact, it wasn't my vineyard. It was his. I needed to attend to what God was doing. I needed to let God be God for me, too.

I returned to that ecclesial vineyard with my head just a bit above water, with my eyes a little more open to what God was doing, to the idea that whatever it was that was happening or going to happen wasn't all up to me. It was God's doing. God's timetable. God's agenda. I had scattered some seeds, asked some questions, opened God's word anew. Now to wait, to watch, to attend.

As if this weren't enough, there was a larger meaning to my own struggle, my own dark night. I realized that in some sense I was living in my own life the drama and narrative of the congregation itself. On one hand, I was bound and determined to keep on as before, as if nothing had happened, onward toward ministerial success. They, for their part were determined to be "cutting edge," and "a leading church," one that took on the world's most vexing challenges even though unable to know or sort its own identity and reality. This was the mainline of that time, the '80s. We were on the ropes, but clueless. We would end the threat of nuclear war and achieve ambitious new membership goals all within five years. We would end homelessness and accomplish "church growth" in a decade. We only needed more resolove, more resolutions, more work, new and better leaders.

What had not occurred to us was that what we most needed was not more us but more God. We were not yet, by a long shot, ready for harvest. We were just into the seed casting stage, which would be followed by long seasons of waiting and watching for sprouting here and there, now and then, not knowing how it happened or even quite what "growth" was.

So, ten years later, reporting on *Transforming Congregational Culture* I encountered those who thought this only another program or project for us to do, I wasn't entirely surprised. I had been there. And often enough, still was there. Leadership as a theological practice is not an either/or; it is a both/and. There's a role for us, for human action, even initiative. But not perhaps nearly so large a role as we had thought. To lead theologically is, as Peterson put it, "To say 'God' personally, to say his name clearly, distinctly, uapologetically, in proclamations and in prayers. We are to say it without hemming and hawing, without throat clearing and without shuffling. . . . We have no other task." God drove me, as God has driven us, into a dark night of the soul that we might learn more clearly, more deeply who God is, and who, by the grace of God, we are. We are still learning. God is teaching us, again, that ours is the second word, that ours is answering speech. "The first word is God's word. Prayer is a human word and is never the first word, never the primary word, never the initiating and shaping word simply because we are never first, never primary."[6]

Peterson was a help and a companion in the midst of this. A sometimes comforting, sometimes abrasive counselor. But I was also, and at the same time, thinking about "leadership." Oddly, "leadership," like "God," had often been overlooked or dismissed in my part of Christendom. "Leadership" was even a bad, suspect word. It sounded, somehow, authoritarian. We preferred other words, words like "facilitator," or "enabler," or "companion." I wasn't so sure about this suspicion of leadership. I intuited that leaders are important. Even as I was driven by my dark night deeper into prayer and Scripture and God, I was simultaneously pondering and studying a whole new literature on "leadership."

Some of this was prompted by the vocation of my spouse, who became a school principal. In that world, at that time, one thing was clear: the principal was to be an educational and building leader. Her or his presence was not merely important, but decisive. Could the same be true in the church? I thought so. I observed it to be true. I also observed what happened in churches when leaders failed to lead, when they failed to "show up." How to hold these two—attending to God and effectively leading—together, seemed a challenge. Could it be done? Should it?

On those rare occasions when Peterson mentioned "leadership" it was with a slightly disparaging tone and a note of scorn. He tends to see "leaders" and "leadership" as they are defined by the wider culture, as (his words), people "who get things done," and "make things happen." In this respect, we have imbibed leadership models "that seep into our awareness from the culture—politicians, businessmen, advertisers, publicists, celebrities, and

6. Ibid., 33.

athletes. But while being a pastor certainly has some of these components, the pervasive element in our two-thousand-year pastoral tradition is not someone who 'gets things done,' but rather the person placed in the community to pay attention and call attention to 'what is going on right now' between men and women, with one another and with God."[7] But can we do both?

While I concur with Peterson's emphasis on "paying attention to God," I also want to put in a good word—a better word than I think Peterson is himself willing to do—for the importance of leadership and leaders, particularly at this juncture in the church's life. Peterson can help us to think about and enact leadership as a theological practice, a God-centered endeavor and not merely another iteration or expression of human drive and initiative. I want to push back on Peterson's overly simple consignment of "leadership" to the worldly realm, to the realm of a bastard "can-do" culture. Leadership is not that simple. It is more nuanced and complex.

In particular, I note the work of Ronald Heifetz and his seminal distinction between "technical problems" and "adaptive challenges." When dealing with the former, says Heifetz, we deal with a problem that is clear and known. We apply existing technique. Moreover, it is experts and authorities who do the work. This is a familiar sequence, one that has its place and value. The problem comes when every issue is construed as a technical problem, amenable to a problem/solution framework. When this happens, a minister is assigned the role of expert, who is to come up with the right technique to solve or fix our problem. So our problem is named "membership decline." The solution is "church growth techniques." The good minister/leader is an expert or authority on such techniques. She applies those and our problem is solved. No fuss, no muss.

But Heifetz introduces the notion of the "technical problem" largely to dismiss it or at least to argue that this is not the province or work of leaders. Leaders deal in the more complex and fraught realm of "adaptive challenges." Here the problem or challenge is not even something we are capable of understanding or describing, at least initially. We don't know what we're up against. We don't understand what God is doing and we probably don't like it. Call it "Wilderness" or "Exile," or "Crucifixion," it entails confusion and lostness. It requires learning and change. It means loss and grief, for the world is not as we thought it to be or wished it to be. Moreover, when facing

7. Peterson, *The Pastor*, 5.

"adaptive challenges," there are no easy answers (The title of Heifetz's first book, his masterwork, is *Leadership Without Easy Answers*).

If naming and describing the challenge before us requires time, learning, grief, and change, discovering fitting responses is also not simple. It too requires learning and change, the kind of learning and change—transformation—God's people experienced in the Sinai wilderness, in the Babylonian exile, and in the liminal time of Crucifixion/Resurrection/Pentecost. And perhaps most significantly, it is not experts or authorities who do the work for us when we are dealing with an "adaptive challenge." It is the people who face the challenge who must engage the work. The leader's role is to walk with the people, as did Moses and as did the Risen Jesus, to inspire people to engage the work themselves, and to give the work back to the people at a rate they can stand. For many, Heifetz's framing of leadership as helping people to identify and engage adaptive work has proven enormously helpful. Moreover, what he describes as "adaptive work," I would call "spiritual work," for it entails the dynamics of confusion/loss, deeper self-awareness and risk, growth and change in hearts and minds. This is a dying and being raised to new life. Leaders, so construed, are not simply experts who "make things happen" or "get things done," in Peterson's somewhat dismissive terms. True leaders do something deeper, richer, and far more complex. So, as grateful as I am for Peterson's many calls to ministers to attend to God and God's word, I also believe leadership to be important, and I find at least some of the contemporary literature and theory about leadership to be helpful for clergy and churches to take seriously.

The task is leadership as a theological practice. This is a paradoxical task, involving both our watchful attentiveness and our decisive action. Leaders do, like the person in Mark's parable, scatter seed. They ask worthy, hard questions. They cast the seeds of possibility. They also know that the miracle of growth is not theirs to effect. It is of God. "[T]he seed would sprout and grow, he does not know how." Such leaders are humble. But they are also passionate. They know when to wait. And they know when to act. They know when the moment has come and the time is at hand. "He goes in with his sickle, because the harvest has come."

PART TWO

institutions

All Who Follow Jesus?

THE TROUBLE WITH PETERSON
AND THE WIDER CHURCH

Tee Gatewood

The Church is not a building,
The Church is not a steeple,
The Church is not a resting place,
The Church is the People.

I am the Church,
You are the Church,
We are the Church together,
All who follow Jesus,
All around the world,
Yes, We are the Church together.

—RICHARD K. AVERY

I GREW UP SINGING this song. Week after week we repeated it as the prelude for the children's sermon. In the repetition I learned a simple but deep ecclesiology: the church is the community of people who follow Jesus.

More than any other pastor or theologian, Eugene Peterson has helped me grasp the truth of this song and its implied ecclesiology. Peterson makes it clear that the church is a people called together by God to follow Jesus in a specific time and place. He is also clear that pastors are called to do personal, relational, and local work among the people. Pastors are "the people who share the majestic reality of God within the immediate significance of each personal and local detail in the story of redemption."[1] This definition has guided me in my pastoral work as I try to hold together the vast story of grace with the mundane details of life on the ground in the here and now.

Peterson has helped me believe and sing and live out the line "I am the church, you are the Church, we are the church together." What isn't clear to me as I read Peterson is how pastors relate to the line, *"All who follow Jesus all around the world."* As a result, it isn't clear how Peterson would lead pastors into the reality that "Yes, We are the church together."

This leaves me asking these questions: How do pastors love and relate to and work with the followers of Jesus around the world? How for Peterson do pastors share the majestic reality of God within the less immediate yet still personal details of a presbytery or even within a local community where Baptists, Pentecostals, non-denominational and mainline churches share a common life?

In *Five Smooth Stones, Working the Angles,* and *Under the Unpredictable Plant* Peterson provides foundational resources for answering these questions. Most importantly he identifies and describes a pastoral identity that is shaped by the call of the Lord. After tracing the outlines of this pastoral identity I want to look at possible reasons that Peterson doesn't address the wider catholic context of the pastoral call. Finally, I want to suggest a few ways of moving from the local church to the universal church that continue to be personal, relational, and faithful.

The Pastoral Calling

Five Smooth Stones for Pastoral Work, Working the Angles, and *Under the Unpredictable Plant* form a trilogy of sorts. They are written to subvert, to restore, to challenge, and to inspire pastors who work in a context that is antithetical to the gospel. The trilogy can provide a starting point and a practical foundation for pastoral work in this troubling time.

1. Peterson, *Five Smooth Stones for Pastoral Work*, 2.

I have come to this conclusion by reading and thinking about these three books backwards. I start with *Under the Unpredictable Plant.* Peterson's reflections on the pastoral vocation focus on just that, the call of God that is the starting point for faithful ministry. The triune God calls and pastors are called into being. This call initiates the pastoral life where pastoral work follows in God's train. Recognizing this lets pastors rest in the truth that God has been out in front of us, is on the move before us, and is in all things anticipating our participation in his work. Because the Lord speaks, there is a life to be had for pastors in the revolutionary gospel work of announcing and practicing the kingdom of the Lord.

Peterson develops his notion of calling in response to the story of Jonah and in reaction to ministerial careerism. The risk to be avoided is developing a religious career that we can take charge of and manage.[2] Because of personal sinfulness and our ecclesial context this is a real risk. Pastors are praised when they are effective and efficient, sharp and ambitious. They are rewarded for success with bigger churches and bigger budgets, both institutionally and personally. In this way of life we can use the call of God to avoid the presence of God. We hear the call to go, but like Jonah we can choose the destination and means of getting there. Here the risk is that in hearing the call of God, we are tempted to be like God. We are tempted to start our own ministry under our own power with our own goals.[3]

To avoid this temptation Peterson uses the story of Jonah to "pull [pastors] into the dry dock and scrape off the ponderous false dignity, the fantasy-bloated ambitions."[4] After scraping off professionalized obedience and program directing, Peterson is left with the living, calling, using-us-in-grace Lord. What is left for the pastor is a "recovered vocation." Peterson writes, "What pastors do, or at least are called to do, is

> really quite simple. We say the word God accurately, so that congregations of Christians can stay in touch with the basic realities of their existence, so they know what is going on. And we say the Name personally, alongside our parishioners in the actual circumstances of their lives, so they will recognize and respond to the God who is both on our side and at our side when it doesn't seem like it and we don't feel like it.[5]

2. Peterson, *Under the Unpredictable Plant,* 4.

3. Ibid., 12.

4. Ibid., 11.

5. Ibid., 172.

This clarifies that pastors are conversation partners who need to speak clearly and faithfully. This speaking occurs within a conversation where the Lord speaks and pastors respond. This calling and responding happens in the lived reality of a local community gathered in worship and scattered afterwards to respond to the speaking God of grace. Pastors are being pastors as they overhear the conversation of the triune God, respond in worship, and help people repeat that response in the details of their lives.

Near the end of *Under the Unpredictable Plant*, Peterson suggests that faithfulness to God's calling results in a paradigm shift away from program directing to spiritual directing. He explains that it is the imagination that must shift so that the interior of our lives can take a specific form. This form has a specific angle and corresponding space so that we can deal with the vast expanse of God working in people's located and limited lives.

Peterson develops this form or framework in *Working the Angles*. The middle book in the pastoral trilogy is about this interior shift to prayer, Scripture, and spiritual direction. These three ways of responding to God are so basic, according to Peterson, "That they determine the shape of everything else. . . . Besides being basic, these three acts are quiet. They do not call attention to themselves and so are often not attended to."[6] Peterson imagines a basic shift in the heart of the pastor out of which will flow a new way of listening to God and the other.

One by one Peterson attends to the disciplines of prayer, reading, and relating. At each point Peterson is about the way we practice our calling. Prayer is the starting point. It is what pastors do in relationship to the talkative God of the Bible. Not just what we do, but the *first* thing we *must* do. Peterson explains, "Anything creative, anything powerful, anything *biblical*, insofar as we are participants in it, originates in prayer."[7] In his encouragement to pray, Peterson is both humorous and helpful. The humor comes in the form of irony as he diagnoses the common understanding of pastoral prayer as getting things started by saying little prayers. In contrast to this way of using prayer to frame the real work of secular life, Peterson describes prayer as the big work. Prayer is answering the God who always has the first word. This work is big because sinful people are so good at putting ourselves, our needs, and our work, first. To avoid this, Peterson calls pastors to restore prayer to its context in the conversation where God is always the first speaker. The previous word of God, spoken in Christ and

6. Peterson, *Working the Angles*, 3.

7. Ibid., 40.

in Scripture, is what we must listen for and respond to with our people if we are going to be pastors who have a common life shaped by God's call.

Peterson is ruthlessly honest about the temptations of the pastoral life. When he turns his attention from prayer to Scripture, Peterson immediately identifies and describes an ubiquitous temptation: "In reading, teaching, and preaching Scriptures it happens: we cease to listen to the Scriptures in the first place."[8] Once again, Peterson centers the pastoral life in the act of listening, not on technique or skill, passing on information or insight. It is about listening. Reading is not listening. Studying is not listening. What is missing in reading and studying is the talkative other, the triune God on whom the pastor depends and at whose mercy she lives.

If pastors are praying and listening to Scripture, then Peterson suggests they will approach their people with a different kind of attentiveness. This attentiveness allows the pastor to be a spiritual director who notices the small, perseveres in the commonplace, and appreciates the obscure. Peterson explains that "Being a spiritual director means noticing the familiar, naming the particular."[9] This kind of noticing can happen only when we have listened to God and Scripture and have learned the deep truths of sin, grace, atonement, and judgment. This is not mere knowing in the abstract. Instead, Peterson is calling pastors to know these truths in the details of the particular, in the weeds of life, where the task is to name sin, grace, and faith with love. Here the pastor becomes the helpmate of sorts that we were all created and called to be. The pastor names, like Adam, the things in the world that must be known and appreciated if we are to live before and with God as the image of God.

Peterson describes a transition of attention within a pastoral call from the self to the people with whom God calls pastors to worship and serve. This attentiveness to the other in response to the call also leads to the pastoral works described in *Five Smooth Stones*. In his discussion of the works of counsel, guidance, comfort, prayer, administration, and community building, Peterson's goal doesn't change, neither does his method for reaching that goal. His goal is to build a solid foundation for pastoral work that can connect the work pastors do between Sundays to the life they share with the congregation before God on Sundays. The method for doing this is to listen to the antecedent word spoken by God that pastors can hear and with which they can live and work.

8. Ibid., 87.
9. Ibid., 157.

As pastors listen to the Songs of Songs, Ruth, Lamentations, Ecclesiastes, and Esther with Peterson, they can begin to take seriously the act and word of God. Again, it is the first word of God that calls them to the work of directing prayers, making stories, sharing pain, saying no, and building community. At each turn, the task is to hear and know and speak the word of God while naming the response of faith. This naming and noting happens as we listen to Scripture and speak in the dialect of the local, the specific, and the personal. Pastors have a task and a hope because the God they serve is loquacious: God speaks to create and to call, to save and send, to make and remake pastors and all of us.

Clarifying the Call

Pastors become pastors, within Peterson's framework, because God calls. God calls, individuals and communities discern, and then affirm it in ordination. The definition of a pastor given within Peterson's own Presbyterian tradition is of ordination to a ministry of word and sacrament.[10] Pastors are ordained by the Presbytery and receive a call to specific congregation where they speak the word of God and enact the sacraments. This distinction between local congregation and presbytery places a pastor in a congregation that is a part of the wider denomination that is a part of the universal church.

The distinction between congregation and the wider church is assumed in the ordination vows of this tradition. These vows describe an obedience to Jesus Christ, under the authority of Scripture, guided by the confessions, governed by the church's polity, within a collegial ministry. After vowing to live within this structure, pastors promise to further the peace, unity, and purity of the church and to serve the people with energy, intelligence, imagination, and love. The call is to be a faithful minister, proclaiming the good news, teaching the faith, and caring for the people, as well as serving in the governing bodies of the church.

These vows assert that pastors are called to serve the church as a local people. Peterson's pastoral identity takes us a long way towards faithfulness to this call. These vows also recognize that the Lord calls pastors to serve the one holy, universal, or catholic church. There is one body and one Spirit just as there is one call to one hope, one Lord, one faith, one baptism, one God and Father of all (Eph 4:4–7). Peterson's pastoral identity

10. Ibid., 22.

does not explicitly lead pastors to faithfulness in this aspect of their calling. Peterson fails to clarify that Christ calls pastors to serve his people, and that while this begins with the local it must continue into the wider body of the church.

The writers of *In One Body Through the Cross* clarify this call with precision and brevity: "this Christian vocation to community has been realized not only in local gatherings, but in awareness of a deep, if less visible bond with saints in other regions (2 Corinthians 8–9), with a family of communities throughout the known world or *oikoumene*." They continue and explain that "visible Christian unity is thus not a modern dream, but a permanent and central aspect of Christian life. . . . It continues to call us beyond differences of theology and worship that have developed over centuries, to a deeper unity of common prayer, common witness, shared conviction, and mutual acceptance."[11] Pastors who are called to serve the body of Christ commit themselves to a vocation where true unity isn't an option but is the will of the one who prays "that all of them may be one, Father, just as you are in me and I am in you" (John 17:21).

Missing the Call

Why doesn't Peterson's vision of the pastor echo his own vows to serve the wider church? Why doesn't he help us respond to the call of Christ to uphold a visible unity between local congregations within the universal church? There are at least two potential reasons. First, Peterson is a strident critic of the gnostic temptation within the Christian tradition. He writes that "Gnosticism is the ancient but persistently contemporary perversion of the gospel that is contemptuous of place and matter. It holds forth that salvation consists in having the right ideas and the fancier the better. It is impatient with restrictions of place and time and embarrassed by the garbage and disorder of everyday life."[12] Peterson's pastoral theology, from beginning to end, is about the garbage of everyday life and the way pastors are called to bring Christ into the local and specific. As a reader of Wendell Berry, Peterson affirms and assumes the insight "that the more *local* life is, the more intense, more colorful, more rich it is, because it has limits."[13]

---

11. Braaten and Jenson, eds., *In One Body Through the Cross*, 12.

12. Peterson, *Under the Unpredictable Plant*, 130.

13. Ibid., 137.

While I want to affirm this insight and live it out among a people, the affirmation of the local cannot be made in separation from the catholic character of the church. The local community is the body of Christ and is but a member of the body of Christ; we must distinguish these two things while not separating them from each other. Reacting against gnostic temptations should prevent us from accepting vague notions of a universal brotherhood of believers, but should not prevent us from recognizing the catholic character of Christ's body. Instead, the movement of the Spirit within the limits of our time and place must lead us back in history as well as out into the wider fellowship of Christ's people.

The second reason Peterson might not address the catholic character of the pastoral life is his personal experience of that catholicity. One of Peterson's best stories told and retold through his corpus details the prevalence and depth of institutional sin.[14] Peterson was required to prepare a monthly report of his church plant for a denominational review. The report included statistics and narrative descriptions of life in the congregation as well as reflections on his pastoral ministry. When Peterson got the impression that his superiors were not reading beyond the numbers, he began to narrate a slide into depression, an inability to pray, a drinking problem, and an affair. After not receiving any feedback Peterson reported "innovating" with the liturgy and made requests for advice. Month after month Peterson sent in the creative dramas. Month after month no one replied. Finally, when the day of reckoning came Peterson confronted the denominational board that was charged with reading and responding to these reports. Excuses were made, the buck was passed.

One wonders if Peterson's belief in the catholicity of the church passed as well. He writes, "the laughter and fun of those days [of writing fictitious reports], though, was cover for a deep disappointment: I had discovered that spiritually and vocationally I was on my own. The people who ordained me and took responsibility for my work were interested in financial reports, attendance graphs, program planning. But they were not interested in *me*. They were interested in my job: they cared little for my vocation."[15] Because we are failed by our institutions, our denominations and our colleagues in ministry we do often experience the wider church as a disappointment. However, the sense of being left on your own does not warrant describing the pastoral life as if it should be lived on your own. Pastors are not called

14. Ibid., 77–80.
15. Ibid., 80.

out to be left alone in a congregation with a few mentors on the shelf and a spiritual director in the wings.

Called to Serve the Body, the Temple, and the People

In the rest of this essay I want to make a few brief suggestions about hearing the call of Christ and living as a pastor with a catholic identity. To develop this I want to think briefly about the church as the body of Christ, the Temple of the Spirit, and the people of God.

As we begin to think about the body of Christ, I want to go back to a basic commitment that Peterson expresses with conviction and clarity. In *Under the Unpredictable Plant*, Peterson calls pastors to a life of stability. He explains that

> American pastors, without really noticing what was happening, got our vocations redefined in the terms of American careerism. We quit thinking of the parish as a location for pastoral spiritual- ity and started thinking of it as an opportunity for advancement. . . . The moment we did that, we started thinking wrongly, for the vocation of a pastor has to do with living out the implications of the word of God in community, not sailing off into the exotic seas of religion in search of fame and fortune.[16]

Many suggest that it is necessary for faithful pastors to set sail and lead "their" congregation to calmer seas, to places where the kingdom of Christ can be more easily advanced. The temptation is to seek a place where the conditions are more apt to lead to growth instead of staying in a place of decline and death. The siren call, in my tradition, is to change your church's denominational affiliation and discover a place where faithfulness is more convenient.

For Peterson, the pastoral life is a refusal of any view that makes God and kingdom work dependent on human skill or external conditions. Tak- ing a call at a different church or changing denominational affiliation can suggest that external factors are determining our faithfulness and God's ability to work. Learning from Peterson we need to resist this false assump- tion and flawed journey. We need to be committed to the body of Christ as we receive it from the Lord.

---

16. Peterson, *Under the Unpredictable Plant*, 20.

Ephraim Radner in *The End of the Church* and R. R. Reno in *In the Ruins of the Church* make this same argument and call pastors to a life of stability. As much as I would rather seek more convenient places to serve, both call pastors to endure a broken form of life in the body. Reno writes,

> To see the church in ruins has not led me to despair, and it certainly has not led me to curse God for failing to provide me with a triumphant and splendid church in which to dwell. These reflections, then, seek to bring you to see the spiritual imperative of redemptive suffering that is, I think, the only proper response to the ruination of the church. . . . There is no hope in detachment or separation, whether in the form of critical judgment, hesitant loyalty, individualistic faith, theological abstraction, or self-protective spiritual illusions.[17]

We must be clear that it is the crucified and risen Jesus who calls us to serve his body. This means that we must live close to the broken people for whom he suffered. Like the suffering servant, we must love his sinful bride and resist the temptation to judge and withdraw.

Graciously, Christ does not call us into this life within the body as lone ranger pastors. We don't work in corn fields or on a mountainside by ourselves. There are others that Christ has called as pastors within the body. This is a blessing because pastors need fellowship and accountability, encouragement, and inspiration. This is given to us within the body and yet we can only receive this as we move out from our local congregations to form relationships with other pastors who have received this call. This must mean moving out into our denominations and even across denominational lines to form relationships that can sustain us where we serve the body of Christ.

If we continue to focus on the nature of the church as described in the New Testament, then we might also come to a deeper understanding of the church as an eschatological community. This means that the church is the people of God, called to anticipate the coming kingdom of their risen Lord. We are a people united to a savior whose kingdom is now and not yet. A decisive part of that not yet is the gift of unity that will come through the Spirit. There will be one and only one community of the Lamb around the throne of God. There will only be one bride of Christ at the heavenly banquet. There will be one temple of God filled with the Spirit proclaiming praise to the risen King and the God who is over all and in all.

17. Reno, *In the Ruins of the Church*, 15.

If we glimpse this vision of God's future, then we are called to live into that reality in the present. Robert Jenson suggests that this should have definite consequences for the way we do theology.

> The church must regard waiting as the most creative of activities, since she apprehends fullness of being only in the coming Kingdom. And God may act tomorrow. In the meantime, it is a great blessing specifically to theology that we need not wait for the church to be undivided to do theology for and even of the undivided church. For theology is itself a form of the waiting we must practice.[18]

For Jenson the implication of this kind of eschatological waiting is that we must resist doing "Lutheran" or "Reformed" theology for only a part of God's people.

In the same way, we must resist doing merely local pastoral theology. Pastors are called to love the people where they are in the mundane details of their life. At the same time, we are called to love them with the love that is of the coming kingdom. If we do so, pastors will love the local people of their church as part of a universal church and will also love the universal church. The coming Lord calls each pastor to know and love and bless the communion of saints.

Practically this must include serving with other congregations, serving other congregations through denominational structures, and giving up oneself to groups and individuals beyond the boundaries of the local church. This service to the church that will be one can happen through institutional structures or renewal communities or simply within the local community.

Regardless of how it happens, pastors are called to serve the church that is coming into its future unity through the work of the Spirit.

The church is the body of Christ. It is the temple of the Spirit. It is also the people of God. The people are those united to Christ gathered by the Spirit who pray to the God and Father of the risen Lord. Within the New Testament, the phrase "people of God" means several different things. It refers to the people of Israel as a nation as well as the eschatological people who will enter their Sabbath rest. It can also refer to the people gathered by the Spirit from among the Jews and Gentiles. Taken in this sense the people of God are those gathered from every nation and tribe and tongue who will one day worship in the new Jerusalem. Those who will be one are now

18. Jenson, *Systematic Theology, Volume I,* viii.

scattered across the globe. These people spread around the world constitute the whole church that pastors are called to serve.

The implication of this broad ecumenical vision is that pastors are called to love and serve and care for people as they meet us across racial and cultural barriers. Churches remain divided by racial and class divisions that are undercut by the gospel and overcome by the power of the Spirit. To be a pastor exclusively to a local congregation of people who are of the same race or class or place risks minimizing the gospel and tailoring it to our culture and its needs.

In response to this risk we must first notice that the church is a missionary community whose mission expands across cultural lines and national borders. Baptism makes and marks the community as a people brought in through repentance and sent out with a mission. The narrative of Acts describes how radical this call was, for both Jew and Gentile, as well as their leaders, the apostles and elders. The call was radical and it still is today. As pastors recognize this, they can lead the people in a common mission that requires creativity and diligence, two things Peterson helps us value and develop. Mission organizations that facilitate and help maintain these kinds of universal connections can help as pastors, churches, and communities, grow into their identity as the one people of God.

Last Call

In the Introduction to *Five Smooth Stones for Pastoral Work*, Peterson asks this question: "Is there a biblical foundation providing solid, authoritative underpinning for what I am doing so that my daily work is congruent with the ancient ministries of prophet, priest and wise man to which I am heir?"[19] After reading Peterson and recognizing the centrality of God's call and the form life to which the call leads, we can answer in the affirmative. There is within the Bible a witness to the living, talkative God who can make our interior life and life among the people congruent with the work of the prophets, priests, and pastors who have served the local and the universal church with faith and humility.

---

19. Peterson, *Five Smooth Stones*, 4.

Eugene Peterson

AMERICAN PASTOR

William H. Willimon

I hear it was charged against me that I sought to destroy institutions;
But really I am neither for nor against institutions;
(What indeed have I in common with them?—Or what with the
    destruction of them?)
Only I will establish ...
in the fields and woods ...   5
Without edifices, or rules, or trustees, or any argument,
The institution of the dear love of comrades.

—WALT WHITMAN, *LEAVES OF GRASS*, 1900

North American culture does not offer congenial conditions in which to live
vocationally as a pastors.... Pastors in America today find that they have
entered into a way of life that is in ruins. The vocation of pastor has been
replaced by the strategies of religious entrepreneurs with business plans.... I
love being an American.... But I don't love "the American way." ... I don't love
the rampant consumerism that treats God as a product to be marketed. I don't
love the dehumanizing ways that turn men, women, and children into impersonal roles and causes and statistics.... I wanted my life, both my personal
and working life, to be shaped by God and the scriptures and prayer.

—EUGENE PETERSON, *THE PASTOR*, 2011

ONCE AGAIN I ASSIGNED *Working the Angles* to my course, "Introduction to the Theology and Practice of Ordained Leadership." Once again the class dubbed Eugene Peterson the course's most helpful writer on ministry, easily eclipsing my two books that they also read. I treasure that Peterson once blurbed me as "the most interesting writer on preaching today." I now trump the compliment: Eugene Peterson is our best writer on ministry.

Peterson's is a wonderfully nitty-gritty view of church and ministry. Pastors dearly love his candid, realistic portrayals of North American church life and recognize themselves in his accounts of his work as founder and then as pastor for three decades at Christ Our King Presbyterian. Although he was a church-planter before we coined the word, early on he saw the dangers of church expansion mimicking the consumer-driven practices of the secular world. In his later writing, two terms are used with equal vitriol: consumerism and church growth.

In nearly all of his books, Peterson advocates a theologically authorized church that is free from the world's allures, a church that unashamedly stands and delivers its gospel without snazzy mass media tricks or church growth quick tips, a church untethered to the world's standards of success. He advocates and embodies a ministry that is local, personal, prayerful, and eloquent.

Through a succession of books, Peterson displays a warm, positive, generous spirit toward the church and its leaders—with one notable exception—his scorn for the institutional framework for ministry.

Peterson versus Institutions

For Peterson, the institutional church doesn't extend far beyond the local congregation. "The visible lines of pastoral work are preaching, teaching, and administration."[1] While eloquently commending preaching and teaching, he barely mentions the ministry of administration. He delights in depicting his entrance into Presbyterianism as haphazard luck,[2] a quirk of someone's having tapped him to be the basketball coach at Madison Avenue Presbyterian Church. "I gradually became accustomed to what, previous to seminary, had been a church word I could not have defined. I was

---

1. Peterson, *Working the Angles,* 3.
2. Peterson, *The Pastor,* 86.

welcomed. I was affirmed; I almost felt like a Presbyterian. Then I made it official. I became a Presbyterian."[3]

As a young pastor he was disillusioned that "The people who ordained me and took responsibility for my work were interested in financial reports, attendance graphs, program planning. But they were not interested in *me*. They were interested in my job: they cared little for my vocation."[4] Peterson aspired to the sort of ministry "that can't be measured or counted, and often isn't even noticed."[5] Above all sins, he fears being "a bureaucrat in the time-management business for God."[6]

will choose agenda,

He scorns the way we pastors have allowed leadership models to

> seep into our awareness from the culture—politicians, business-men, advertisers, publicists, celebrities, and athletes. But while being a pastor certainly has some of these components, the per-vasive element in our two-thousand year old pastoral tradition is not someone who "gets things done," but rather the person placed in the community to pay attention and call attention to "what is going on right now" between men and women, with one another and with God.[7]

He is more a poet than a professional. His description of the founding a growth of Christ Our King Presbyterian makes the new congregation sound like an inexplicable miracle. Of course, the birth of any congregation is necessarily miraculous, but aren't we correct in presupposing that Peterson's exceptional (and professional) competence, prudence, and brilliance also help explain the birth of this church?

"American pastors, without really noticing what was happening, got our vocations redefined in the terms of American careerism. We quit thinking of the parish as a location for pastoral spirituality and started thinking of it as an opportunity for advancement. . . . The moment we did that, we started thinking wrongly, for the vocation of a pastor has to do with living out the implications of the word of God in community, not sailing off into

---

3. Ibid., 91.

4. Peterson, *Under the Unpredictable Plant*, 80.

5. Peterson, *The Pastor*, 5.

6. Ibid., 8.

7. Ibid., 5. I'd like to know how Peterson's reading of church history has revealed to him that pastors have historically had little interest in "getting things done." John Wesley? Gregory the Great? Augustine? Perhaps I'm revealing that I'm part of the problem that Peterson is trying to solve.

the exotic seas of religion in search of fame and fortune."[8] Peterson's vision of the pastorate knows no formulae but the narrative world of Scripture. He stands in fierce opposition to much that passes for pastoral leadership these days, and he shows almost a disciplined inattention to results. The quietly ordinary is more important than the publicly celebrated. People over programs. Dignity over function. Don't ask "how?" ask, "what?" Leisurely spiritual direction over ministerial busyness. Prayer over a PR campaign. The quietly balanced spiritual leader versus the showy cheerleader who is jerked about by events.[9]

Judged by the fruits of Peterson's scholarly life, his seminary did a wonderful job on him, but he barely mentions his seminary in *The Pastor*. From his Pentecostal background he got the conviction that "everything, absolutely everything, in the scriptures is livable,"[10] though his conviction of the ubiquitous livability of the faith does not extend to mechanisms like denominations or ecclesiastical hierarchy. God speaks through Scripture for Peterson, but not through the institutions that birthed Scripture.

Though Peterson is a remarkable blend of erudition and passion, advanced linguistic ability and fluency in language, there is scant knowledge of or praise for the ecclesiastical institutions that produced him. In Montana, as a boy, Peterson says that his Pentecostal church home was giving him, without his knowing it, "a sacred imagination strong enough to reject and resist the relentlessly secularized and ghettoized one-dimensional caricature that assigned American pastors to jobs in a workplace that markets religion . . . hiring pastors to provide religious goods and services for a culture of God consumers."[11] He doesn't seem to appreciate the irony that this Pentecostal congregation, as haphazardly organized as it may have been, was an institution that gave him the skills to resist good old American

8. Peterson, *Under the Unpredictable Plant*, 20.

9. I presume that Peterson's Reformed theology makes him suspicious of human effort and leads to his view of the church as an almost exclusively divinely wrought miracle. Perhaps my critique of Peterson on institutions is attributable to my own Methodism. John Wesley had the highest regard for the pietistic Moravians, but broke with them fiercely over their (according to Wesley) "quietism." The Moravians taught that human effort in pursuing the divine life was dangerous; one ought quietly and effortlessly await the advent of God into life. Wesley's synergistic view of the human life, his stress that God's grace not only works for us but energetically works in us, led him to castigate Moravian "quietism" as a rejection of the active, transforming, synergistic grace of God that enlists us in divine activity.

10. Peterson, *The Pastor*, 214.

11. Ibid., 13.

institutionalized commercialism and consumption. His memoir makes his father's butcher shop (a business seeking profit, I might note) a more formative influence upon his pastoral leadership than any exemplar in any church.

As a seminarian and church basketball coach in New York, he sounds more like Saint John exiled on the Island of Patmos than Saint Paul, always on the road and slugging it out with various poorly formed Christians in the tough, grubby organizational work required to establish new churches in a culture that did not want churches.

The American Religion

Though Peterson despises the instrumentalist, pragmatic "American way," and eloquently, fiercely calls pastors back to the peculiarity of our vocation, in a curious way Peterson is more American in his construal of the practice of ministry than he acknowledges, particularly in his good old American disparagement of the institutions where ministry is both done and undone.

As I read American church history, the American church was born in 1835 during Ralph Waldo Emerson's Harvard "Divinity School Address"— the apotheosis of American, philosophical romanticism.[12] Emerson defined "religion" as "sentiment," a sensibility that makes life worth living. Through religious sentiment, a person comprehends the goodness within and enjoys direct communion with God through intuitive Reason, a virtue that cannot be attained "at second hand" by borrowing from the past or by copying the spiritual paths of other people. Alas, corrupt religious institutions have all but destroyed our original oneness with the divine through their concoction of religious rituals and requirements. Emerson admits that, "Miracles, prophecy, poetry, the ideal life, the holy life," are sometimes present in institutional religion, but only historically, in its ancient, more spiritual forms, not as religion currently exists.

The major illustration of the perversion of religion, says Emerson, is the established Christian church. Jesus "belonged to the true race of prophets," fully living out the inherent relationship between God and humanity. Unfortunately the church quickly denied Christ's humanity and replaced our innate, inner perceptions of goodness with externally imposed commandments. Religion has been formalized and codified. The personal,

12. Emerson, *Divinity School Address.*

innate, intuitive connection with God has been lost, stolen from each individual by a lifeless church.

Emerson urged graduating seminarians (only a couple were there for his address) to lead creative pastoral careers to restore truth, the soul, and intuitive revelation to the church. The barrenness of inherited religion must be acknowledged and ministers must accept their true and exalted function. The preacher's particular office is to express the applicability of moral sentiments to the duties of life, to help parishioners see that each of them possesses "an infinite Soul; that the earth and heavens are passing into his mind; that he is drinking forever the soul of God." Emerson even speaks of the Eucharist as having irretrievable significance, now lost to the sensitive mind because of the rite's "hollow, dry, creaking formality," which is "too plain." He exhorts his hearers to abandon institutional Christianity, "to go alone; to refuse the good models . . . and dare to love God without mediator or veil." Doing so will allow them to inspire their congregations to break from conformity, and thus to "acquaint men at first hand with Deity."

It would be horribly unfair of me to link Peterson with Emerson's Transcendentalist drivel. I'm sure that Peterson would condemn Emerson's arrogant dismissal of Scripture and sacraments. However, I do want to point to the decidedly naïve, romantic, anti-institutional polemic of the Divinity School Address as setting the tone for much of American Christianity. The popular American Christian response to the dead, cold formality of our inherited religious institutions? The turn inward. Emerson made the lone individual, plumbing the depths of his or her individual spiritual sentiments, the uniquely American way to God. If I seem to have attributed more to Emerson than he deserves, note Reinhold Niebuhr,[13] who in his quintessentially American work *Moral Man and Immoral Society* gave modern, sophisticated, allegedly historically based rationale for the American notion that we are at our best and our most humane as role-free individuals rather than as those trapped in servitude to immoral institutions and societies.

One of the reasons why Eugene Peterson is so revered by pastors is his biblically derived, God-centered view of church and ministry. Only in his scorn for the institutional and social embodiment of church and ministry does Peterson seem to succumb to the "American way" that he otherwise deplores. When he rails against the secularization and commercialization of contemporary Christian ministry in North America, how can he be sure

13. Niebuhr, *Moral Man and Immoral Society*.

that he is not practicing another form of cultural accommodation—Ralph Waldo Emerson in homespun, earthy, Montana garb?

The church is an institution that shares many of the characteristics (sins?) of other institutions—a tendency toward self-aggrandizement, a greater love of survival than of purpose, boring protection of the organizational status quo, to mention a few. To be sure, the church claims a self-transcendence that makes it a different sort of institution, but the transcendence that is the church of Jesus Christ is embodied in a human institution. The church must never be more spiritual than Jesus. We cannot claim a transcendence that sets us free from the limitations and sinful tendencies of all human institutions. Still, in what's become of mainline Protestantism, I judge that squeamish docetism is a greater temptation than worldly ecclesiastical triumphalism. As Bonhoeffer said, we must never dream a church that imagines a corporate identity that has never existed. We must resist the tendency to make the Christian life something that is inward and spiritual rather than primarily visible and historical.[14]

I suspect Peterson might say that the only faithful canon for judging these matters is Scripture. Fair enough. But on the basis of Scripture—itself a product of a succession of institutions—I do not believe that Peterson sufficiently accounts for the power and the inevitability of institutional Christianity (is there any other form of Christianity?). Nor does he sufficiently guard against the abuse of his ecclesiology by those of us who may be tempted to use his anti-institutional scorn as a rationale for freedom from any institutional responsibility or accountability for the fruit of our ministry. *ahem! yes!*

Incarnation and Countercultural Ministry

Karl Barth—Peterson's acknowledged theological mentor—was unrelenting in his criticism of the church. Barth contrasted the "real" church, the

14. Here Lesslie Newbigin is my teacher in stressing the historicity and visibility of the church. Newbigin criticizes the Reformers' conception of the church as having "no real place for the continuing life of the church as one fellowship binding the generations together in Christ. It makes the church practically a series of totally disconnected events in which, at each moment and place at which the word and sacraments of the Gospel are set forth, the church is there and then called into being by God's creative power." Lesslie Newigin, *The Household of God*, 48. In these same lectures, Newbigin criticized Barth's ecclesiology of church as "event" for allowing the eschatological "completely push out the historical" (49).

church that is never actualized by human effort, with the "sham church" in which we exist.[15] Barth sounds like Peterson when he readily admits that the church is at best an "equivocal witness."[16] Barth famously said that to be in the church is to be a bird always beating its wings against the bars of a cage.[17] "The world would be lost without Jesus Christ . . . the world would not necessarily be lost if there were no Church."[18] Peterson couldn't have said it with more pathos and scorn.

The church's ministers are peculiarly fit subjects for the wrath of God, says Barth, because we have done more to "narcotize than to stimulate."[19] Ouch. No one would accuse Peterson of narcotizing homiletics. Yet I think he is vulnerable to the charge that he fails to acknowledge how dependent he is upon the bodily form of the body of Christ and how responsible we clergy are for leading in the practice of corporeal Christianity.

True to the Reformed tradition of "visible saints," even as Barth excoriated the church and its ministry, at the same time he warned that we must never "overlook the visibility of the church, explaining away its earthly and historical form as something indifferent, or angrily negating it, or treating it only as a necessary evil, in order to magnify an invisible fellowship of the Spirit and of spirits," in order thereby to flee the real church into "a kind of wonderland."[20]

Peterson does a fine job of showing the friction with and the seduction by American consumerist culture (come to think of it, how much of American culture isn't "consumerist" to some degree?). But the church has, from the first, had friction with and tendencies toward idolatry in every culture in which it has been present. From my angle on Scripture, the way to resist the allures of pagan culture is not to presume that God will miraculously extricate us from culture but rather by the typical, God-given means of resistance to godlessness—enculturation by a community strong enough to raise godly children and to give us the grace to say, "No!" That is, *baptism* into the countercultural people called *church*. The lures of American

15. Barth, *Church Dogmatics*, IV/2, 614–18. Peterson says he was introduced to Barth not at New York Theological Seminary (of course) but rather by a *Jewish* graduate student on his basketball team at Madison Avenue Presbyterian (Peterson, *The Pastor*, 89–90). I'm certain that Barth would have loved that.

16. Barth, *Church Dogmatics* IV/2, 617.

17. Barth, *Dogmatics in Outline*, 147.

18. Barth, *Church Dogmatics* IV/3, 826.

19. Barth, *The Word of God and the Word of Man*, 54.

20. Barth, *Church Dogmatics* IV/1, 653–54.

consumerism are too great to resist as lone individuals, even as biblically well-formed individuals.

"I didn't want to be a religious professional whose identity was institutionalized," Peterson says.[21] Just how does one pull that off unassisted by institutions? Institutions enable most of us to aspire to Peterson's wonderful "long obedience in the same direction" through the muck and mire that must be endured and vanquished in those same institutions.[22] It is clear enough in the "Company of Pastors," those fifteen pastors with whom Peterson met regularly enabled Peterson to stay centered, passionate, and theologically attentive. That group, and its willingness to regulate itself and to hold one another accountable, was an institution. So was Sister Genevieve, who proved to be so helpful in Peterson's ascent from his time in the "badlands."[23]

You are a pastor who aspires to Peterson's vision of the pastor living "patiently," "locally," and "personally"? I can't figure out any way to live such a countercultural life except through the culture called "church." Indeed, I would say that there's not much wrong with most of us pastors that couldn't be cured by a church willing to stand up to the dominant culture that robs the church of some of its best leaders.

I don't hear much Christology in Peterson's memoir, though perhaps it is simply assumed in a man who is so well formed by Scripture. While his writing is so wonderfully incarnational, is he overlooking the incarnation when he thinks about institutions? In his advocacy of inwardly turning, contemplative, non-activist pastors, how does he know he is not playing into the hands of those aspects of the American culture he deplores? I wish he had not chosen to speak of the move that he thinks pastors ought to make as "interior." He calls us pastors "stewards of the mysteries,"[24] but surely one of the most miraculous of divine mysteries is the determination of Christ to incarnate in the poor old, compromised, bride of Christ: the church.

I hope that I make these criticisms from christological reasons rather than from my anxiety about the future of ecclesiastical institutions. One could argue that because Jesus is always on the move, we don't have to be, but that seems to me specious reasoning. They said many things about Jesus

21. Peterson, *The Pastor,* 242.
22. Ibid., 247.
23. Ibid., 227.
24. Peterson, *Working the Angles,* 4.

but who accused him of "stability"? When Peterson urges us to be still and to locate, he sounds like Wendell Berry, not Jesus. I know this is a prejudiced Wesleyan statement, but I must remind you that Jesus's last words to us, before ascending and taking charge (Matt 28:20) was not "stay put" and "pray," but rather, "Go! Make! Teach! Baptize." The body of Christ is a body in motion.

Most of us pay attention to what God is doing in the world not because of our strong, meditative commitment to Christ but because, on a regular basis, the poor old church keeps grabbing our attention, forcing us to focus upon the God we would avoid if left to our own devices. If prayer were a solitary exercise, I'm sure I would never obediently pray for my enemies if the church did not routinely, ritually make me do so.[25] And though the mission of the church seems to be overshadowed in Peterson's urging the church to be still and know God, I'm sure that I would have little inclination to join in the *missio dei* without the church pestering me to do so.

I heartily agree with Peterson when he says, "There can be no maturity in the spiritual life, no obedience in following Jesus, no wholeness in the Christian life apart from an immersion and embrace of community. I am not myself by myself. Community, not the highly vaunted individualism of our culture, is the setting in which Christ is at play."[26]

If Peterson had said that more often, then I would have even more reason for proclaiming that Eugene Peterson is our best writer on ministry.

25. In Marva Dawn and Peterson's *The Unnecessary Pastor*, it is interesting that Dawn, and not Peterson, wrote chapter nine, "The Call to Build Community." Dawn praised the liturgy of the church, and the continuity and sustenance gained through participation in ritual.

26. Peterson, *Christ Plays in Ten Thousand Places*, 226

Hunter and Peterson on Institutions

Kristen Deede Johnson

I was recently asked to identify five books that I would recommend to someone who wanted to understand the sort of work I do.[1] As I named books by Eugene Peterson and James Davison Hunter, I found myself wondering yet again if there is a tension in the degree to which the ideas of Hunter and Peterson have shaped me. This tension goes back to my very first extended conversation with my soon-to-be husband when we discovered that while we shared many of the same concerns about the church and contemporary culture, he, having been deeply shaped by Peterson, and I, having been deeply shaped by Hunter, approached those concerns quite differently. He tended to emphasize the significance of micro-level engagement, focused on the local church. I was more inclined to macro-level thinking, concerned about how to mitigate the impact of culture on local churches. Thankfully we have managed to reconcile those differences. Since that time I have also been significantly impacted by Peterson's ideas as they provide a perspective on culture and the church that seems to complement Hunter. Nevertheless, I have continued to feel some tension between these perspectives in my own vocational life.

I have come to believe that Peterson and Hunter need each other for their respective visions of the church to be realized. Peterson's call to the church to be faithful amidst the immense cultural pressures it faces needs to incorporate Hunter's sense of the significance of institutional engagement by Christians, rooted in Hunter's understanding of how culture

1. Johnson, "Patience, Trust, and Vision."

works. Hunter, in turn, needs the type of *pastors* that Peterson is calling for in order for the church to be all that he thinks it needs to be in this cultural moment. To put this more strongly, not only do Peterson and Hunter need each other, but the American church needs both Hunter and Peterson, as it seeks to live faithfully within the dynamics of American culture.

Let me support these contentions by exploring ways in which Hunter and Peterson have helped me both to question and envision anew the relationship between culture and the church in contemporary America. As a new convert to Christianity in my teenage years, I found myself particularly concerned with integrating the Christian faith into the entirety of one's life. Based on my own experience and those of others around me, I sensed that the call to discipleship was not easy to heed even for those who were well-intentioned and sincere in their desire to be faithful Christians. During my undergraduate years I discovered the category of "culture," which helped me to begin to make sense of the larger dynamics at play within American Christianity. During Christmas break of my first year of college, I came across Robert Wuthnow's *God and Mammon* at the public library and received my first glimpse of the collision between the consumeristic components of our culture and of contemporary Christianity. During my senior year, in a small and riveting graduate-level course with James Davison Hunter, I learned more about the nature of contemporary culture, including the degree to which the therapeutic had triumphed in our culture at large. Through my own subsequent research, I saw that this triumph was likewise pervasive within American Christianity. After graduating I continued to explore the significance of culture through my work as the research assistant to Hunter and the Institute for Advanced Studies in Culture at the University of Virginia that he directed.

I began to think that something had gone awry in the American church at large. The degree to which the Christianity I knew so uncritically reflected both the consumerism and the self-help therapeutic nature of the larger culture left me searching for a different vision of discipleship. When I discovered Peterson's writings, they provided both a diagnosis of the problem and a vision for how the church could move forward. Reflecting on the problematic nature of the church that he encountered as he was first entering the pastorate, Peterson writes,

> The church was no longer conceived as something in need of repair but as a business opportunity that would cater to the consumer tastes of spiritually minded sinners both within and without

congregrations. . . . This is the Americanization of congregation. It means turning each congregation into a market for religious consumers, an ecclesiastical business run along the lines of advertising techniques, organizational flow charts, and energized by impressive motivational rhetoric.[2]

This incisive critique also pointed to some deeply troubling theology that places humans at the center of the Christian life rather than God. The "motivational rhetoric" that Peterson observed in the church was rooted in a vision of Christianity in which we are saved by God's grace, but after that we are expected to find the zeal and strength to worship, serve, witness, and generally live as disciplines on our own. As Peterson describes this prominent mentality, "Salvation is God's business. It is what God does. And then he turns it over to us."[3] Fleshing this out further, Peterson reflects that after Jesus's ascension, American Christians "let Jesus slip into the background and proceed to understand the story of church as what we are doing for God. Doing for Jesus to be sure, doing in the name of Jesus certainly. But *we* are in charge. *We* are now making the decisions. *We* have Jesus's commands; *we* have Jesus's example. But now it is up to us: *we* take responsibility for the church."[4]

This human-centered, action-oriented vision of the Christian life was one that had been emphasized in my early Christian formation. It had worked for me for a few years. But I had begun to encounter its limitations and was starting to see these for the larger church when I began to read Peterson. Through essays like "Teach Us to Care, and Not to Care," I was given a vision of what it looked like to believe that God is alive and active in others.[5] Learning to trust that God is *always already* at work in others' lives and in the church significantly altered how I approached ministry. Likewise, learning to believe that God is always already at work in our own lives significantly altered how I approached the life of discipleship. Through books like *Answering God*, I began to see that acts of prayer and worship are not rooted in my actions but in God. Like Peterson, and in part through Peterson, "I was embarked on a steep *unlearning* curve . . . the unlearning that was necessary to clear the ground for learning that God at work—not

---

2. Peterson, *The Pastor*, 111–12.

3. Ibid., 117.

4. Ibid., 116–17.

5. See Peterson, *Subversive Spirituality*, 154–68.

I—was the center of the way I was going to be living for the rest of my life."[6] This was personally freeing, but it is also freeing for those churches that can take it to heart. Peterson describes his own church as it learned this lesson:

> As we let Luke tell the story, it became clear that being the church meant that the Holy Spirit was conceiving the life of Jesus in us, much the same way the Holy Spirit had conceived the life of Jesus in Mary. We weren't trying to be a perfect or model or glamorous church. We were trying to get out of the way and pay attention to the way God worked in the early church and was working in us. We were getting it: worship was not so much what we did, but what we let God do in and for us.[7]

This theological vision of God always already at work in our lives and ministries is counter to the dominant American emphasis on *our* work and efforts, an emphasis that is uncritically incorporated into much of American Christianity. James Hunter was instrumental in opening my eyes to the powerful influence of culture on all of the institutions of society, the contemporary church included. Eugene Peterson then gave me more specific language to diagnose the church's acquiescence to some dominant cultural themes and a theological vision that enabled God to return to the center of the church's life and ministry. For these reasons, I see a great deal of synergy in the thought of Peterson and Hunter. Yet in some ways they are dramatically different. This difference is particularly manifest in the attention they give (or fail to give) to institutions within their writings.

Peterson's relationship to institutions is ambiguous at best. Most noticeable is probably the fact that beyond the local church, Peterson does not generally engage with institutions in his writings. This includes the relationship between the local church and the larger denomination. While it is understandable that denominational relationships and "politics" might not be at the forefront of his passions, many pastors in America have to tend to their church's governing structures and denominational commitments—so a bit of guidance from Peterson on this relationship might be useful. Peterson's own story, growing up in Montana in a Pentecostal church, presumably contributes to his non-institutional spirit. Despite having spent decades serving a Presbyterian church, his own relationship to the denomination developed rather accidentally (or might one say providentially?). As a requirement of his seminary education, he had to do field

---

6. Peterson, *The Pastor*, 44.

7. Ibid., 172.

work. He was, in his words, "lucky in my assignment."[8] He was assigned to be the basketball coach at Madison Avenue Presbyterian Church and decided to worship there the first Sunday that his responsibilities began. He freely admits that he knew no Presbyterians prior to this point, nor did he know anything about the denomination. He appreciated what he discovered within that church in the preaching of George Arthur Buttrick. During seminary he was assigned to Presbyterian churches all three years and eventually joined the denomination. ("I gradually became accustomed to what, previous to seminary, had been a church word I could not have defined. I was welcomed. I was affirmed; I almost *felt* like a Presbyterian. Then I made it official. I became a Presbyterian."[9]) The pastor of his final placement urged him to become ordained in the Presbyterian church and Peterson heeded his advice. At that time Peterson was headed to graduate school so he did not realize the implications this decision would have. When he eventually discerned his call to congregational ministry, he and his wife were given the task of planting a church for the denomination on the outskirts of Baltimore.

Reflecting on his decision to become Presbyterian, Peterson notes that it didn't seem like a big decision or transition and it was not something that would be considered a renunciation of his Pentecostalism. He continued to appreciate the Pentecostal conviction that "everything, absolutely everything, in the scriptures is livable,"[10] while he found in Presbyterianism "the gift of a living tradition."[11] Through his Presbyterianism he also discovered people who took the calling of pastor seriously and offered him a different vision of ministry than he had encountered in his Pentecostal roots.[12]

These were important discoveries, to be sure, but Peterson's reflections on Presbyterianism do not address the institutional implications of his membership and ordination in the denomination. The primary place in which he addresses his connection to the Presbyterian denomination lies in his discussion of the monthly reports he had to submit to the office of the New Church Development (NCD). Acknowledging that he owed the institution a great deal for ordaining him, entrusting him with the call to organize this new church, and helping to provide his salary and mortgage

8. Ibid., 86.
9. Ibid., 91.
10. Ibid., 214
11. Ibid., 215.
12. Ibid., 216–17.

payments for the first three years of these efforts, he notes that at first he was eager to write the reports. Gradually, however, he began questioning whether those at the denominational office actually read all of the reports, so he began inserting fictionalized accounts of personal problems into the report, asking explicitly for help addressing the problems, and never receiving any response. His stories became more and more outlandish, but were never noticed.[13] This is certainly an indictment of those charged with his supervision. It also serves to reinforce a sense of institutional irrelevance, at best.

Institutions feature much more prominently and positively in the recent thought of James Davison Hunter. Indeed, Hunter goes so far as to argue that institutional engagement is of "essential importance" and that unless Christians intentionally engage the institutions of which they are a part, we will end up with "the same individualism and idealism that so fatally undermine Christian life and witness at present."[14] Peterson and Hunter share many similar hopes for and convictions about the contemporary church, including the significance of separating "the life and identity of the church from the life and identity of American society"[15] and reclaiming worship as the most defining practice of the church.[16] The church stands as the prominent institution in both of their visions, with pastors singled out for the contributions they can make to help the church to live faithfully in this cultural moment. This may be more obvious in Peterson's writings, but it is also present in Hunter. As he writes of the church, "What has been missing is a leadership that comprehends the nature of these challenges and offers a vision of formation adequate to the task of discipling the church and its members for a time such as ours. . . . By admonishing Christian lay people for not, in effect, being Christian enough, they shift responsibility for their own failures onto those that they lead."[17] What Hunter means is that pastors have failed to take seriously the degree to which their congregants are shaped by the larger culture and have correspondingly failed to provide the leadership needed to enable their churches to be places of faithful worship that truly form disciples who have a vision of shalom. Put more strongly, Hunter argues that:

13. Ibid., 196–200.
14. Hunter, *To Change the World*, 270.
15. Ibid., 184.
16. See ibid., 244, 286.
17. Ibid., 226.

As a community and an institution, the church is a plausibility structure and the only one with the resources capable of offering an alternative formation to that offered by popular culture. What I am arguing simply reiterates points made earlier: the depth and stability of formation are directly tied to the depth and stability of the social and structural environment in which it takes place. Formation into a vision of human flourishing requires an environment that embodies continuity, historical memory, rituals marking seasons of life, intergenerational interdependence, and most important of all, common worship. . . . At all levels, formation into a vision of human flourishing requires intentionality and the social, economic, intellectual, and cultural resources of a healthy, mutually dependent, and worshipping community provided for Christians by the church.[18]

Perhaps we could put it this way: Peterson and Hunter both long for the church and its pastors to be distinct from the larger culture of which they are a part. Peterson calls for this as a pastor, emphasizing how pastors can live, think, and minister differently. Hunter calls for this as a sociologist, articulating the conditions that will be necessary for the church to provide a genuine alternative to the dominant cultural frameworks. If Hunter is right, Peterson's desire for pastors to be set apart can only be fulfilled if we pay attention to the larger institutional realities that make up the culture and the church.

Hunter's argument in relation to pastors and the church stems from a larger theory of culture. In presenting this theory, Hunter argues that institutions have largely been neglected in common conceptions of culture, including those held by most people of faith. Focusing specifically on Christians, Hunter notes that the operating assumption held by most Christians and the organizations they have established is that culture is made up of values or of worldviews (understood to be wide-ranging understandings of the world primarily informed by great ideas), both of which are thought to reside in the hearts and minds of individuals.[19] Underlying this sense of culture is a problematic form of idealism, in which ideas and the mind are thought to have greater ontological significance than the material world. This focus on ideas as the dominant force shaping culture misses the significance of institutions and structures of power.[20] Hunter ar-

18. Ibid., 282–83.
19. Ibid., 6–9.
20. Ibid., 24–26.

gues that we need to recognize that culture is intrinsically dialectical, in two ways. Culture exists at the intersection of ideas and institutions. As Hunter writes, "Ideas are not free-floating in consciousness but are grounded in the social world in the most concrete ways. To put it bluntly, culture is as much infrastructure as it is ideas. It takes shape in concrete institutional form."[21] Culture, then, is not generated solely by great ideas or by individuals putting forth and adhering to those great ideas, but by institutions and the elites who lead the institutions that have cultural consequence. These institutions include the market, the state, education, the media, scientific and technological research, and the family.[22]

The second dialectic identified by Hunter is that of the relationship between institutions and individuals. Just as institutions would not exist without the individuals who comprise them, so individuals have to be understood in light of the institutions that shape them and their activity. This dialectic, it should be noted, is not evenly balanced: "While individuals are not powerless by any stretch of the imagination, institutions have much greater power."[23] To connect this back to Peterson, if we would like to see pastors and the Christians under their care living differently, we have to grapple with the degree to which they are shaped by the institutions of this culture. Good intentions and sincere calls to faithfulness are not enough in the face of the powerful influence of institutions and the ideas generated by and embedded in those institutions. When we consider the state of things today, Hunter argues that the problem is not a matter of inadequate faith but inadequate recognition of the influence of the larger culture and its institutions on that faith. As he writes, "In contemporary America, Christians have faith in God and, by and large, they believe and hold fast to the central truths of the Christian tradition. But while they have faith, *they have also been formed by the larger post-Christian culture,* a culture whose habits of life less and less resemble anything like the vision of human flourishing provided by the life of Christ and witness of scripture."[24]

This is why local churches are so significant in Hunter's vision. In the face of the formative role of cultural institutions, the church needs to heed the calling to be its own formative institution. If the church, and its pastoral leadership, were to take this calling seriously, it would be a place in which

21. Ibid., 34.
22. Ibid., 35.
23. Ibid.
24. Ibid., 227; author's emphasis.

people could be deeply formed by the realities of the kingdom of God instead of being primarily formed by the (seeming) realities of the culture at large. In the current cultural context, this will take significant intentionality. Central to the formation of its people will be the task of giving them a vision of shalom, a vision of the "order and harmony, fruitfulness and abundance, wholeness, beauty, joy, and well-being" that God intended for creation, that God will fully bring about in the eschaton, and that God in Christ calls Christians to embody within every part of their lives and in every place they inhabit.[25] Central to this vision is another dialectic, one of affirmation and antithesis. Christians need to affirm the goodness of creation, the calling given to humans to bring forth life, and the existence of truth, beauty, and goodness in this creation despite the fall. This, for Hunter, is connected to an affirmation that culture, and the human call to create culture that "brings forth life," remain valid even after sin enters the picture. The reality of sin is what necessitates the second part of the dialectic, antithesis. All human achievements and all culture-making fall short of God's original vision. This means that the church is called to engage the world by affirming and even contributing to its truth, beauty, and goodness, while it is also called to be a "community of resistance" that highlights the degree to which cultural institutions and ideals fall short of the shalom of God. It is important to Hunter that this antithesis does not consist simply of denouncing the culture but that it is creative and constructive as it embodies and points towards ways of living and being that defy the dominant modes and pictures.[26]

This vision of the church plays out on different levels. On one level, the church itself is called to be an alternative to other cultural institutions. This means that the church needs to be a community in which disciples are formed into the people of God, given a vision of the shalom of God, and enabled to live according to the true reality of the kingdom of God. On another level, but concomitant with the first, the church is carried with people into their individual vocations, and here too Christians need to live as the people of God in light of the reality of the kingdom of God, fostering the shalom of God. Hunter believes this calling of the church is "every bit as important" as the church's role as a formative community in and of itself, writing that "the church, as it exists within the wide range of individual vocations in every sphere of social life (commerce, philanthropy,

25. Ibid., 227–30.
26. Ibid., 231–36.

education, etc.), must be present in the world in ways that work toward the *constructive* subversion of all frameworks of social life that are incompatible with the shalom for which we were made and to which we are called."[27] In other words, as Christians go out from the worshiping community of the church to their different callings, they are to carry God's vision of human flourishing with them and to let that guide all that they do. This means that they are to care about not just personal piety or evangelism, but also about how all the spheres of life in which they are engaged and all the institutions of which they are a part reflect God's shalom and promote the flourishing of all people (not just Christians). Through their faithful presence in the church alongside their relationships and callings inside and outside the church, Christians can help to promote "the welfare of the city."[28] In our families, neighborhoods, volunteer commitments, and work, in whatever spheres of influence that have been entrusted to us, we are to "seek new patterns of social organization that challenge, undermine, and otherwise diminish oppression, injustice, and corruption, and, in turn, encourage harmony, fruitfulness and abundance, wholeness, beauty, joy, security, and well-being."[29] This means that we are to engage the institutions with which our lives intersect, bringing shalom to bear not just in our individual workplaces, but also to the larger institutional realities that surround those workplaces. In so doing, we are not just trying to escape the negative influences of the culture at large, but to enrich and enliven that culture for the benefit of all who inhabit it.[30] That is a way of fulfilling the Great Commission, in which Jesus's call to "go into all the world" can be understood not only in terms of geography, but also in terms of social structure:

> The church is to go into all realms of social life: in volunteer and paid labor—skilled and unskilled labor, the crafts, engineering, commerce, art, law, architecture, teaching, health care, and service. Indeed the church should be *sending people out* in these realms—not only discipling those in these fields by providing the theological resources to form them well, but in fact mentoring and providing financial support for young adults who are gifted and called into these vocations. When the church does not send people out to these realms and when it does not provide the theologies

27. Ibid., 235; author's emphasis.
28. Jeremiah 29:7.
29. Hunter, *To Change the World*, 247–48.
30. For more on faithful presence, see ibid., 243–48, 255–72.

that make sense of work and engagement in these realms, the church fails to fulfill the charge to "go into all the world."[31]

In order to further support and make possible this "going out," Hunter believes that the church needs to help Christians form networks across churches and geographic locations. Those with a common interest in education, business, and the arts, to name but a few, can collaborate, support each other, advance the welfare of the city, and help each other faithfully to engage the tensions that arise when dealing with the power and status dynamics within their respective realms. Christians need this networking to be able creatively and faithfully to live within the structures of this culture in such a way that they are "instantiat[ing] a vision of human flourishing in the wide range of circumstances and spheres of social life."[32]

In Hunter's vision, the church is called to be a community of worship that significantly shapes its people while simultaneously equipping them to go into the many different areas of our culture with a strong sense of vocational vision. Peterson has focused more on the former, shaping, than the latter, sending out, in his writing. He has written often to ask how the American church and its pastors can faithfully embody their callings in this cultural context. But could it be that for the church and its pastors to be able to be faithful in the ways Peterson hopes, Peterson needs more of Hunter's vision? If Hunter is right, Christians need the church to be distinctive *and* they need to be given a distinctive vision for living out their various callings. This includes taking personal callings and institutional realities seriously. Without these components, the larger culture will continue to be more toxic than life-giving, while Christians will continue to be influenced by this toxicity while failing to live out significant portions of God's vision for their engagement with this world. Although he has not given much overt attention to issues of vocation outside those of the pastor, to the call to engage culture, or to the significance of institutions, I don't sense that Peterson would disagree with these aspects of Hunter's thought. In his memoir, Peterson describes the welcome discovery made through his uncle, a pastor in Seattle, that the church could care about the "welfare of the city" (a phrase taken from Jeremiah 29:7 that also informs Hunter's vision). Having grown up in a sectarian church, Peterson appreciated seeing his uncle serve his church in such a way that "the windows and doors of

31. Ibid., 257; author's emphasis.

32. Ibid., 270.

this church didn't enclose; they opened out."[33] Peterson carried this vision into his own pastoral life and his larger sense of the pastoral calling. That being said, he does not flesh out in concrete ways what this "opening out" looks like for the church generally and for church members as they seek the welfare of the city. Hunter's vision, while in keeping with the spirit of Peterson's, provides more direction for how people can let their faith convictions inform the vocational and institutional realities of their lives.

Hunter's emphasis on the importance of networks is another place where Hunter unpacks something academically that Peterson has personally experienced as significant. Peterson articulates the significance of a "Company of Pastors," a group of pastors with whom he met weekly for twenty-six years, almost the entirety of his time as a pastor at the church he helped to plant and nurture. Peterson recognizes that this group became critical "for maintaining a pastoral vocation in the cultural conditions of our time." It was "a place to form and nurture a pastoral identity that had theological and biblical integrity. We knew it was a rare thing. And we knew that none of us could have done it on our own. We needed one another. There was too much in American culture that was hostile to who we were."[34] This Company of Pastors provides a case-study of the type of networks Hunter is describing—people united by a common vocation, exploring together how to faithfully and creatively live out their callings within institutions amidst the tensions of this cultural moment. This group helped Peterson to figure out what it meant to live out his calling as a pastor. They published a book that described what the Company had discovered together in a way that it could serve other people exploring that vocation.[35] This is just the type of networking that Hunter believes can and should happen across the wide array of callings that Christians share, resulting in fruitful creativity that can sustain Christians in their callings while also reinvigorating institutions and promoting human flourishing within and outside the church. Although Peterson does not present his Company of Pastors as a model for all to follow or probe its application for other callings beyond the pastorate, I would suggest that this type of collaborative networking is something Christians need as they try to live faithfully in this cultural moment.

I have been arguing that for Peterson's vision of the church to be realized it needs to be supplemented by some of Hunter's ideas. I would also

33. Peterson, *The Pastor*, 68.

34. Ibid., 159.

35. Peterson, *Five Smooth Stones*.

suggest that Hunter's vision needs a little "Petersonian" supplementation. Hunter articulates the crucial role to be played by pastoral leadership in creating churches that can withstand cultural forces and encourage faithful presence, but he does not provide detail on how these sorts of pastors can be nurtured and formed. Here is where Peterson's corpus can help to give pastors a more concrete vision of how to fulfill their callings while withstanding the pressures that American culture places on the church and its leadership. Peterson has spent a lifetime discerning how to be a faithful pastor amidst these very real pressures and he has shared this wisdom through his wide array of writings. By drawing on this wisdom in conjunction with Hunter's ideas, churches may come closer to finding the pastoral leadership they need to live faithfully and creatively within this cultural moment.

Peterson dreams of churches that are truly forming disciples to live integrated, holistic lives, lives in which the grace of the triune God, the narratives of Scripture, the sacramental practices of the church, and the rhythms of everyday life, are all interconnected. Peterson dreams of pastors who are strong enough to withstand the forces of the larger culture that have so deeply shaped many pastors and churches today. If we combine Peterson's vision for the pastoral life with Hunter's vision for the church, which involves forming disciples with a robust sense of calling and institutional engagement, we just might see these dreams come true.

The (Scholar-) Pastor

Jason Byassee

THERE ARE MANY REASONS to read Eugene Peterson.

His broadest readership may come from those who want translations of the Scripture that are rhetorically accessible while remaining faithful to the biblical languages. Pastors I know approach him for spiritual theology that is totally, blessedly without piety or cliché (I love the line he reports from the Scottish preacher Alexander Whyte when asked what a young person should do to become a preacher: "relieve yourself often and take a long vacation"). Some, I suspect, have gone to him to learn about the venerable church practice of spiritual direction, long taboo in evangelical circles, resurrected almost single-handedly by Peterson's work. One of Peterson's own favorite points of praise for an author like Barth or Dostoevsky is that their work has "juice" in it. Peterson's own work hangs so heavy with juice it's dangerous to cut into.

I read Eugene Peterson because he smudges lines that need smudging. For example, he's a pastor in a mainline liberal denomination who comes from Pentecostals and still belongs to them in some ways. He's an academically trained pastor who straddles the division between the parish and the academy. He's theologically orthodox and evangelical without throwing elbows at those to his left for being insufficiently orthodox and evangelical. Peterson unites in his person and ministry things God never intended to be divided. What sort of crazy nonsense says that you have to choose between the life of the mind and the life of worship? What sort of silliness is it that says love for evangelism and the long roots of tradition are mutually

76

exclusive? Who ever came up with the ridiculous idea that treasuring tradition makes you enemies with those who treasure it differently?

I am a pastor who has spent time in both the academy and parish and who wants to continue living in both worlds. I come from evangelicals, I now serve mainliners, and I want to maintain commitments to both in tension-filled relationship. I've often had students tell me they want to have a foot both in the academy and in the church. I tell them they were born in the wrong century. It was common, default really, for theologians in the early church also to be ordained as pastors. Now, both the academy and the church are jealous of people's time and do not want professors or pastors with divided attentions and loyalties. In a way they're right to be jealous. Both vocations take all the time and attention that very smart, very holy people can muster just to be done adequately, let alone expertly. Peterson's work shows it is possible to do both to some extent. My own academic work has also been an effort to blow the dust off of forgotten treasures from the church's history for a new day. In fact I remember coming across a section of one of Peterson's books entitled "Liturgical Exegesis" and banging my head on the table: I thought I invented that term for my own book, *Praise Seeking Understanding*. Doesn't any truly good idea have to be totally original?

Peterson's work is, blessedly, strikingly, unoriginal. Or if it is original it is the practiced originality of a virtuoso who has so totally imbibed the spirit of the music she plays as to become part of it, living it and interpreting it anew.[1] Maybe it's best for him that he never went to Yale to write that Old Testament dissertation he was set to do for Brevard Childs. Theological education, especially at the doctoral level, is often a process of grinding the curiosity right out of its students. Peterson belongs to the blessed ranks of those in the theological stratosphere who never earned a terminal degree, among whom are also Karl Barth and Reinhold Niebuhr. One could argue Peterson's the most important biblical theologian living. No one combines the reading of Scripture and the living of the Christian life between church and academy in quite the form he does. That's not to say he's often read in the theological academy, which prizes originality and narrowness of subspecialty more than Peterson's studied unoriginality and broad vision. St. Augustine believed that teachers teach by what delights them more than by the content of their catechesis. If that's right, Peterson's work is primarily

---

1. The analogy is Peterson's own, from *Eat This Book*, 76.

one of reigniting the church's delight in Scripture, community life together, the life of the mind, and the countless intersections in between.

In this essay I would like to treat the way Peterson dances back and forth across the line between the church and the academy. Both come off as good, Godly, grace-bearing institutions in his hands, even as he has hard words for both.[2] Although he has spent his career trying to lead a faithful church amidst conditions that would ordinarily make for despair, I wonder what it would have looked like for him to charge into academia with teeth and knives and carve out a space for a faithful life there? What would a Petersonian vision for an institution of theological education to look like?

Hard Words

Despite what I wrote earlier about Peterson not throwing elbows, he does hammer his audience in both the church and the academy. To read Peterson you must take your lumps. His prophetic voice is leveled against false forms of the pastoral or Christian *life*, not so much against incorrect doctrinal beliefs. Peterson is an equal-opportunity critic, screeching at pastor, church, and theological academy alike. This may be the Reformed thinker in him, who lights fires that he hopes will clear the underbrush and make way for genuine growth. You can almost tell what Peterson is *for* in each case by listening to what he rails against.

A favorite target among pastors is the effort to fake ministry by meeting people's false expectations of us.[3] Congregations pay us and we do what they want us to do: we perform, they applaud, success happens (I wish it were as easy as Peterson makes it out to be, but bear with me). He confesses in one place that he used to joke we could churn out pastor robots from degree programs that would provide scripted services guaranteed to produce success. "Used to," until he started seeing advertisements that promised that very thing. He compares pastors' offices to illegal "stills" that squeeze all of the local and the particular out of community life as they squash a specific place into a one-size-fits-all mold.[4] In another place, commenting on the book of Esther, he notes Mordecai's famous speech to

2. I am partly reading Peterson from my own vantage as one charged to recover a theology of institutions as grace-bearing instruments of the gospel. See my and others' work on this at www.faithandleadership.com.

3. This from *Working the Angles*, 9.

4. Ibid., 135

his niece. God *will* deliver his people, by some other means than her if necessary, but if she's willing, God will use Esther's position and courage. Our ministries, by contrast, often fail to assume God's prior action. We are often in a frenzy of activity, trying to create or build or buy something like Babel rather than receiving and responding to God's grace, a grace that runs downhill to us and can only be received. When he's done hammering away at us in that passage he concludes with this devastating, two-word sentence: "Prostitute pastor."[5] Peterson summarizes his lament against:

> Pastors who don't pray, pastors who don't grow in faith, pastors who can't tell the difference between culture and the Christ, pastors who chase fads, pastors who are cynical and shopworn, pastors who know less about prayer after twenty years of praying than they did on the day of their ordination, pastors with arrogant, outsized egos puffed up by years of hot-air flattery from well-meaning parishioners.[6]

One senses he could go on, and would perhaps rather like to.

Lest we think Peterson has it in for his fellow pastors alone, he also has harsh words for congregations. Echoing Scripture, he notes that when two or three believers gather, there they construct an idol (and in fact, that idol-making proclivity is part of what makes it so hard to be a faithful pastor).[7] Preaching among his suburbanite parishioners was like "talking to my dog"—they were kindly, but the content of his words meant little.[8] His primary target in the local church is its submission to consumerism. A consumer church is an anti-Christ church.[9] To try to discern needs and meet them—the standard church growth model in America—is so much Baalism, harlotry.[10] In his recent memoir he compares church growth to other sorts of growth, like the growth of a cancer, or an oil spill.[11] Elsewhere he calls the self-aggrandizing mania of church building, passing under the guise of evangelism or mission, "the crassest kind of bitch-goddess

---

5. Peterson, *Under the Unpredictable Plant*, 60.
6. Peterson, *Working the Angles*, 166.
7. Peterson, *Under the Unpredictable Plant*, 4.
8. Ibid., 27.
9. Peterson, *The Jesus Way*, 6.
10. Ibid., 110.
11. *The Pastor*, 158–59.

nonsense."[12] Here we have an implicit argument for a lifetime of soaking in biblical language: better cursing.

Peterson praises, by implication, ministry that is local, patient, leisurely. His antidote to ministry purchased from a glossy mailer, imitated by a charlatan, and applauded by canines is that which is done by indirection. One enters into it as a community together with Jesus, gnawing on Scripture together like a dog gnaws a bone (canine references *can* be more positive than bitch-goddess nonsense!). Scripture ought not be bowdlerized, packaged, bought and sold, but rather it addresses us, calls us to worship, leads us to live in community in a specific place, and holds over us an eschatological promise and warning (more on each of these points below). In Peterson's hands, eschatological urgency does not disqualify pastoral leisure.

Another Lover's Quarrel

When Peterson turns his prophetic ire against the theological academy, his tone is still critical but much more circumspect. When he criticizes the academy, it is with polite distance—more like the way one smacks one's lips while reading the paper about a politician's misdeeds rather than the intense proximity of a lover's quarrel. It is as though after he dropped into the mailbox his refusal of Yale's invitation into its PhD program and put his hand to the plow of the parish, he hasn't turned back.[13] I'm interested in the combination of peculiarly academic and pastoral gifts in Peterson and curious what his witness has to say to institutions and persons who wish to have a foot in both camps.

On the one hand, Peterson would not be Peterson without institutions of higher learning. He comes from Pentecostals who, he regularly reminds us, did not value erudition. He served among people in the suburbs for whom, he regularly says, *TV Guide* was the most sophisticated reading material in their homes. In several places he describes beautifully and

12. *Five Smooth Stones for Pastoral Work*, 211. Peterson does have criticism for his fellow academics, but their tone and degree of harshness seems to me by contrast to be much more muted, respectful. He does decry biblical scholars who write commentaries that are without interest in God, and warn against interpreters of the text who are mere "text-nicians," in *Eat This Book* (55 and 65). But even the most godless commentators can be of some use. He saves his most contemptuous language for ecclesial rather than academic prostitution.

13. *The Pastor*, 19.

succinctly the good in the Enlightenment traditions from which modern historical criticism comes: "People lie a lot."[14] No critical scholar and no Christian could disagree (though perhaps for different reasons—the former in hopes of a previously undiscovered historical layer, the latter because we are sinners). His biography describes him as something of an autodidact, for whom only the library at the great Johns Hopkins University could compete with the local library in his Montana hometown. Perhaps he learned to appreciate the university but not to need it. Interestingly, in *The Pastor*, Peterson doesn't name an institution of learning he attended until he mentions, almost in passing, the name of his seminary (now called New York Theological Seminary). He never tells us where he attended college, only that it was in Seattle. And as he attends Hopkins he doesn't dwell on being at Hopkins. He dwells on his teacher, the great William Albright, among the most important Bible scholars of his generation. For all Albright's brilliance, Peterson praises him most highly for his humility. In Peterson's story, Albright listens to a graduate student's dismissal of a theory of his. Albright pronounced the student right, at his expense: "Forget everything I have said."[15] Fortunately Peterson did not. At its best the academy is an electric place of learning—one of dialogue, engagement, and expanding of the imagination. Academia does not escape Peterson's scathing eye for critique. Interestingly, his language is not as harsh here as when he condemns congregational leadership. At times he's almost gentle. When discussing the church's worshiping life as the matrix for interpreting Scripture he notes, parenthetically, some scholars' disagreement or obliviousness: "I have little regard for the opinion of the university in these matters."[16] Tough words, but not to the level of "prostitute." Over against historical critics' penchant for finding the patchwork behind the biblical text, he responds with the criticism of a writer, noting how most are "highly offended when people get more interested in the contents of their wastebaskets and filing cabinets

---

14. *Working the Angles*, 33, and *Eat This Book*, 68. In the latter he proposes as an antidote for the "hermeneutic of suspicion" approach to texts, as always complicit in corruption or mendacity or oppression, a Christian hermeneutic of "adoration." That has to be right. For adoration to *work*, we have to apply all the tools of criticism at our disposal. Then we also must stand before God and heed God's call to worship and love neighbor. Without the latter, criticism is not genuine criticism. For incorrect approaches to any text or idea can only be discerned vis a vis correct ones, and a right reading of the Bible is meant to draw reading communities toward worship of the God of the Bible.

15. *The Pastor*, 63.

16. *Working the Angles*, 112.

than in the books they write."[17] He hammers on certain scholars for the "breezy arrogance" with which they elide the genuinely erotic love poem of Song of Songs into a document "as interesting as a sex education chart in an eighth-grade hygiene class."[18] More seriously still, too much is excluded from academia: it's too tidy, leaving out "too much life, too much of the world, too much of the students, the complexities of relationships, the intimacy of emotions." At one point in the memoir Peterson says, baldly, "My seminary professors had no idea what pastors were or did."[19] They were ignorant. Tough thing to say about an academic.

But they were also indispensable. And here Peterson's language, otherwise so rich and textured, may be underdeveloped. Andy Crouch points out in his book on culture that his Harvard students were experts in the language of subversion, for the kingdom and against their school.[20] But they were unpracticed in the language of praising the glories that Harvard offers. So too with Peterson. He simply would not be who he is without the theological academy. He'd be further along than most of us—his skill as an autodidact is clearly at the genius level. But he did learn in company. For example, he regularly stops and praises Karl Barth as the epitome of a pastoral theologian. This is not normally how Barth is praised by his friends or cursed by his enemies, but Peterson is, of course, right. And I'm told as Peterson labored away as a pastor all those years he repeatedly reread the *Church Dogmatics*, planting seeds that would bear fruit much later in his work once publishers couldn't get enough of him. Peterson rarely tells us details about what Barth does for him or should do for us. Yet his praise is extravagant, and biblically shaped: "At a time and in a culture in which the Bible had been embalmed and buried by a couple of generations of undertaker-scholars, [Barth] passionately and relentlessly insisted that 'the child is not dead but sleeping,' took her by the hand, and said, 'Arise.'"[21]

17. *The Jesus Way*, 61.

18. *Five Smooth Stones*, 39.

19. The last two quotes are from *The Pastor*, 21–22 and 162.

20. Crouch, *Culture Making*, 96–97. Crouch writes, "We had a very hard time acccounting, in the language of faith, for the delights of a place like Harvard: the thrill of research in a well-equipped library, the ineffable joys of the library stacks, the exhaustion and exhilaration of rowing a six-man boat on the Charles at 5:30 in the morning. I suspect that many students who visited our fellowship, oriented as it was toward critiquing the culture, simply moved on, puzzled at our diffidence or even annoyed at our apparent hypocrisy."

21. *Eat This Book*, 6.

However, we might ask how most of us learn to read Barth if not in the academy—even if according to his memoir Peterson first heard of him from a secular Jew at the gym? I heard Peterson quote Barth in a talk on Sabbath saying, "Only where there are graves can there be resurrection." Yet in *Five Smooth Stones* Peterson attributes the line to Nietzsche, to whom Barth was responding in his *Epistle to the Romans*.[22] Peterson praises Barth in Franz Kafka's words, "If the book we are reading does not wake us, as with a fist hammering on our skull, then why do we read it? . . . A book must be like an ice-axe to break the sea frozen inside us."[23] How are most of us inducted into the multi-generational conversation about Scripture and life that Peterson engages so effortlessly? Through the effort of academic study in institutions of higher education.

Peterson can be at his most lyrical, mystical, writerly self when praising the fruits born of academic erudition. Writers may not like when their garbage dumps are probed but the long-dead people of the Bible yielded their treasures from these very places. Papyri discovered at Oxyrhynchus in Egypt in 1897 showed people writing out grocery lists and conducting other everyday business in koine Greek. Suddenly the everyday, unlearned, market-place Greek of the New Testament seemed appropriately more commonplace—"daily bread" in the Lord's prayer is the same thing a child is fortified to demand from the baker instead of the day-old ripoff variety.[24] In several places Peterson himself gives the best description of the need for Enlightenment-informed, skeptical scholarship: "People lie a lot." Top that, in punchiness, brevity, wisdom! Here we are close to the heart of Peterson's work. He has learned the glories of the academy. At its best it can hand out pick axes to crack the ice inside us. Yet it does this best when combined with the glories of the parish. For example, a parishioner in an apocalyptically bad family situation kept him from reading Revelation in superficial, sentimental ways. Theology (my term more than his) is God's address of us in the present tense. It best not be relegated to historical, past-tense speculation (my term, but I hope faithful to him).[25] The living God is breaking into his beloved but alienated cosmos—it's the only good news that will lift such pastoral luggage. Professors get to ask "what happened?" Pastors get

22. *Five Smooth Stones*, 148.

23. *The Pastor*, 90.

24. *Eat This Book*, 141–43.

25. This from ibid., 52, quoting Hans Urs von Balthasar.

to be *in on the happening* as a new generation of God's people live out the same story.

No wonder Peterson's work in translation on *The Message* was like strolling through a field of ripe fruit trees plucking heavy fruit as it bends its branches toward him.[26] He'd done the hard work of pastoring that makes Scripture yield its treasures. But mixing academy and parish need not mean the choice of one or the other. Pastors apply the same skills in intensive study of texts to patient study of souls. These are not two motions in tandem—they are one and the same.

Go Thou and Do Otherwise

There is a canned prototype for pastoral success in America that Peterson works hard to detonate. It's a model without place—it claims to work as well on either coast or in the middle, in towns large and small. It depends on an efficient, corporately minded pastor. It also depends on a theology that is buttoned-up, unproblematic, and clear. Folks arrive at church in droves and just keep coming, and people are treated as statistics, not souls. As one burgeoning megachurch in my part of the country has painted in enormous letters on the exterior of their building (!), "Catch, Release, Repeat."

At every turn Peterson undoes this model of ministry "success" in America. For him, all ministry is geographical and eschatological (two words the church growth movement would discourage us from using).[27] God comes to us in specific places on the map, named places, irreducibly particular places. No one-size-fits all gospel here, but one as local as Nazareth and Bel Air. And God comes to end the world. The gospel is not a comfort for the relatively-already-comfortable. It upsets everything, especially when we try to use it to achieve something else, or use others in an attempt to serve the gospel. To offer a bit more detail, Peterson's vision of ministry is more art than technique. It trades on being a pastor at play, in leisure, rather than a manager looking to manipulate others to his (sic) ends. It explores the spacious country of Scripture and the God who must never be pondered in a hurry. And it insists that we buckle before the mystery of every other person, especially those in the churches we serve. Peterson may have hard things to say about congregations in America, but for all that,

---

26. *The Pastor*, 303.
27. *Under the Unpredictable Plant*, 148.

they are the place where the *shekinah* of God dwells, the people with whom the incarnate God pitches a tent.

When Peterson reads Scripture like an artist, not a technocrat, he doesn't force it to yield its treasures. Instead, he steps into it and marvels at its most fulsome sense, its greatest depths. In his memoir he says it was artists—with jobs that supported their real work—who helped him see his work as a vocation.[28] And it was when reading Dostoevsky that he discovered a holy person could change society from its margins simply by being holy—and that a novelist could unlock scriptural and personal depths at the same time as a pastor. When Peterson moves into Scripture he finds ever greater depths there, noting how St. Mark ends with the dangling participial *gar* (an academic observation if there ever was one) because the Gospel wants us to write its ending with our lives (a participatory, churchly observation if there ever was one).[29] Scripture is not a source for information; it is an engagement, more akin to a wrestling match or a quarrel than a milquetoast handshake or embrace.[30] Reflecting on Naomi as a world-class kvetcher, Peterson suggests pastors can help their congregations learn how to formulate complaints with appropriate biblical gusto.[31] Ruth's inclusion in Jesus's family tree suggests that our work is to help our parishioners find themselves included in the same collection of questionable saints. Scripture, in the church, is not read so much as joined.   *Yes!,*

Joined to these themes of patient attention to depths is the theme of unhurried pastoral pace. Here Peterson draws most deeply from Wendell Berry: the pastoral life is one of countless small fidelities. Sure, one can travel in this life, but it's best to travel only in one's backyard. Why hurry farther when one can stagger under the weight of holiness of one inch in the ground? Peterson marvels that farmers work hard. But are they in a hurry? So too we pastors should strive not to be in a hurry. We should pay careful attention to the ground, then plant, steward, and wait. Prophets strive to say God's name "correctly, accurately, locally." And that requires a patience willing to buckle the knee at the beauty on the text in front of us and in the face across from us.[32] People are mysteries to be contemplated—not problems to be solved. Scripture too.

28. *The Pastor*, 161.
29. *Under the Unpredictable Plant*, 196.
30. *Eat This Book*, 105.
31. *Five Smooth Stones*, 99.
32. *The Jesus Way*, 119. The other themes sounded in these sentences come from

It would be hard to imagine being farther from the church growth movement of the last quarter century than in the work of Peterson. Yet I'm left wondering what sort of institution we're trying to build here, and what sort of institution of theological education might serve it. Peterson, like all of us, is clearer saying what he is against rather than what he is for. One thing he claims to be for is the monastery, which in church history has managed both to interiorize and socialize the holiness to which God calls us.[33] He's in favor of the posture of the Pentecostals of his youth for being "sin conspicuous and God aware."[34] He is outwardly disdainful of his own chosen mainline tradition at times, but at other times deeply respectful of iconic liberal preachers, of institutions of higher education, and above all for the life of the mind one can cultivate in mainline institutions. How do we create more Petersons, short of growing them in Pentecostal Montana with a revivalist mother, a butcher father, sending them to great east and west coast universities, having them fail at church planting, go back into church leadership, and thrive by attention to Scripture, to the local, and to people's particular souls?

Such an institution will advocate reading fiction as avidly as theology. It will teach an artist's eye, a farmer's patience, an exegete's Greek, a spiritual director's discernment. And even so there is a touch of divine whimsy when God touches one life and uses it in such spectacular, challenging, deepening ways.

God has done precisely that among us in the life and work of Eugene Peterson.

Eat This Book.

33. *Under the Unpredictable Plant*, 98.

34. Ibid., 119.

PART THREE

PEOPLE

Leadership and the Christianity and Culture Dance

Carol Howard Merritt

SITTING IN THE CLAY hut, I admired how my hosts had suspended flowers on a string that lined the walls so that the buds looked like tiny clothes that were hung out to dry. The same type of flowers clustered to make a beautiful arrangement in the middle of the table. Sweltering in the August heat, I reached inside my purse for my trusty tissue to dab the sweat off my forehead. Grace, a woman wrapped in colorful swaths of fabric, stooped to serve me tea. I smiled broadly and thanked her as I accepted the hot liquid, hiding the fact that I wasn't really interested in anything that might elevate my body temperature.

High tea in the afternoon heat was a long-standing tradition that this tribe held. As a guest of the Anglican Church, I participated each day. Aside from the heat, I loved the ritual because it gave me a chance to chat with my hosts and the other church leaders. I also silently ruminated on how disconnected the tradition seemed from the festive, dancing African culture. When the British colonized Uganda, they brought along their religion, language, and customs. Even though teatime seemed more at home in the frigid drawing rooms of British society, the priests had transported the custom to these clay huts, where the inhabitants were situated so much closer to the equator.

My host brought me cookies. I thanked her and thought about the strange dance of religion and culture. I had been in the presence of many anthropologists who cursed missionaries for destroying cultures. The students of human behavior often condemn Christianity for baptizing a people's dress, art, and festivities, until there is nothing left, except a Westernized mutation of the indigenous. Stirring the sugar into my tea, I could see what they meant. The afternoon ritual seemed as out of place as the untouched prayer books in the church of members who could not read.

In the World but Not of the World

From Africa to North America, culture and Christianity often fumble with one another in an awkward dance. Sometimes culture and Christianity work against one another, stepping on each other's toes or fighting for the lead. Other times, religion adapts the corrosive rhythm of culture, taking on its materialism or pounding the drum of military patriotism. Still other times Christianity can purge a region of its celebrations, myths, and rituals in order to replace it with WASP-y "civilized" values.

In its best stance, religion is a faithful corrective of culture, a voice calling out against the world's destructive forces. As spiritual leaders, it is often our job to confront that potent cultural power that has no problem preying on the weak and poor as we give voice to the voiceless. In the United States, we stand up to our voracious capitalism that instigates the business of war, as we call for peace and reconciliation. We resist a culture that disregards the environment when there is a profit to be had, as we plead for resources of the next generation. We withstand the backpatting we receive when we work too much, as we remember the Sabbath as an act of resistance.

Of course, I thought as I dabbed my forehead with the tissue once again, perhaps religion should not *always* be working against culture, especially if the church is going to change the afternoon menu choices of an African tribe. I wondered if the missionaries imagined that they were bringing a more mannerly culture along with their religion. Or perhaps they were just trying to recreate the comforts of their home. Whatever the case might have been, the missionaries were gone and high tea remained. It made me wonder if my anthropologist friends were correct when they criticized the church for destroying cultures through their global outreach.

In a strange way, I think about those beautiful afternoons, spent with fellow African Christians, sipping tea inside the clay hut when I read about Eugene Peterson's leadership. Peterson calls out against the general consensus of our culture and forges a new way as he takes to heart what *The Message* proclaims in Romans 12:2:

> Don't become so well-adjusted to your culture that you fit into it without even thinking. Instead, fix your attention on God. You'll be changed from the inside out. Readily recognize what he wants from you, and quickly respond to it. Unlike the culture around you, always dragging you down to its level of immaturity, God brings the best out of you, develops well-formed maturity in you.

In seminary, pastors preparing for ministry learn about binary forces in our introductory courses. We study H. Richard Niebuhr as he attempts to navigate the relationship in his slim but foundational work *Christ and Culture.* He outlines different postures that a Christian takes when it comes to the larger milieu. Then pastors work in the midst of the tension for the rest of our lives, allowing them to pull us in interesting directions.

When it comes to leadership, Eugene Peterson forcefully swims against the cultural tide, especially when he speaks for long-term, intuitive leadership. But when it comes to the contemporary translations of the Bible, Peterson may not have understood the ways in which he participated with our culture and the impact that he would have on the world at large. Through his words and language, Peterson may not have fully understood how his leadership would shape a generation in deep and meaningful ways.

A Cultural Crisis: The Short-term Career

Fred inspected his hands as he told me the news. He didn't look like himself as his eyes avoided contact. Shame overwhelmed him. Like so many people in the workforce that year, the economic downturn pummeled Fred's company. As a result, he was asked to leave his job. As the markets plunged, companies downsized like weak, crumbling rocks rolling down a jagged slope. Fred, who had been a stellar employee, ended up battered as the financial indicators toppled.

As a pastor in D.C., I learned quickly that any professional inside the beltway had to be adept at changing jobs, especially since so many positions changed with the political will of the country. Still, the flailing economy exacerbated the already volatile situation until it became unbearable for many in our congregation. Lay-off victims became so common in my office that I had already done a great deal of research. I counseled Fred on the practical matters at hand, like making sure that his financial position was secure enough to handle a transition. I spoke to him about his future, brainstorming how he could hone his resume and rely upon some of the networks in the church. We talked about finding spiritual strength in the fact that God loves him, instead of allowing his identity to become wrapped up into his career. I prayed for him daily during the next couple of weeks.

The next time I saw Fred and we had a quiet place to talk, I asked how the transition was going. He replied, "It's not. I told my boss 'no.'"

"What?" I asked while noticing that Fred's confident smile had returned.

He shrugged, "I just explained to him that I refused to leave." Evidently, his employer was trying to bully him to take a smaller salary or step down, but the boss didn't actually have the will to fire the employee.

I thought about how different his response was from my own reactions. Like many people in my generation—those who were born in the '70s—I had been an anxious worker, always looking for signs of the next downsizing. By the time I finished my seminary education, it was the turn of the millennium. The employment culture in our country seemed to have drastically changed since my father began his thirty-year career in one job. The rise of temp-work and internships began to change our expectations as workers. We were only expected to stay at our jobs for two to three years. In fact, we were told to expect about *five* careers in our lifetime.

Pink slips became common, businesses were routinely eaten up by bigger businesses, pension promises were broken, and company loyalty became an alien concept.

Along with the shattering of company loyalty, employee loyalty eroded as well. The Internet seemed to make job searching easier, as companies began to switch to online tools that made discerning a vocation feel a lot like computer dating. When the economic downturn occurred, the frenzy heightened.

When I entered the pastorate, I brought that desperate mentality with me. It seemed like the wise thing to do because pastors were not faring much better than other employees in our country. We stepped into denominational churches that had been in decline for four decades, and the older generation of members who had invested the most into mainline life were now dying. Many congregations were passing away with them.

Our churches budgets began to shrink, congregations closed more rapidly, and some members turned to the pastor as the cause of the decline, not seeing that the whole body was part of a greater decades-long trend.

Each month I heard about another friend who was forced out of his or her ministry position.

To exacerbate matters for seminarians entering the ministry, many congregations, who were full of members over the age of sixty, found they enjoyed a retired pastor's easy efforts and sage advice far more than the young graduate's green preaching and ambitious ideas. Retired employees could work for less money than the starting pastor who was burdened by student debt. Congregations began to rely on retired ministers and lay people instead of calling trained and active ministers.

The economy had changed so that most households were dependent on two salaries, rather than one. Many of us had professional spouses, who often made more money than we did, so we had strategic geographic navigating that we had to do. We not only had to leave our positions when our calls were not working out, but we also had to leave them when our spouse needed to find another job.

But it wasn't just a fear of pastoral downsizing or the two-career conflicts that forced us to become nimble in position switching. I had always been counseled in the ways of business: "If you want to move up, then you need to change jobs every three to four years."[1] This was common knowledge for the brazen careerists of my generation. We learned that having a healthy dose of discontentment was a good thing. We had our full-time jobs, and we understood that our unofficial part-time job was to keep our vitae jittery at the starting gate so that it would be ready for the next thing that came along. We needed to be smart about it all, which meant that we needed to be ready to move.

Even with all of that in mind (or *especially* with all of that in mind), I wish I had read Eugene Peterson's *Under the Unpredictable Plant* when I started in ministry. Peterson describes his commitment to start a congregation and stay at the church for the long term. In the midst of a sprawling suburb, with heels as itchy as the next person's, Peterson made a lifetime commitment to the ministry.[2]

What would happen if pastors stayed rooted in our congregations? I wonder if the church would have a different form or shape if women and men counteracted our culture's short-term career crisis. What if we stared down pressures to leave with a steady, "No"?

1. See, for example, Kamenetz, "The Four-Year Career."
2. Peterson, *Under the Unpredictable Plant.*

Would it help disempower bullies? Too often the genial nature of our congregational life caves to coercion. People don't go to church to get into arguments. We're too nice to fight and we confuse love with spinelessness. So when a cantankerous person moves into power, we learn to appease them, soothing them by letting them have their own way. After years of a community placating small demands, the dictates become louder, until one person begins to affect how the entire body makes decisions.

One case in point was when Clara, a colleague and friend, was under terrible pressure to leave her congregation. The presenting issue was that Clara clinked the communion ware too much when she served the Eucharist. Every time I presided over the table, I wondered how it was even possible to make a racket from clanking cups. But that didn't stop the superb frustration of an adamant church member who didn't appreciate Clara's grace and choreography, and wanted her ousted because of it.

If that was the only issue (and just like in a divorce, there is always something more), the church seemed to be in the clutches of a bully. We have seen how men and women take over, using the power that they have available to them—money, history, or time—to badger a congregation. When a minister begins to threaten their power, they can put a great deal of pressure on a congregation to get rid of the pastor or stir up discontent. The rest of the congregation becomes frustrated with the nastiness, and the body caves to get rid of the cause quickly. In these situations, it's usually much easier to get rid of the pastor than it is to get rid of the noisy patriarch. The leader, who feels battered and frustrated, graciously decides that he or she would probably be better off somewhere else. Anyone who might be new to the community backs off right away. The bullies remain in charge while the church dwindles in size.

But what if the scenario was different? What if the pastor borrowed Fred's instincts and just said "No"?[3] The minister could explain, "I'm not going to leave my position because of my lack of grace when I preside at the table. I'm going to do the best job that I can while you work on your control issues. But I plan to be in this congregation for thirty years." How would things change? I imagine that we might have some healthier congregations. Not only would bullies begin to have a less destructive place in our bodies,

3. I'm speaking from my particular tradition, the Presbyterian Church (USA), where we have a call system. I assume that much of this discussion would be different among my United Methodist friends who work with an appointment system. However, the wisdom of longevity can be helpful for all traditions.

but pastors would have the chance to do the meaningful relationship building that can only come with time.

Of course, there are occasions when a pastoral relationship *should* be severed. Sometimes a minister's wrongs are too drastic to overlook and forcing the pastor out is the best thing for the church. Likewise, some churches become so critical and demanding that a pastor who stays serves to prolong and exacerbate an abusive relationship.

Those exceptional cases aside, Peterson calls out amongst the discontent that surrounds us and encourages pastoral leaders to set aside the careerism that can engulf us—that drive for more prestige, for more members, and for bigger steeples. He encourages passion, even in the midst of the mundane.[4]

If we had more of a covenantal aspect to our commitments together, would churches and pastors be healthier? If pastors did not feel like they had to get all of their work done in less than five years, would we have more patience with our congregations? If we learned that we needed to negotiate with one another, for the long term, would we learn how to communicate better? I'm sure as church leaders, we would certainly be able to hone our intuition.

Intuition and a Dog's Nose

When it comes to working as a leader in a pastoral context, one of Peterson's metaphors stands out for me more than any other: a dog's nose.[5] When he describes the discernment process and the call to ministry, Peterson talks about Denise Levertov's poem "Overland to the Islands:"

> Let's go—much as that dog goes,
> intently haphazard. The
> Mexican light on a day that
> "smells like autumn in Connecticut"
> makes iris ripples on his
> black gleaming fur—and that too
> is as one would desire—a radiance

4. Peterson, *Under the Unpredictable Plant*, 41–46.

5. Peterson explains the dog metaphor in an interview with Raz, "Eugene Peterson Chronicles Memories in 'Pastor.'" In *The Pastor*, Peterson emphasizes "every step, an arrival," a line Levertov echoed from a Rilke poem.

> consorting with the dance.
>
>   Under his feet
> rocks and mud, his imagination, sniffing,
> engaged in its perceptions—dancing
> edgeways, there's nothing
> the dog disdains on his way,
> nevertheless he keeps moving, changing
> pace and approach but
> not direction—"every step an arrival."[6]

I have plenty of chances to think about the comparison when I walk my own pet each night. My dog is a mutt, but her herding instincts clearly dominate her personality. Her salt and pepper fur curls on her back in rebellious waves until the strands of her unruly hair settle in a determined order when they get to her nose.

Like the dog in the poem, she focuses on the ground, moving from the grass to the tree to the mailbox, and back to the tree. A smell awakens her to a shrub. A sound perks her senses and she suddenly bolts up, looking to hunt. There does not seem to be any order to the process; the scent of any sort of dog seems to get her off track. But then the determination comes back, and she goes back to sniffing and finding just the right spot to do her business. That dog's nose, that sense that every step is an arrival, is not only about the initial recognition that God is calling us into ministry, but about each day of ministry.

We open ourselves and remain aware of the smells and sounds around us. We may even seem like we are going off course, but underlying all of it, there is that determined drive to do what we were made to do. What God intends.

I think of this as intuition because it points to the driving force that underlies whatever senses might surround us. The truth of the metaphor speaks clearly in the midst of our hyper-fad, commercialized culture.

About a year before I'm writing this, the entrepreneurial co-founder of Apple computers died. As a businessman, Steve Jobs did a great deal to change the way we communicate with one another and helped Apple amass an incredible fortune, but Jobs had many personal failings and used immoral employment practices in China.[7] In spite of all that, in the last

6. Levertov, *Selected Poems*.

7. Austen, "The Story of Steve Jobs." Steven Thrasher, in "Steve Jobs's Death and the

months, instead of ministers decrying the abuses in the workplace, I have read articles, posts, and sermons imploring pastors to be like Steve Jobs and the church like Apple computers.

Of course, the church could use a good dose of creativity, but why should we emulate a man who pays his workers a miniscule fraction of what he made? Why would we aspire to be like someone who provided working conditions that would never be allowed in the United States? Are we so enamored by success that we would strive to emulate someone who kept sweatshops operating?

I chafe under the advice and I'm happy to read Peterson alongside the pleas that we ought to become as tech gurus. Peterson reminds me that we cannot become fully occupied by the sights, smells, sounds, and successes of those around us while abandoning our underlying intent.

Another way in which we can have less focus than a dog's nose is when we see the *tools* of ministry become the *purpose* of ministry. Right now, as our world shifts the ways in which we communicate, we have all sorts of tools at our fingertips—ways in which we research, talk to one another, and form community. We have shifted from writing memos to sending emails, talking on the telephone to texting, and pulling out our paper calendars to syncing dates. We have moved from personal invitations to sending Facebook notifications and organizing Meetups. We have moved from newspaper announcements to Yelp reviews. And much of our social justice outreach is done with Twitter hashtags.

While all of these tools and shifting ways of doing things might be sights and sounds that surround the dog on her walk, they are not the dog's intent. The tools entice us with the promise of speed and efficiency. Yet the drive of our church has been the same for thousands of years: to love God and to love our neighbors as we love ourselves. No matter how much shifts and changes, that remains the underlying motivation.

Peterson's voice is a welcome call to reject the consumerism, lust for success, and greed that seeps into our ecclesial lives. He points out the slithering serpents that entice us to confuse the tools of ministry with the goal of ministry. Peterson reminds leaders to go back to that singular drive.

Legacy of the Foxconn Factory Suicides" (*The Village Voice*, October 6, 2011) recounts the suicides at the factory where iPhones and iPads are made.

The Language of Culture

Even though Peterson's religious tradition of origin did not allow for women ministers, his Pentecostal mother found a way to minister amongst the coal miners and lumberjacks, bringing her passionate voice into song and storytelling.

I smiled as I read the account. Likewise, I've also come from a succession of women who have found ways to minister in spite of their tradition's bans. My charismatic/Baptist mother and aunt serve Special Gatherings, an organization that gathers communities of mentally challenged people in Florida and South Carolina. On Saturday afternoon, buses and vans transport men and women from their group homes and houses to the fellowship hall of a Methodist church, where they keep the out-of-tune piano. After a time of singing, they read from *The Message*.

My mom encourages the families to read, study, and memorize *The Message*. The accessible language allows parents, siblings, and her mentally challenged members to find resonance and meaning whatever their particular intellectual capacity might be. A part of what makes the language of *The Message* comprehensible, the reason why it has such depth, is because of its language. And so our dance between religion and culture begins again, keeping a rhythm and beat. Just as religion has to be an important component of culture, so does language. And the words of our faith, as we read them, speak them, memorize them, and allow them to form us, become a part of the cadence of our lives.

Many experts point to the King James Version of the Bible as one of the most significant forces in keeping the particular cadence and rhythm of the English language intact. To have our vast country reading one book week after week shaped our culture so much that many of our common idioms comes from the poetry of the KJV and we hardly recognize them.

The one way in which Peterson confounds my expectations is with his declaration in an interview with *Christianity Today*, "It's very dangerous to use the language of the culture to interpret the gospel. Our vocabulary has to be chastened and tested by revelation, by the Scriptures."[8]

Now to be clear, Peterson is writing in the context of using intimate language regarding our spiritual lives (like having a "personal relationship with Jesus Christ"). He suggests that in our American vocabulary, this type of language has a sexual tone that connotes completion. Yet it sounds

8. Galli, "Spirituality for all the Wrong Reasons."

strange to have Peterson scolding us not to use the language of the culture to interpret the gospel, because it seems to be a hallmark of what he does.

In another part of the *Christianity Today* interview, Peterson talks about not bending to the whims of culture. He explains, "When you start tailoring the gospel to the culture, whether it's a youth culture, a generation culture or any other kind of culture, you have taken the guts out of the gospel. The gospel of Jesus Christ is not the kingdom of this world. It's a different kingdom."

Then he goes on to explain how a minister did not wear a robe, because he wanted to relate to the culture of a new generation. Yet, the pastor ended up putting back on the robe.

What frustrates me about this story is the assumption that an academic robe is truer to the gospel of Jesus Christ. I wear a robe each Sunday, but I do not assume that the big black garb makes me more like Jesus. I realize that it's expected from my Presbyterian heritage that values education and wants me garbed as a reminder that I went to seminary. When I get my doctorate, I'll have some velvet chevrons to sew on my robe. But that will not get me any closer to doing ministry like Jesus. It just makes me more civilized and palpable for the traditional Protestant members whom I serve.

And so the dance begins again. From the cool clay huts of the African village, to the fearful crisis of employment, to our infatuation with success, to the cold-tiled Methodist fellowship hall, we learn from Peterson how Christian leadership calls for confrontation and a bit of resonance with our cultural surroundings.

Enough with Little

THE PROPHETIC PASTOR

Kyle Childress

He koude in litel thyng have suffisance.
—CHAUCER, *THE CANTERBURY TALES*

My task was to pray and give direction and encourage that *lived* quality of the gospel—patiently, locally, and personally.
—EUGENE PETERSON, *THE PASTOR*

WE WERE SITTING ON the tailgate of Wilson's pickup after sharpening and oiling chainsaws when he held out a bag of chewing tobacco and said, "Preacher, you can't cut wood without a chaw." I took a small, almost dainty, three-fingers-full while he stuffed what looked like the entire bag in the corner of his mouth and we hopped down and proceeded to cut wood on a crisp winter afternoon. The very young and newly minted pastor of a small rural Baptist church in central Texas was helping saw firewood for the oldest member of the congregation, a widow who still heated her tiny frame house with an old fashioned pot-belly wood stove. Wilson was a quiet leader in the congregation, a tough old leather-skinned surveyor by trade who was as tender-hearted toward children and widows as any man

I've ever known. Later I would learn that the real reason I was there was so he could get to know this young preacher who was preaching so hard on race and racism and stirring up trouble. I thought I was a prophet; they wanted a pastor. And I began to learn that day that I couldn't be the first without becoming the second.

What Wilson and others were beginning to teach me was reinforced and deepened when I began to read the books of Eugene Peterson a few years later. But not at first. When introduced to Peterson, my first response was that he was no prophet. He was the pastor of a congregation in the midst of the turmoil of the '60s and '70s who never said a word about the issues of that turmoil. He made no denunciations of injustice, said nothing against racism or poverty or war or any number of other issues that, from my perspective, the white church, especially in the South, had too long been silent about or, worse, had actually supported. I was a young preacher who had watched the southern white church oppose most of what was good coming out of the civil rights movement of my childhood. From my point of view, if the American white church said anything about Vietnam it was to wave the flag; this was not the Way of Jesus Christ. We—the church—were called to do better; we were to follow Jesus Christ, not the status quo. I saw Eugene Peterson as good and gentle, loving and attentive to God, to the Bible, and to his people, but I heard him as much too like what I had heard growing up. I wanted to make a difference in the world and Peterson seemed to settle for simply being different as a person. I dreamed of being a part of something Big while he wrote of making small talk with parishioners; I wanted to change things now while he worked quietly, behind the scenes, planting seeds and tilling the soil.

My testimony, however, is that after more than thirty years of being a pastor my reading of Peterson has changed along with my understanding of being prophetic. A pastor can be as prophetic sitting around the coffee table in quiet conversation as she is when in the pulpit. Even more, it is usually the small and mundane work of visiting parishioners, listening to them, and paying attention to their lives that not only allows us to speak a hard, prophetic word when preaching but also allows the congregation to hear us. They hear us when they respect us, and they respect us because we've done the detailed work of being their pastor.

Eugene Peterson is emphatic that most pastoral work is "little" work—small acts patiently and quietly done over a long time. In his memoir, *The Pastor*, Peterson says he realized that his role as a pastor was to encourage his people to live the gospel: "Patiently: I would stay with these people; there are no quick or easy ways to do this. Locally: I would embrace the conditions of this place—economics, weather, culture, schools, whatever— so that there would be nothing abstract or piously idealized about what I was doing. Personally: I would know them, know their names, know their homes, know their families, know their work—but I would not pry, I would not treat them as a cause or a project, I would treat them with dignity. . . . [and I would] see to it that these men and women in my congregation become aware of the possibilities and the promise of living out in personal and local detail what is involved in following Jesus, and be a companion to them as we do it together."[1]

That small country church where Wilson was a member started growing me into becoming a pastor who worked patiently, locally, and personally. They called me to be their pastor, but only after a couple of months of listening to me and watching me did they invite me to be ordained. According to their low-church Baptist polity I could be ordained by my home church or by them, and since I was discovering through these people whether I was truly called to the gospel ministry, I decided that I wanted them to put their hands on my head and set me aside as a pastor.

Brother Starnes, an eighty-eight-year-old retired pastor from my college church, among the wisest veteran pastors I knew and gentle in spirit, was invited to give the ordination sermon (rumor had it that he had the King James Bible memorized). He preached a simple sermon telling me to love God, love the Bible, and love God's people. When he sat down, our deacon called me forward and I knelt as the people lined up to put their rough-hewn hands on my head and tell me I was called of God to preach and pastor. Then we proceeded to one of those country church suppers of which legends are made, with lots of homemade food fresh from the garden, good conversation, storytelling, and laughter. As the evening wore on, people began to drift toward home and I escorted Brother Starnes to his car, where he leaned against the hood and told me that in addition to what he had told me in the sermon there were two other things I needed to know in order to be a faithful pastor. "You need to learn to be able to say 'No!' and 'Hell no!'" This sounded like "sic'em" to a young pastor eager to be a prophet.

Already aware of the racist jokes and comments all too prevalent among some church members, I had recently learned that no one of any

1. Peterson, *The Pastor*, 247.

skin color but white had been inside the church doors in its 125-year-history; suddenly, my calling had a clarity. If I were going to say "No!" and "Hell no!" then I would say it over racism.

A few weeks later I had a college friend from Nigeria come and fill the pulpit, which set off a firestorm of conflict and confrontation—a twelve-gauge shotgun was shoved in my face, I was cussed out, and I learned that a few were determined to run me off. That was when Wilson called me and asked me to help him saw wood.

In between chain-sawing we made small talk, and I listened to some of his stories of the congregation. Eventually, my preaching on race came up. I found it instructive that he never suggested that I quit talking about race but he did suggest that I needed to visit the members of the congregation more and learn to listen to them. Furthermore, he would be willing to go with me. What I didn't learn until later is that Wilson and most of the congregation had already had several conversations concluding that it was time for the church to begin to change, including on race; they also needed to quit pulling guns on the pastor, and they needed to give me a chance.

Meanwhile, I had heard from some of my pastoral heroes about the importance of visitation and listening to church members. Browning Ware, of the First Baptist Church, Austin, Texas, told me to "visit, visit, visit. There never has been a pastor fired for visiting too much, so you go see your people and sit in their kitchens with them and listen to them and pray with them." Around this time I heard Ernest Campbell, the former senior minister of the Riverside Church in New York, speak at a conference. Campbell modeled for me what a prophetic pastor looked like, so I wanted desperately to hear him and speak to him if possible. After his address, in between people tugging at his sleeves reminding him of the flight he had to catch, he patiently listened to me as if he didn't have another thing in the world to do. His response I'll never forget: "Remember the words of the Apostle Paul to the troubled church at Corinth, 'I have for you a more excellent way.' Go show your congregation the more excellent way of the love of Christ."

So reinforced with the advice of wise prophetic pastors, I set off to visit, listen to, and get to know every single member of the congregation, sometimes with Wilson or a couple of other members going with me. Over the next nearly five years I hoed weeds in gardens and picked tomatoes, learned how to drive a tractor, sat on porches and sipped sweet iced tea, sat around a quilt frame while three elderly women performed intricate needlework, fished, helped re-roof a house, ate barbequed alligator, changed out a carburetor on a pickup, and numerous other duties never mentioned in seminary, and all the time I listened and learned about these people's lives as we talked about Jesus, the Bible, growing in Christ, and about race, too.

Instead of the large and dramatic "thus saith the Lord" pronouncements from the pulpit, I was practicing the little work of prophetic and pastoral conversation. In the General Prologue to *The Canterbury Tales* Chaucer tells of the Parson, "poor but abounding in goodness . . . he was humble, gracious" and "he was able to live on little," or "he had enough with little." And though Chaucer specifically is referring to the Parson's modest income and simple lifestyle, it is also an apt description of the Parson's ministry. He had submitted himself to the modest and little ways of good pastoral ministry, including prophetic ministry. The Parson visits far and wide everyone, high or low estate, but he also would "chide and scold, sharp and straight from the heart" if needed.[2] He was pastoral; he was prophetic, but everything he did was little, or in Peterson's words, patient, local, and personal.[3]

The Parson's ministry and Peterson's are for the long haul. It is slow work. No fast-food, instant Christians here. I've been in my present congregation twenty-three years and it was only as I passed the six- and seven-year mark that my counseling began to pick up. People began to come and see me because they began to realize that I was going to stay with them and not move on to the next bigger opportunity. Trust was built and friendships grew. During our eighteenth year, while we were away on sabbatical, the congregation built a porch onto our house. After it was complete I had people call me and ask if I was going to be on the porch; they wanted to stop by and talk. I soon learned that just sitting on the porch and "talking among friends" was much more significant than "counseling with the pastor" in my study at the church. Another time, while at the church I had a fellow stop by and ask me to go look at fishing boats with him. I didn't

2. Chaucer, *The Canterbury Tales*, 15–16.

3. It is interesting to study the analogous work of the civil rights movement, contrasting the working styles of the Southern Christian Leadership Conference (SCLC) with that of the Student Nonviolent Coordinating Committee (SNCC) and the Mississippi Freedom Movement. The SCLC organized for the "big" events of marches and mass meetings with Martin Luther King, Jr. coming to town at the "big" moment. On the other hand, SNCC did the "little" and "slow" work in the "backwaters," sitting on porches, picking cotton alongside field hands and farmers, listening, learning, and discovering what needed to be done and how to do it. See Marsh, *The Beloved Community*; Payne, *I've Got the Light of Freedom;* and Hauerwas and Coles, *Christianity, Democracy, and the Radical Ordinary*, 57–78.

have time to spend the afternoon driving around to boat dealers but I had known this person for ten years and sensed that there was more going on than just looking at boats. So I dropped what I was doing and climbed into the pickup with him. Only after an hour and a half of looking at more boats than I knew existed, the conversation turned to his relationship with God and him asking me to teach him to pray. It took three hours, four boat dealers, and ten years of friendship to have that conversation.

Growing Christians is highly relational, or as Peterson puts it "personal," and that is why he says he is committed to being a companion to his parishioners. One of Peterson's mentors is farmer and writer Wendell Berry, who said, "A farm can be too big for a farmer to husband properly or pay proper attention to."[4] It is the same with a congregation; there can be too many people, too much going on, and too many meetings to properly know in detail the lives of one's members. Even the clergy of large congregations tell me that the real work of church goes on in small groups of various types within their church, so this is not a criticism of large churches as much as it is a statement about the personal and relational nature of the gospel ministry.

Back in my first congregation, when I listened to them and got to know them as real persons—their struggles, fears, history, and hope —I became their companion, or friend. It did not mean I ceased being their pastor, a lesson I had to learn, as well. When I walked into a room full of people in the hospital where someone was dying, they did not want simply a friend, they wanted their pastor. But they wanted a pastor who knew them and loved them, would pray and grieve with them, and walk alongside them. Becoming their pastor who was their friend was not about "becoming one of the guys," which was impossible. Friendship was about mutual, self-giving love for each other and becoming a community of friends, in which Charles Campbell says members "give themselves in love for each other by engaging in these kinds of mutual encouragement, support, and correction."[5]

---

4. Berry, *Standing by Words*, 70. Peterson says, "Wendell Berry is a writer from whom I have learned much of my pastoral theology. Berry is a farmer in Kentucky. On this farm, besides plowing fields, planting crops, and working horses, he writes novels and poems and essays. The importance of place is a recurrent theme—place embraced and loved, understood and honored. Whenever Berry writes the word 'farm,' I substitute 'parish': the sentence works for me every time." In *Under the Unpredictable Plant*, 131.

5. Campbell, *The Word Before the Powers*, 161.

This changed the entire dynamic of my relationship to the congregation. As their companion and friend, they weren't the enemy any longer, and therefore my preaching changed. Instead of "you" language, I used more and more "we" language. I encouraged more, became more loving, and talked about the love of God that casts out all fear. Charles Campbell, in his remarkable book *The Word Before the Powers*, says, "The preacher does not stand over against the congregation but rather stands with them as one who also struggles with complicity in the face of the powers; all stand together in need of redemption. . . . In this kind of preaching, to put it another way, the distinctions between the 'pastoral' and the 'prophetic' begin to lose some of their sharpness."[6]

Campbell goes on to say, "Such an approach shifts the attention away from the twenty minutes of the sermon to the communal relationships within which the sermon occurs. . . . When a friend speaks to us, we are willing to listen. We know we share a common purpose with the friend, and we know the friend cares for us and seeks our good. Within this relationship, we are even willing to listen to strong words from a friend—words of critique and challenge as well as words of comfort and support."[7]

In becoming their friend and companion and listening to them, I learned that the issues of race and racism were more complex than I'd thought. Many of them knew it was time to change but didn't know how, and they found themselves caught in something much larger than their individual choices and willpower. They were caught in generations of ignorance and systems of fear.

I didn't know how to express it theologically at the time, but I was experiencing locally what Campbell, and Walter Wink and William Stringfellow before him, calls the Principalities and Powers, that "'something larger than ourselves' within which many of us often feel trapped and against which we often feel powerless."[8] These spiritual Powers are embodied in institutions, systems, and ways of being corporately and socially, extending over time. Racism, as a Power, was more than an individual's choices or perspective. My church members were responsible for their racist attitudes, habits, and practices, but it was important for them and me to know that

6. Ibid., 92.

7. Ibid., 162.

8. Ibid., 10. See also Walter Wink's important work on the Powers. His most concise and summary work is *The Powers That Be: Theology for a New Millennium*. And William Stringfellow's groundbreaking *An Ethic for Christians and Other Aliens in a Strange Land*.

we were caught in a web of something larger than our individualism and particular choices. To deal with such racism was going to take deeper spiritual resources than I realized at the time, and it was going to take the whole community of faith living and working together.

As I grew into the realization of what the church was up against with the Powers, I also grew in my appreciation of Eugene Peterson. Peterson continues to be unparalleled in returning pastors to the deep wells of spiritual communion with God through prayer and the Bible, thus helping us cultivate and nurture a church capable of that same deep communion. This, in turn, empowers us to be capable of resistance to the Powers. In his classic reflection on the pastoral office through the lens of the Jonah story, *Under the Unpredictable Plant*, Peterson speaks of "a man here, a woman there determined to live nobly: singing a song, telling a story, working honestly, loving chastely. Pockets of resistance form when these men and women recognize each other and take heart from one another."[9] And while Peterson is primarily speaking in this context of clergy, the same holds true of the church becoming a "pocket of resistance." This is exactly what Brother Starnes told me at my ordination, as I look back over many years in retrospect, when he told me to "love God, love the Bible, and love God's people," and also "learn to say 'No!' and 'Hell no!'" His words were less about my preaching on racism and more about forming an entire congregation, a community in Christ, able to love God so clearly and deeply that they are able to say "No!" and "Hell no!" to the Powers. Ordination was not so much about becoming a prophet as it was pastorally forming a prophetic community.[10] As Moses said, "Would that all the Lord's people were prophets, and that the Lord would put his spirit on them!" (Num 11:29).

This did not mean back in my first pastorate that I quit preaching on "issues." In the face of the Powers, social issue preaching can be superficial with its assumption that the congregation simply needs to make different choices or change its mind. At the same time, it is important for the congregation to know what it's up against, and naming and exposing the Powers is part of a pastoral ministry that seeks to form pockets of resistance.[11]

It also does not mean that everyone in the congregation is in agreement or at the same place as they talk, study, pray, and struggle over what

9. Peterson, *Under the Unpredictable Plant*, 37.

10. See Campbell, *The Word Before the Powers*, especially 92–94 on forming what he calls a "non-violent community of resistance."

11. Ibid., 107–10.

it means to be the body of Christ, a pocket of resistance in the face of the Powers. One Sunday night during a congregational meeting, one big and angry man stood up on the back row and said, "I'm sick and tired of the preacher preaching on race and I'm going to whip his ass right here, right now!" A gasp went up from the entire congregation; they were upset that he said "ass" in church! He tried to get past the people sitting on the pew but couldn't get out fast enough so he started climbing over the pews as he came at me. I was standing down at the front thinking to myself, "What in the world am I going to do?" But by the time he got down front, Wilson and three other men stood in front of him, blocking his way, and said, "If you're going to whip the preacher you need to take it outside." I didn't know it at the time, but apparently there was a protocol about not whipping preachers inside the church house. Outside was another matter. Well, the man promptly turned around and went outside and stood in the yard while the rest of the congregation followed him out and formed a large circle with him in the middle. I stepped out onto the front porch of the church and kept thinking, "What am I going to do?" and "I can't believe this is going on." Meanwhile, when he started coming at me again, the same four men, led by Wilson, stepped out between him and me and said, "If you are going to whip the preacher, you're going to have to whip us first." The man hesitated for a moment, turned, and left.

I stayed at that church for another year before leaving to do other things, including finishing my seminary work before returning to the pastorate in another city some three hours away. Over the next twenty-five years I stayed in touch with Wilson and other members of the congregation and occasionally stopped to see them when I passed through town. One day I got a call that Wilson had died, and since the church was in between pastors, the family asked if I would perform the funeral.

When I arrived the church parking lot was full and inside, scattered throughout, were many familiar faces. But what was particularly striking to me were all of the unfamiliar faces in the service, black faces and a few brown faces mixed in with the white faces. Who were these people and what were they doing here?

"Oh, didn't you know? About half of the membership of the church is black now," someone told me after the graveside. I suppose they could see the puzzled look on my face because they explained, "Since you've left we've had probably four preachers but every one of them showed us that God is no respecter of persons. A couple of preachers started picking up kids who weren't in church anywhere else and bringing them here to church on Sunday mornings, and they happened to be black children. We saw the future: either we were going to be black and white together or else the church was going to die. Anyway, after awhile the kids' parents started coming and one thing led to another and, well, now we have lots of black members and even a Hispanic couple."

Patiently, locally, and personally—five pastors working with one small church over thirty years, drinking gallons of iced tea and coffee, eating home-grown tomatoes, listening to lots of stories, marrying and burying, praying and preaching, helping grow a prophetic community of faith that is a witness to the gospel of Jesus Christ. My testimony is that Eugene Peterson is right.

Eugene Peterson Saved My Ministry, and Ten Ways He Can Save Yours Too, with Jesus's Help (Not)

Lillian Daniel

TWENTY YEARS INTO MY life of ordained ministry, I decided to spend our church's entire 150th anniversary year preaching my way through the Gospel of Mark, from *The Message* translation by Eugene Peterson. There were moments when the congregation laughed out loud at some of the readings, either from delight, or sometimes shock, to hear biblical characters saying things like, "Shut up."

I found myself telling them about the enormous difference that Peterson's work had made to the wider church, across the theological spectrum. But that year with Mark also gave me a chance to pause and remember the difference this translator had made in my life as a pastor, nearly two decades earlier. Long before *The Message* had changed the way we hear Scripture, Peterson's writing changed the way I heard my early call.

New to the ministry, straight out of Yale Divinity School, I found myself an associate minister at a large and historic New England church where my five bedroom colonial parsonage sat next to a white wooden meeting house from the 1800s. In the Congregational tradition, the church windows were clear, to let the gospel light shine out into the world and to allow the concerns of the world to be always visible from within the church. In this case, the "concerns of the world" were things like misbehaving dogs straining at the leash, children picnicking, or the entire village delighting in the annual strawberry festival on the town green.

"Town green" was what the newer upwardly mobile residents called the lovely emerald gem in the center of the village. But the older residents, who remembered the town not as a suburb but as a farming community, called it by its real name: the *church green*. And a thriving church from the 1800s stood at the center of it, looking over the town, presiding like a proud and aged matriarch.

It was 1993 and this was my first parish, in the town of Cheshire, Connecticut, where apparently no one had gotten the word that Christendom was over. But all around us, in circles that no layperson was a part of, we ministers were talking about it. Loren Mead had written *The Once and Future Church,* a call to arms to mainline Protestants to do something before they became old line, or even worse, spent down the principal on their endowments.

The field of Congregational Studies was producing real data about our churches, and a few brave souls were telling the truth that no one had told me at Yale Divinity School. My school had not yet discovered, or more likely, not yet noticed, that burgeoning field. But writers in the *Christian Century* magazine trumpeted the statistics that our denominations were in free fall, and my own United Church of Christ was a contender to win the race to bottom.

In the news media at the time, conservative megachurches dominated the public imagination of the future of Christianity, and that was a conversation that laypeople were a part of. Members of my historic Congregational Church wondered at such stories, but there were few examples of churches like that near us. Those megachurches seemed to exist in mega places, like Texas, California, and that great mega mystery to New Englanders, the South. But one church in our denomination, in a neighboring historic town (now a wealthy suburb) had a pastor enamored with the teachings of Robert Schuller. That old New England church had boomed using the principles of the Crystal Cathedral, which was an enormous televised ministry born in a drive-in theater.

Our church in Cheshire had over a thousand members, two services with two full Sunday schools, and a senior minister who had been there for over thirty years. But the budget never flowed in like milk and honey, and some worried that we just weren't as "with it" as we might be. The church leaders looked to their twenty-four-year-old, newly-minted pastor for cues, asking me about "best practices," "deliverables," and "takeaways" from what they assumed was a master's degree as practical as their own MBAs.

I had spent four years as a religion major at Bryn Mawr College, where my specialty was viewing medieval mystical nuns through the lens of feminist theory. That was followed by three years at Yale Divinity School, where I had fallen in love with Paul, Augustine, Calvin, and Jonathan Edwards. I realized to my horror that my first congregation had two—and only two—areas they expected their new young associate minister to be proficient in: fundraising and church growth.

The lay leaders, having no idea that I must have skipped those two days of class at divinity school, asked me to devote my attention to these matters. The sixty-four-year-old senior minister, who had mentored (or in some cases suffered through) more associate ministers than most clergy, was hardly threatened by such a request of me. In fact, he appeared to welcome it. That should have been my first clue.

I had learned enough at Bryn Mawr, my little liberal arts womb with a view, to know this: that I knew absolutely nothing about the two things the congregation wanted me to know a great deal about. So in good liberal arts fashion, I took the bull by the horns and took action, which meant that I went out to look for some books to read on the subject. In the days before the Internet, I headed to the book table at every clergy conference I could sign up for. I was going to solve this problem in the only way I knew how. I was going to read about it. Look out world, Lillian is heading to the bookstore.

I soon discovered that my own people in the more liberal Protestant churches were long on books about the decline in members and money. They just didn't seem to be writing about what to *do* about it, other than to criticize those more conservative churches that had the bad manners to be booming.

I took some comfort in those books for a while. Yeah, who wants to be a megachurch, you big bullies? I'd rather be small, shrinking, and right, than big, booming, and wrong. That could have been our denominational motto in those days.

But after a while that fare grew thin. I took a group of lay leaders to visit the mainline church nearby that was Crystal Cathedralizing itself, and it was impressive. They still had a lovely historic church building, but they also had things like greeters in the parking lot, friendly ushers who actually tried to assist newcomers, multiple services—some of which were not on

Sunday. And, in a bold move, they had thrown aside the lectionary in favor of something I had been taught to fear above all other sins at Yale Divinity School—the topical sermon series. That last sin was greatly troubling to me in those days, right up there with refusing to contribute to NPR and throwing recyclables into the regular trash, but there you have it. They were mavericks at the growing church, mainliners who were learning from the evangelical world of church growth.

Church growth? Who knew there *was* such a category? In the United Church of Christ circles in which I ran, on the rare occasions when we did speak about growth, we were always careful to add: "by which we don't just mean numerical growth but spiritual also." All of this was meant to reassure us that small, shrinking, and right, was a form of growth as well.

After all, the early church was full of small churches. The disciples were only a band of twelve. Perhaps soon we would join them in faithfulness with average church sizes of a dozen or less. Our denomination's ecumenical motto was "That they may all be one," but sometimes I wondered if that was really our aspiration for the perfect church size: just one lonely, faithful, politically correct member with no one to squabble with about preserving the endowment.

Getting cynical within my own shrinking tribe, I threw myself headlong into the evangelical growth gurus. I learned about purpose-driven churches long before there was a purpose-driven life. I followed the freewheelers who told us those sacred cows made great hamburgers with powerful stories of how they had grown their fabulous churches, with Jesus's help. And with the help of their lovely wife. There was always a lovely wife.

No women ministers of course. But always a lovely "I-couldn't-have-done-it-without-her" wife, a veritable equal partner in the ministry, who in these narratives always chimed in at some moment of her husband's despair ("Oh no, the billboard we ordered is too small for our vision!") with words of comfort to the weary leader that reminded him of a) his humility and b) his designation as God's anointed to not only save the church but to write a book telling the rest of us how to do it. In ten steps. Always a list of ten steps. Or twenty ways to do one thing or another.

I discovered *Leadership* magazine, aimed at evangelical pastors, full of tips from the charismatic men who back then didn't wear hipster glasses but were hip in the way of the day, in Hawaiian shirts, khaki pants and portable mikes. They were interviewed to inspire the rest of us with their humility and humble beginnings. ("Yes, I can remember when we were meeting in the old high school and the PowerPoint died in the middle of the message and I really thought, right then, it was all over. But God did not abandon us.")

After awhile, I found myself getting depressed with this genre as well. I started skipping the growth-oriented articles because they always left me with a long to do list ("No time to write the sermon this week. I have to recruit a parking lot ministry team").

Gradually, I found myself drawn instead to the small church stories in the magazine, about treasurers who had run off with the mission money, and the inevitable "ten steps to prevent it from happening to you." I lingered over the anonymous articles, because I had learned that those were the ones that were comfortingly depressing: pastors who felt discouraged, pastors who gambled, pastors who pretended to pray but didn't really. But the truth is, between the mainline decline books and the ten steps to church growth articles, I was stumbling ten steps at a time, downhill, to the blues.

It was at this juncture that I discovered Eugene Peterson. His name seemed to come up in both camps, from the mainline to the evangelical, not usually at the center of the conference book display but somewhere off to the side, a little pile of small books. In a moment of vulnerability, I confided to a more seasoned pastor that I was thinking of quitting the ministry after only a couple of years. He recommended that I read *Under the Unpredictable Plant*.

In the early nineties, the Lilly Endowment reported that a disproportionate number of new clergy were leaving within the first few years, and my friends were already starting to quit. They were leaving frustrating positions with oppressive senior ministers who did all the weddings, funerals, and baptisms, leaving the associates to play the fruit game in the basement with the youth, but still somehow work every night. My young clergy friends were starting to say things like, "I went to grad school for this?" and "I could have gone to law school. In fact, I could *still* go to law school."

Peterson framed my problem on the very first page of *Under*: "Then this chasm opened up, this split between personal faith and pastoral vocation. I was stopped in my tracks. I looked around for a bridge, a rope, or a tree to lay across the crevasse and allow passage. I read books, I attended workshops, I arranged consultations. Nothing worked."[1]

How long had this Eugene Peterson been spying on my life?

---

1. Peterson, *Under the Unpredictable Plant*, 1.

Peterson explained that most clergy leave their parishes due either to boredom or ambition. When I read that, it convicted me. I had a good senior colleague and a good church. I was frustrated that I could not meet their expectations of success, but I didn't have an alternative vision for myself, other than more school. I was thinking about going back to get a PhD to return to church history, back before the church had any problems of the momentous nature I was encountering (studying the Spanish Inquisition seemed more appealing than listening to the predictable howl at yet another denominational meeting: "Where are the young people?"). I wanted to go back to a world where I could keep my scholarly distance both from the church and the culture, and recapture some of my idealism about both. I also wanted to do something I was good at. I didn't feel particularly good at serving a church full of soccer moms and yuppies looking for "deliverables" and "takeaways."

Elsewhere in this volume on Peterson's work, you will read about how this very same book has helped long term pastors to stay in one place. I would later learn that *Under the Unpredictable Plant* is about encouraging experienced pastors to stay in their churches for two or three decades. But I read it as a call to stay in for longer than eighteen months. For me, as a brand new pastor, it seemed to be exactly what I needed.

Today, twenty years later, I am the senior minister at a church that statistically resembles the church I served as an associate: 1200 members, two services, two full Sunday schools, in a quaint affluent village that has not yet received the word that Christendom is over. This one is outside Chicago, rather than in New England.

But the congregations feel very different to me, mostly because I am different. I'm still cynical, striving, seeking for answers, ambitious, easily bored—in other words, human. But I feel that I learned a few things from Peterson early on that remind me to resist my baser instincts to be a "just let me meet your needs" chaplain on a Love Boat church docked in a suburban port.

I recently rediscovered my original copy of *Under the Unpredictable Plant,* and went back to see what I had underlined in pencil—what had mattered so much to me in those early years. I was struck by how much I needed to hear it again.

"Somehow we American pastors, without really noticing what was happening, got our vocations redefined in the terms of American careerism. We quit thinking of the parish as a location for pastoral spirituality and started thinking of it as an opportunity for advancement. . . . The moment we did that, we started thinking wrongly, for the vocation of pastor has to do with living out the implications of the word of God in community, not sailing off into the exotic seas of religion in search of fame and fortune."[2] I recall that I underlined that section while I was putting my pastoral profile together.

The profile is what we call the giant clergy resume full of self-aggrandizing essays that masquerade as humble sharing ("What is my greatest weakness? Perhaps that I just give too much of myself"). It even includes our own top twelve ministry skill lists, filled out by anonymous references, i.e., consumers of our pastoral products. I was working on my profile in the hopes of moving from the role of associate to being a solo minister at my own church. And I wanted it to be "a good one," whatever that meant, so I was sure to include my "success" in membership development as well as my vast fundraising experience based upon two years of attending annual fund meetings when the senior minister didn't want to go. But I still underlined that passage in the book, as a corrective. Peterson was looking over my shoulder.

"A successful pastor will discover a workable program and repeat it in congregation after congregation to the immense satisfaction of the parishioners. The church members can be religious without praying or dealing with God. Prostitute pastor."[3] Prostitute pastor? Who talks like that? I loved that part, and still do, but I understand it more deeply. Now at my third church, I have had time to develop my own workable programs, and run the risk of hating myself in the morning.

When I graduated from divinity school, I thought you needed a PhD to write for the church. After immersing myself in the church growth genre, I thought you needed a megachurch. But then I discovered that my most valuable reading in those early years was produced by someone without either one. To heck with credentialing, this writing pastor was moving on to the project of translating the Bible. To this day, I love Peterson's holy chutzpah, his refusal to have his vocation as a pastor, or a writer, be defined by the rules and expectations of others in the guild.

In those early years of my ministry, it was pastor writers who were immersed in the church, like Barbara Brown Taylor, Martin Copenhaver, Heidi Neumark, Anthony Robinson, Will Willimon, and Eugene Peterson,

2. Ibid., 20
3. Ibid., 60

who kept me in the work when so many of my friends left. These writers appeared to me like an oasis in the desert, a watering hole between the desert of decline on one side and mega success on the other. And they could *write*. They loved ministry, they loved words and they loved the Word, bringing their sense of beauty, mystery, and humor to my day-to-day work. And of all of them, it was Peterson who convicted me in my excuses and impatience. Especially when he told the unforgettable story of how he almost left the ministry. But by keeping the Sabbath, by recovering his role as spiritual leader and lover of the Word, and by leaving the lay leaders to run the business of the church, he was able to stay.

Certainly, there were times when Peterson's truth seemed too good to be true. I never did learn to take a Sabbath. I never had a spouse willing to take a day off each week to walk in the woods with me. I never got out of all those committee meetings. And I'm not sure I would have wanted to. Holiness and prayer can be a part of those as well. I find that in doing that work together, we bond in ways we would not if I were absent.

In the end, what I took from Peterson's narrative was that it was exactly that: a narrative. Not a ten step, one-size-fits-all plan, but one man's story, bravely shared with a reader he trusted to have the intelligence to sort through the details rather than be spoon fed a list of rules. He gave me the courage to try to write that way myself.

In my early days of ministry, I kept looking to outside forces and fixes for my congregation. We didn't pray enough because the mainline was declining. We didn't pray enough because the evangelicals did it better and had ruined it for the rest of us. We didn't pray enough because Christendom was over and those people who used to pray probably didn't really mean it anyway.

Peterson prompted me to look within myself as a pastor. Maybe we didn't pray enough because I didn't pray enough.

I was shocked that anyone had the nerve to admit this: "The only reason we aspire to holiness is that the alternative is so insipid."[4]

Refusing to allow the pastor to finger wag, whine, escape, or wriggle out from God's hard call, Peterson raised the bar so high that suddenly it seemed worthwhile to try to stay in the game. And so I did.

4. Ibid., 53.

WWED?

Trygve David Johnson

The Contemplative Pastor

IF IT HAD NOT been for the writings of Eugene Peterson, I don't think I would be in pastoral ministry. More than any other writer, Peterson's voice has been as reliable as a compass, orienting my way in the expansive landscape of salvation. His wisdom has kept me encouraged to pursue a "long obedience in the same direction," keeping my attention off myself, and onto another, namely, God.

I was first introduced to Peterson when I was a sophomore in college. I arrived at a small liberal arts college in the middle of America with an intuitive sense that the pastoral vocation was my calling. This was not a natural path. Christian faith was a part of our home, but God was not a subject any of us felt comfortable talking about. So when I began to sense a pull in my mind and heart towards this odd kind of work, I was unprepared to talk about it.

I was going to have to drill down deep into a faith that I knew only at a surface level. I was going to have to plumb down to the water table of the human condition; I would need to exercise with long walks into the wide-open country of salvation and map out the source that is also the spring from which all things flow. I took lots of philosophy, English, religion, and history courses.

I remember making a confession to my college chaplain, "I don't think I fit being a pastor." I wasn't looking for an out. I just seemed different from those around me who were thinking about doing this kind of work. Matt listened to me patiently, and then his eyes narrowed knowingly like a doctor making a diagnosis. He went to his bookshelf, and pulled a thin volume from the shelf and placed it in my hands. *The Contemplative Pastor.* "Read this," he said.

I read. Something deep within me stirred and quickened. I kept reading. I was pulled in. Here was a voice that was articulating all the things I felt but didn't have the words to express. This is a rare experience—when it happens it is critical to pay attention. Sometimes the right book at just the right time is the work of the Holy Spirit.

The author was, like me, a broody Norwegian with an intense interior life, who expressed feeling out of place in the cultural conditions in which he worked, prayed, and wrote the book. He named some of the same fundamental tensions that I was feeling. Reading made me feel less alone. Rather than always trying to "connect" with the culture, the author invited me to a life of study, of writing, of imagining the consequence of the grace out of solitude as the necessity to form someone called to this odd vocation. He understood these instincts to be a gift to be embraced, rather than an obstacle to overcome.

I was soon devouring all of Eugene Peterson's books. Later, Peterson would become a household name in the church for his translation of *The Message*, but I still contend that his most significant work has been calling the church to reimagine the office of the pastor as a vocation worthy of a life. The Petersonian vision of the pastoral life is fundamentally relational. Peterson writes of the Triune God's grace as cosmic in scope, while locating this large grace in our own backyard.

WWED?

Ever since my introduction, Peterson's has been the voice that has shaped my understanding of what it means to be a pastor. I have adopted an internal questioner that is constantly wondering, "What Would Eugene Do?" "What would Eugene do in response to this ecumenical crisis?" Or, "In response to the technology and the church?" Or, "What would Eugene do with his time in the study?" I contemplate, "What would Eugene do with criticism from those who didn't like his last sermon?"

Peterson is not always an easy conversation partner. For example, Peterson writes that he would never pastor a church with more members than names he can remember—about 150 people. Because Peterson wants the pastoral vision to stay personal, it requires a context where one can know and be known personally. I perpetually feel anxious that I have betrayed the vision. One of Peterson's fundamental critiques is that Christianity in America has been shaped more by American values than by Christ and his kingdom. Chief among the cultural values that tempts a pastor is a preoccupation with size, prestige, and power.

In America this game takes on all kinds of forms, but the aim is always the same: to win, whether in one's chosen position as a plumber, a professor, a politician, or a pastor. Winning is really what our culture values. Winning requires one to become a competitor and to view others the same way. So we begin to treat our charge—and the people in our charge—as functions that we have to manage successfully, in order to get the next promotion. For a pastor, winning means a large church.

The unintended consequences are severe. Relational intimacy, a threat to upward mobility, is sacrificed for pragmatism. We grip people's hands only for a moment as we stretch to reach the next rung on the ecclesiastical ladder. The higher one climbs, the larger the audience, the more prestige and power. This cultural instinct is what Eugene warns us corrupts the pastoral soul.

Eugene gives voice to this warning in a letter to a pastoral friend named Phillip, who confided that he was thinking of leaving his pulpit for a call to a larger church. Eugene describes the growing trend of trading up as "the devil's temptation to Jesus to throw himself from the pinnacle of the temple." Peterson writes as a wise and watchful elder: "Every time the Church's leaders depersonalize, even a little, the worshipping/loving community, the gospel is weakened. And size is the great depersonalizer. Kierkegaard's criticism is still cogent: 'the more people, the less truth.'"[1] Peterson concludes, "Your present congregation is close to ideal in size to employ your pastoral vocation for forming Christian maturity. You talked about 'multiplying your influence.' My apprehension is that your anticipated move will diminish your vocation, not enhance it."[2]

"Size is the great depersonalizer." I fear he may be right. And I don't work in the context in which Peterson encourages Phillip to remain. I am a Dean of a Chapel at a modest liberal arts college in the upper Midwest. We worship four times a week, sing the songs of the faith (old and new), listen

1. Peterson, *The Pastor*, 157.
2. Ibid., 158.

to and wrestle with the Word, do pastoral care and counseling, and arrive every week at the table of Jesus on the Sabbath. The size of the college is about 3,200 students, with about 700 faculty and staff. This is a modest size. It is big enough for a student to get lost, but small enough to be found. It is a size where you get to know a lot of names, but not *everyone's* name. My pastoral context gathers a number of people that I will never get to know personally.

Feel the tension? I fear I have bought into one of the classic temptations Eugene warns Phillip (and all pastors) to avoid. Eugene warns that it is the temptation to crowds where the American pastor is most vulnerable.

Why are pastors vulnerable to crowds? It *is* a visible verification that we are doing something people value, in a work that is predominantly invisible. In our culture, the vocation of pastor has the feel of being pushed to the margins. Just read the tension in someone's eyes when you tell them "I'm a pastor." But if we tell the cocktail party crowd that we are a pastor of a *prominent* church, or a dean of a respectable college, maybe we can be understood as a success. Or maybe crowds allow us a chance briefly to escape ourselves. Peterson argues, "The religious hunger [for crowds] is rooted in the unsatisfactory nature of the self. We hunger to escape the dullness, the boredom, the tiresomeness of me."[3]

Peterson's warning honors the small and local church (and, by implication, the small and local college) in a cultural atmosphere that glorifies the large and prominent. In such a cultural space, the latest fads are pursued at the expense of a theological vision, where celebrity is confused with spiritual authority. Peterson's vision is an antidote to this misdirected desire.

I wonder to myself, have I betrayed the vision? Should I quit my job and find a small church in order to be a more faithful pastor? Can I even call myself a pastor if I don't know everyone's name? Am I shaped more by the dominant values of America than I am by the kingdom of God?

I have wrestled with these questions for a long time. There are days that I think yes—the only way to be faithful is in a small and intimate context. There are also days when I confess, "Yes, I want a crowd," and my motivation really has little to do with Jesus.

I usually feel this way when I get tired of the stress, and my calendar seems to be scheduling me. I imagine a picturesque church, with a modest steeple, near a large lake or ocean, or near a mountain somewhere in the

3. Ibid., 157.

Pacific Northwest. Something like Rivendale.[4] I'll know all the people by name, and they will know me, and we'll all get along, and I'll preach, and visit, and study, and write, and live a small but beautiful life.

But then I stop and think. Rivendale is fiction. I don't know where that church is. More to the point, I have not been called to it even if it does exist. I have been called here to this place, to stand alert at this post, not an imaginary one. I know, as Peterson knows, that there is no utopia. There is no perfect church or pastoral setting.

This is where I wonder whether Peterson's vision is a romantic one that creates an unnecessary counter-reaction. Is Peterson promoting his own idealization of the pastoral life? What if one *is* called to serve in a place that is larger than 150 people? Was Peterson's "vow of stability" an effort to justify his own decision to stay at Christ our King for nearly thirty years?

A more charitable reading of Peterson will consider the whole cannon. In his chapter "Fyodor" in his memoir, Peterson acknowledges how those who read his biblical translation *The Message* grow into a kind of congregation: "I had no way of knowing it at the time we said our good-byes to our congregation that seeds sown several years before were going to produce a new congregation, but a congregation that would take us a while to recognize as such."[5]

Peterson himself has been a pastor's pastor through writing. So it *is* possible to pastor people you don't know by name.

To be faithful to do what Eugene would do requires not so much rules about congregational size, but a pastoral imagination about one's context in relationship to who Scripture reveals God to be. We are called to be "masters of imagination."[6] The question is not whether we know all their names, but whether the Triune God of grace knows *ours*.

Working the Angles: A Fresh Triad

Eugene has taught me many things, including how to be faithful even when one's pastoral setting is not ideal.

In *Working the Angles*, Peterson sets forth a triadic pastoral vision. The work of ministry has three lines—preaching, teaching, and administration;

---

4. The home of the elves in J. R. R. Tolkien's *The Lord of the Rings*.

5. Peterson, *The Pastor,* 300.

6. Peterson, *Under the Unpredictable Plant*, 172.

and three angles—prayer, Scripture, and spiritual direction.[7] This is a helpful articulation of the work of a pastor.

I have also imagined an alternative triadic approach to discern whether I am staying faithful to the Petersonian vision. At the end of the day, I ask myself three questions: Did I love my people? Did I love my place? And did I love the Word? If I can genuinely say yes to these questions, I am able to be faithful to the personal ministry Peterson invites, even if I am not on a first-name basis with everyone I serve.

Love the People

My calling is to love the people God has called me to serve. This does not mean that I am only to love the people whom I like, or who like me. Nor am I merely to love what I want people to be. My charge is to love who they are right now.

Is it possible for me to love my people if I don't know them by name? How can you love someone you don't know? Doesn't that make them an abstraction? If there is a singular thing Peterson teaches, it is not to allow God or others to become abstractions. Surely a name is necessary to avoid this?

But it is not possible in this context. So I have to find other ways to learn how to love my people, and for them to see me loving them. One of the ways Peterson has taught me to do this is through a robust theology of Christian prayer: Christ is praying! In his fictional letters to his imaginary friend Gunnar, Peterson reminds us of this first principle of prayer.

> The single most important thing to know about prayer is that Jesus prays, *is praying right now*, and for you. The large revealed fact that Jesus prays is the reality in which you and I learn to do our praying. My life of prayer is not primarily a matter of what I do or don't do, but of what Jesus does—is doing, interceding for us "at the right hand of the father."[8]

Pastoral faithfulness is not about congregation size or name memorization. It *is* about whether the pastor takes seriously the God who knows our names. Right now, Christ is praying for us, by name. This allows us pastors to love and pray for our people "in Jesus' name," even if *we* don't know them by name.

7. Peterson, *Working the Angles*.
8. Peterson, *The Wisdom of Each Other*, 39.

Prayer is the key to keeping our work relational. But prayer can fall prey to projection and escapism. One of the most helpful essays from Peterson is inspired by a line from T. S. Eliot's poem "Ash Wednesday."[9] If the pastor's job is nothing else, he suggests, it is to care for people. But therein lies the rub. How do we care so that our caring does not create more hurt? To do that, we must embrace the humility of our limits. In order to care, we at the same time have to learn how "not to care."

We care, says Peterson, by praying and teaching people how to pray. That is our job. Prayer is the primary way that the pastor keeps the ministry relational. Prayer is how I love my people. Even if I don't know all of what is going on, God does. The Christ who took on flesh, died, and rose again, has the power to take all our broken and frail lives into his life. This offering of vicarious prayer, to a vicarious God, is how we love our people. It is how we keep our ministry relational.

Peterson writes about how he used prayer as an "escape hatch" once when talking to a parishioner named Brenda. When a pastoral meeting goes long, the conversation becomes dull, and we pull out the ace in our sleeves to bring it to a close, "Can I offer to pray for you?" No one ever objects. It was in just this context that he discovered, as if for the first time, what his real job was:

> Brenda's quest, "Would you teach me to pray?" returned me to the country of my origins: God-oriented, mystery-attentive, obedience-ready. My central task among these people was not to help them solve their problems, but to help them to see how their problems could help solve them, serve as stimulus and goad to embrace the mystery of who they were as human beings, and then offer to be companion to them and teach them the language of this world in which we are God-created, Christ-invaded, Sprit-moved, the language of prayer.[10]

Peterson has taught me is to trust, radically trust, that even if I don't have a personal relationship with someone, God does. God's Word precedes our word, so I can be a pastor to people I don't know by name. Before an anonymous student walks into my study, my presupposition is that God has been and will be active in this person's life, even if we will never meet again. I don't have to be best friends with people to be their faithful pastor, but I do have to have a theology of God's faithfulness to them.

9. Peterson, "Teach Us to Care and Not to Care," *Subversive Spirituality*, 154–68.
10. Ibid., 162.

In an essay entitled "Mastering Ceremonies," Eugene asks why pastors are present at occasions where we don't know people by name, such as weddings, funerals, baptisms, and graduations. Peterson offers some wisdom that I have taken to heart.

> We are there to say God. We are there for one reason and one reason only: to pray. We are there to focus the brimming, overflowing, cascading energies of joy, sorrow, delight, or appreciation, if only for a moment but for as long as we are able, on God. We are there to say *God* personally, so say this name clearly, distinctly, unapologetically, in prayer. We are there to say it without hemming or hawing, without throat clearing and without shuffling, without propagandizing, proselytizing, or manipulating. We have no other task on these occasions. We are not needed to add to what is there; there is already more than anyone can take in. We are required only to say the Name: Father, Son, and Holy Ghost.[11]

This is the pastor's real work: holding marriages, deaths, new lives, and lasting achievements before God in a continuing community of prayer. What is important to keep straight is that our prayers are made effective not by knowing names, but by the God in whose name we pray, Jesus Christ.

My job is to take a student's life seriously because God takes them seriously. I may only meet a student once while on campus. Or we might meet once a week. Regardless, the Petersonian vision demands that I trust God's primary initiative in prayer. Eugene writes this about praying the Psalms:

> God's word precedes these words: these prayers don't seek God, they respond to the God who seeks us. These responses are often ones of surprise, for who expects God to come looking for us? And they are sometimes awkward, for in our religious striving we are usually looking for something quite other than the God who has come looking for us. God comes and speaks—his word catches us in sin, finds us in despair, invades us by grace. The Psalms are our answers. . . . The Psalms—all of which listen in order to answer—train us in conversation.[12]

My job is not to fix students. What I am called to do is to create space for them to take seriously the God who takes them seriously. Sometimes, especially at college events, my primary task is to trust that simply saying God's

11. Peterson, "Mastering Ceremonies," *Subversive Spirituality,* 150.
12. Peterson, *Answering God,* 5.

name clearly and without apology can be an exercise in relational ministry. It is God who makes himself personal, not me.

Love Your Place

One of the ways we love our people as a pastor is by honoring and loving the place they live. This can be a challenge. Most pastors are transplants. We often don't have a tacit knowledge of the place, its history, its geography, or its native weather patterns. We don't know the people in their place, and they don't know us. We have to learn how to enter in and not only love the people, but love the place the people live.

In *Under the Unpredictable Plant*, a modern Midrash on Jonah's journey to Nineveh, Peterson articulates the importance of a pastor embracing one's geography.

> It is in the nature of pastoral work to walk into an alien world, put our feet on the pavement, and embrace the *locale*. Pastoral work is geographical as much as it is theological. Pastors don't send memos, don't send generic messages, don't work from a distance: *locale* is part of it. It is the nature of pastoral work to be on site, working things out in the particular soil of a particular parish.[13]

Peterson focuses the pastor's attention not on an abstract system of theology, but in personalized congregations. There are no nameless streets or people. Everything has a name and every name has a connection to a place. The theology that drives all of this is the incarnation. Peterson reminds us again and again that if the incarnation teaches us anything, it is that God makes his ministry personal, even local. As Peterson translates in *The Message*, "The Word became flesh and blood, and moved into the neighborhood" (John 1:14).

Pastors are called to pray and speak in the name of Jesus into their neighborhood, because that is what God has done. If I have learned one cardinal rule of Peterson's vision of the pastoral life it is this: never make fun of where someone is from. Place matters. Every place is someone's place. No one lives in abstraction. No one experiences God or salvation apart from a place. The Christian life has to be embodied in a location, expressed in a culture, played out in a backyard. Peterson is keen on reminding us that we

---

13. Peterson, *Under the Unpredictable Plant*, 123.

are not followers of a gnostic God, but a God who took the time to put on flesh and enter into our place.

This call to a sense of place is one of the ways that I think it is possible to honor the vocation of a pastor, without having to know everyone firsthand. As a college pastor, I don't know everyone's name, but I do share the campus with them. My job as a pastor of transient college students is to honor the soil in which they are planted for this season, so that, like the tree of Psalm One, they might grow deeper.

How does one do this? We tell the stories of the place we serve. We take time to have long conversations with the elders. Each church has a story. Some of them are good ones and some of them are tragic. But a pastor has to know them—to understand the narrative of this people in this place.

Peterson's vision of the pastoral life is rooted in a place. One does not have to know everyone in the place to love it, but one does have to be a student of one's *locale*. When people know their pastor loves their place, they also know that we are willing to love them. This also signals that we are not here to use others for our own ends, but rather to enter and embrace God's ends in our specific geography.

The Petersonian vision calls us to reject the temptation to be someone apart from our locale. Peterson, the son of a Montana butcher, was always conscious of keeping the pastoral economy local.[14] This sense of place is one of the ways that Peterson invites all pastors to keep our ministry relational, no matter how large or small someone's parish or institutional ministry might be.

This pastoral theology of place is the reason Peterson calls us pastors to discover Wendell Berry. Berry taught Peterson the absurdity of resenting one's place. Berry reminds every pastor that without our locale, we could not do our work. Berry taught Peterson that parish work is "every bit as physical as farm work. It is *these* people, at *this* time, under *these* conditions" that we are called to serve in Jesus's name.[15] We are called to work with the realities that are already on the ground.

The place where the people of Christ live has no boundaries. We have to expand our imaginations to see that God's love extends to all people, in all places, at all times—even the places that are in our own backyard. Sometimes the places and the people who are closest to us are the hardest

14. Peterson, *The Pastor,* 35–45.
15. Peterson, *Under the Unpredictable Plant,* 131.

ones to care for. Our place is all the geography of the God's creation. John Calvin had this right: this "place"—all creation—is indeed the theater of God's glory. Every person in this theater, whether we know each character by name or not, is a sign pointing us to the playwright.

Because of the mystery of faith, because of the incarnation, the cross, the resurrection, and Pentecost, this is not a secular place. This is a sacred place—a thin place where heaven and earth kiss. Our place is not a "wasteland"; it is "a rose-garden."[16] *This* is the place—wherever the place one serves—where "Christ plays in Ten-Thousand Places."

Love the Word

Did I love the Word?

On the days I feel anxious that I cannot get to know everyone personally, I am comforted by the knowledge that my primary calling is to not just hang out at the local coffee shop. It is to spend as much time in Scripture as I can. My job is to eat the book.

Jesus is the Word we long to know and to love. The way we know Jesus is not simply by going outside and marveling at God's creation, but through listening to Holy Scripture. Peterson writes,

> The Christian Scriptures are the primary text for Christian spirituality. Christian spirituality is, in its entirety, rooted in and shaped by the scriptural text. We don't form our personal lives out of a random assemblage of favorite texts in combination with individual circumstances; we are formed by the Holy Spirit in accordance with the text of Holy Scripture. . . . Readers become what they read. If Holy Scripture is to be something other than mere gossip about God, it must be internalized.[17]

My anxiety is abated when I realize that we can feast on the Word. My calling is to point people to the Word, to eat the Word, to study and speak the Word, who is Jesus Christ. The reality of our world is shaped by the Word who creates the world. This reality transcends my limited knowledge of people, because the Word is the knowledge that transcends to reveal itself to all people.

---

16. Language borrowed from T. S. Eliot, to describe the change of a conversion vision in "Teach Us to Care and Not to Care," 156–57.

17. Peterson, *Eat This Book*, 15–20.

All that said, many days I think Peterson is right. I should resign my current position, and take up at a small church, and live off the ecclesiastical grid. But then I wonder, who would be here to love my students? Someone needs to be here to love this place, no matter the size.

The primary way I love my people and love my place is by loving the Word.

In a place where people study all kinds of things, my calling is to remember that we have to study the Word written. We learn the language, we translate, and we seek to understand the large narrative scope and consequence of Holy Scripture. Scripture is what invades the citadel of the self and confronts us with a living and speaking God. When we hear this God speak, the pastor proclaims what we have heard. Out of the posture of listening, we speak boldly of the Word that was made flesh, Jesus Christ. The way we love the Word is by pointing, like John the Baptist, to the one true God who has invaded our world. Whether I know everyone by name or not, I do know the name of Jesus, and it is my job to speak that name with clarity.

If I am to keep a relational ministry that loves my people and place, then I have to love the Word in all three of these forms. I have to find ways of expressing this love in work for a specific people in a specific place. I have to trust that if I don't know the people by name, the God of the Word will find them and reveal the Word to them. This living Word is what my students need more than another person to know their name.

Peterson reminds us pastors that it is not about us. It is about God and what God is doing: "The most important thing going on right now is what God is doing. We get in the way, we talk too much. The most important thing being said right now is something God is saying, marvelous things are being done and said right now. Look. Listen."[18]

Loving the Word requires faith in a God who shows us how to love our people and love our place. This faith allows me to trust that despite my imperfect knowledge of the people and place I am called to serve, God always provides enough.

Conclusion

Is it possible to pastor a people one does not know by name, and still be true to Peterson's vision? Yes. But it is not easy. I have to ask myself constantly

18. Peterson, *Subversive Spirituality,* 164

WWED? I have to ask myself each day, "Did I love my people? Did I love my place? Did I love the Word?" This triad of questions keeps my pastoral vocation working the angles of a relational, local, and God-focused vocation. This vision keeps me playing a different game then the one I'm conditioned to play by my culture. I want to play the game of faith—the faith that calls me to "practice resurrection."[19]

19. This is a line taken from a Wendell Berry poem, "The Mad Farmer Liberation Front," that Eugene loves to quote.

Staying with God

EUGENE PETERSON AND JOHN CHAPMAN
ON CONTEMPLATION

L. Roger Owens

A Personal Preface

I'd heard that if pastors leave the ministry it's often around the fifth year, so it was no surprise to me that when I hit the five-year mark I was daydreaming more than usual about going back to school or quitting the ministry to become a writer, and daily checking the academic job openings on the American Academy of Religion website. I was ready to be done.

For five years I'd tried to be the leader I thought was needed to turn around declining churches. I was leading the way John Kotter of Harvard Business School said I should lead in his well-known 1990 article, "What Leaders Really Do"—setting vision, establishing strategies, communicating vision, empowering broad-based action.[1] My problem was that I was doing it well and seeing results. I'd put on the mask of the visionary leader and I wore it convincingly. But after five years of wearing it, the mask was beginning to chafe. I was beginning to discover what Parker Palmer means when he says that soul and role often become disconnected, and that our work, or our way of working, can be done against the grain of our personalities

---

1. Kotter, "What Leaders Really Do."

and our gifts.² I'd been going against the grain for five years, and was suffering because of it—physically, emotionally, psychologically, spiritually. I was contemplating how to get out.

That's when a brochure for a continuing education program called "The Pastor as Spiritual Guide" came across my desk. It promised to introduce participants to a new (actually, old) way of being in ministry: helping a community to be attentive to the Spirit's leading and shaping in its midst. As I read the brochure I saw it as an invitation to enter the space where I could take off the mask of visionary leader, and try a way of ministry that might be more congruent with who I am. I began to think that maybe I should see if there was a way for me to practice this vocation differently before I gave it up altogether. I'd give it one last chance.

Over the next year, through a series of retreats with ten other pastors and two able leaders, I was re-introduced to the work of Eugene Peterson. I'd read his work before, but that was when I was in seminary and graduate school, that is, before I needed it. This time I encountered Peterson's vision of pastor—the resident un-busy, Sabbath-keeping presence, who has the leisure and discipline to be attentive to Scripture and people in order to be attentive to God's Spirit through Scripture and among people—not just as a challenge to the functional atheism of so much leadership literature in general, but to my own functional atheism in particular, my own practicing ministry with the unconscious assumption that if I don't make something good happen here it never will. In other words, I discovered his vision of a contemplative pastor.

Three years later the program is over and I am still meeting regularly with those pastors (Peterson would be proud). And we are committed to supporting one another as we live into what has become a counter-cultural way of ministry. We are accompanying one another on the journey as we become contemplative pastors—pastors with eyes open to the presence of God shaping a congregation in faithfulness to Jesus Christ.

The Democratization of Contemplation

For Peterson, a contemplative pastor is a pastor attentive to and shaped by prayerful engagement with Scripture in order to hear the Word of God through Scripture. Peterson, most well-known for his translation of the Bible, *The Message*, relentlessly calls pastors to allow the stories, images,

2. See Palmer, *A Hidden Wholeness*, 3–30.

and words of Scripture to shape their imaginations—their very ways of seeing the world—so that re-formed imaginations might shape their lives of ministry. To be a contemplative pastor is to embody a particular way of working with the words of Scripture.

This way is perhaps shown most clearly in *Working the Angles*,[3] where he argues that contemplative ministry will be most faithfully practiced when pastors focus their time and attention on prayer, prayerful Scripture reading, and spiritual direction. Each of these angles is grounded for Peterson in what he calls the *word*-ness of the Hebrew and Christian biblical tradition. Prayer is using words shaped by the words of Scripture, especially the Psalms, to address God. The words of Scripture must be exegeted contemplatively, not out of an academic interest in historical matters alone, but out of a perspective that believes God is addressing us through these words. And it's just this attentiveness to words that makes possible spiritual direction—the cultivated attention to the ordinary and obscure in daily life with the conviction that this is where God's spirit is active and attentive. Even a cursory look at Peterson's work will show that contemplative ministry for him is grounded in attentiveness to words of Scripture in order to hear the word of God.

The adjective *contemplative* for Peterson, then, indicates a comprehensive *way* of approaching pastoral ministry. This way is grounded in the activity of contemplation. Peterson sees himself as freeing contemplation from the confines of the cloister and making it accessible to Christians in general and pastors in particular. His task is nothing less than what he calls "the democratization of contemplation."[4]

> The common American stereotype of contemplation is that it is what monks and nuns do in monasteries and convents. Serious contemplation involves leaving the world of family and domesticity, of city and business, and taking vows of poverty, chastity, and obedience in order to live in quiet prayerfulness and reflective study, undistracted in the presence of God.[5]

Against this stereotype, Peterson wants to bring contemplation "into circulation in the world of the everyday."[6]

3. Peterson, *Working the Angles*.

4. Peterson, *Eat This Book*, 111.

5. Ibid., 110.

6. Ibid., 110–11.

He does this in his account of *contemplatio* as one of the movements of *lectio divina*, the sacred, prayerful reading of Scripture. Peterson argues that this fourth movement of *contemplation*, following *lectio, meditatio,* and *oratio*, is not something we self-consciously do. The first three movements of reading, mediation, and prayer are specific activities; you can sit down and *do* them. Contemplation is not like that. Put simply, "Contemplation means living what we read."[7]

> [Contemplation] is life formed by God's revealing word, God's word read and heard, meditated and prayed. The contemplative life is not a special kind of life; it is the Christian life, nothing more but also nothing less.[8]

Though not a discrete aspect of the prayerful reading of Scripture called *lectio divina*, contemplation for Peterson is still clearly *word*-centered. His understanding has the advantage of challenging the Gnosticism of much of American spirituality, for as Peterson argues, *words* are never disembodied. Speech itself is embodied. To live the words of Scripture is nothing less than to participate in the incarnation of the Word, and to embody Paul's dictum that "it is no longer I who live, but Christ who lives in me" (Gal 2:20). These words of Paul's capture the essence of Peterson's understanding of contemplation. Not a discrete activity, but a life so shaped by the words of Scripture that it embodies in the ordinary, everyday world the very life of Jesus.

> Contemplation is not another thing added on to our reading and meditating and praying but the coming together of God's revelation and our response, an unself-conscious following of Jesus, a Jesus-coherent life. It is not thinking about God, not asking continuously "what would Jesus do?" but jumping into the river; not strategizing the success of my life but just being myself, my Christ-in-me-life; not calculating effects but accepting and submitting to on-earth-as-it-is-in-heaven conditions.[9]

If a contemplative life is one that resists "strategizing the success of my life" then we can see how, for Peterson, a contemplative pastor would resist strategizing the success of his or her congregation, but rather help them to simply be the body that embodies Christ's presence in the world.

---

7. Ibid., 113.
8. Ibid.
9. Ibid., 116.

Peterson himself had to be converted from ministry-as-strategizing-success. As his memoir *The Pastor* shows, he had to discover this contemplative life for himself before he could offer this vision to others. And after he discovered it, he did some redecorating in his study to symbolize the shift he had made and to remind himself of the kind of contemplative pastor he wanted to be. He took down his academic diplomas, markers of the very successfully strategized life he was turning his back on. He wasn't abandoning academia altogether, but academic pursuits would move to the margins of his life as he recommitted himself to contemplative ministry in the everyday life of his congregation.

> The diplomas verified my vocation in terms of the world of intellect and learning, classrooms and libraries—professor. I anticipated that my life now as pastor would be worked out in quite different conditions—intimate relationships, a tradition of holiness, and the cultivation of souls. The world of learning was still there in all its glory, but my vocation now was not about the learning itself but about the integrating of learning into prayer and worship and the ordinariness of everyday living.[10]

In other words, he had discovered contemplation, and was becoming a contemplative pastor.

He replaced his diplomas with portraits of three men who embodied this way of contemplation-in-everyday-life and to whom he would continue to look as mentors. Along with the pastors he met with regularly, these three men would companion him, and their portraits would call him back to the vocational identity he was discovering. They were John Henry Newman, Alexander Whyte, and Baron Friedrich von Hügel. Newman's portrait hung in his study because this brilliant intellectual chose to embody his contemplative ministry among the working poor of Birmingham, England. Von Hügel's portrait hung there because von Hügel lived as an independent scholar and spiritual director, who pointed others to how they could be contemplatives in their ordinary lives. And Whyte's, because he embodied the kind pastoral imagination and practice to which Peterson aspired. Each in their own way showed Peterson what contemplation looks like, how attention to the word and the willed allowing of Scripture to shape us, finds flesh in real lives, day by day, hour by hour.[11]

10. Peterson, *The Pastor*, 221.

11. Ibid., 224–27.

And today, pastors might be putting Peterson's picture on their walls for the very same reason.

Another Picture for the Wall

Of course Peterson's impulse to democratize contemplation is absolutely right. He is right to challenge the old contemplation-action dichotomy, and resituate contemplation in everyday life. And he knows that the cloistered contemplatives would cheer, because they would want us to realize their lives are "real life" as well. Their lives are ordinary and everyday, too. If there is any doubt about that, then one should read the Carmelite nun Ruth Burrows's memoir *Before the Living God*.[12] A cloistered nun, Burrows shows that life inside the cloister is ordinary and everyday as well. Nuns eat, dress, argue, clean, weep, worry, fall asleep in church. It's real life. This distinction between the contemplative life—the life lived by people in convents and monasteries—and the active life—the life lived by the rest of us—cannot be sustained, and Peterson is right to point it out. The Christian life, the life of "Christ-lived-in-me," is the contemplative life, wherever this life is lived.

On the other hand, Peterson's definition of contemplation, as helpful as it is, does ignore an important element in the Christian tradition that says contemplation is also something we do, what some writers today are calling "contemplative practice." The end result of this practice might be to discover that in contemplation God is the one doing the work—so to say we "do" it is not exactly right. And yet, there is a *doing* involved. There is finding the time, and sitting still; there is an activity of the will if only the sustained desire to be present to and with God in an intentional way. And this is a practice that those in monasteries and convents have been "doing" for centuries. To democratize contemplation might also mean, along with making the contemplative *life* available to those outside the cloister, also making this contemplative *practice* available as well.

And that recognition leads me to make a humble suggestion: that Peterson add another portrait to his wall, that of Abbot Dom John Chapman. For, as Sarah Coakley has said, Chapman "democratized contemplation" a century ago.[13] He did it by helping everyday people discover that there was a *kind* of contemplative prayer they might be called to, and they could pray this way as well, that this kind of prayer does not belong in monasteries

12. Burrows, *Before the Living God*.

13. Coakley, *Powers and Submissions*, 42.

alone. And this way of prayer lets go of words in order to simply *be* in God's presence.

Chapman (1865–1933) was an English Benedictine monk, abbot, and scholar of early church history best known for his *Spiritual Letters*, the collection of his replies to the queries of the men and women who wrote to him. The people who wrote to Chapman were from all walks of life, but for the most part they were not beginners in the life of prayer. Rather, they had been praying for most of their lives. They were well practiced at what was called mental or active prayer, all the various ways of praying that keep the intellect and the imagination busy—saying rote prayers, reading spiritual books, reciting the rosary, making intercession, imagining oneself in a scene from Scripture after the method taught by St. Ignatius, and many others ways of prayer. These ways of praying were called meditation. Meditation, to Chapman and his interlocutors at the time, referred to devotional activities characterized by mental busyness (unlike the way many of us think of meditation today, having been influenced by Eastern practices). In other words, they were good at *lectio*, *meditatio*, and *oratio*—and probably were living contemplatives in Peterson's sense.

These people knew how to meditate, but they had a problem. Either these ways didn't work for them anymore—they no longer produced the feelings of joy and peace they once produced (often called in the classic literature on prayer *consolations*), or their intellect and imagination literally didn't work when they tried these kinds of prayer. For whatever reason, these people could no longer meditate. Or perhaps they were beginning to recognize a desire for a quieter, less mentally active way of praying, a simpler way of being with God. Chapman recognized that they were beginning what St. John of the Cross called "the dark night of the soul," that time in the life of prayer when God weans us from the good feelings produced by active ways of prayer and moves us toward passive contemplation.

The difficulty of this change in their experience of prayer was compounded by another, more isolating difficulty—few people understood what they were going through. When they approached their priests or other religious leaders they encountered skepticism and sometimes fear. Indeed, this desire for passive prayer sounded to many religious leaders like a form of prayer condemned by Pope Innocent XI in the seventeenth century that was known as quietism. They were told to try harder and persist in the old ways of prayer.

In Chapman, however, they found a kindred spirit. It was to these people from all walks of religious life that Chapman gave the now well-known advice: pray as you can, and do not try to pray as you can't. Chapman was encouraging those who sought his counsel to let go of ways of praying that were becoming burdensome or impossible for them—the ways they had learned since they were children—and to embrace the way of prayer God was leading them to, even if this made others nervous.

Chapman on Contemplative Prayer

This way of prayer Chapman called contemplation, and there are four ways it differs from (though it's not opposed to) Peterson's understanding of contemplation.

First, this contemplative way of prayer is a self-conscious activity, when the word "activity" is understood rightly. Chapman says that "if you are drawn to contemplative prayer, you are also drawn to a passive form of spirituality, in which God does all, while we wait and wonder. Consequently, give yourself to prayer, when you can, and trust in God that He will lead you, without your choosing the path."[14] That in this prayer "God does all" is consistent with the way contemplation has long been understood, at least since John of the Cross, whom Chapman believes he is interpreting. In that sense, this prayer is not an "activity" in the way other forms of mediation are "activity." Nonetheless, Chapman can say to "give yourself to prayer, when you can." He is not simply talking about life, but about engaging in a kind of prayer. That's why he can say that this kind of prayer is "simply giving yourself wholeheartedly into His hands" but also that "you will want some *time* for this prayer."[15] If you can take time for this prayer, then it is an activity of sorts. Thus, his other most famous piece of advice, given to someone struggling (like all of us) with distractions in prayer: "Consequently I can't help advising you to pray. (The longer one prays, the better it goes)."[16]

> On the other hand, the only way to pray is to pray; and the way to pray well is to pray much. If one has no time for this, then one must at least pray regularly. But the less one prays, the worse it goes. And if circumstances do not permit even regularity, then one

14. Chapman, *Spiritual Letters*, 35.

15. Ibid., 45.

16. Ibid., 46.

must put up with the fact that when one does try to pray, one can't
pray—and our prayer will probably consist of telling this to God.[17]

That kind of contemplation, which you can do much and regularly, is a
self-conscious activity.

Second, the kind of attention required in contemplation for Chapman is different from attention as Peterson understands it, though again, not contradictory. For Peterson, contemplation as a kind of life involves a cultivated attentiveness to the ordinary, to whatever is present before one, like the a small child who is "unself-consciously present to the immediate flower, absorbed and oblivious while watching an ant track its way across a log."[18] Peterson would agree with Simone Weil that "prayer consists of attention."[19] Though I doubt Chapman would disagree, contemplation as a kind of prayer, for Chapman, involves *inattention* to life during the period of prayer. That's because this kind of prayer is a willed intention to be present and attentive to God. As he says, "The simplest way of making an act of attention to God, though without thinking of Him, is by an act of inattention to everything else."[20] Chapman calls this act of attention to God having the "will fixed on nothing in particular—which is God, of course."[21] Contemplation as an act of prayer is a cultivated *in*attention to all things other than God, who is not a thing.

Third, words function in a different way for Chapman during contemplative prayer. We already saw for Peterson that words—the words, images, and stories of Scripture—are central to his understanding of contemplation as a life so shaped by Scripture that it is an enfleshment in the everyday of God's Word. Again, Chapman would not disagree with this. But in his account of contemplation as a specific activity of prayer, words function differently. Chapman understands that when the will is making an act of attention to God, the imagination is free to roam, and certainly will, and one's time of prayer will be filled with distractions. This is not a problem, and should be expected. The problem starts when the imagination begins to engage the distractions, which eventually pulls the will from its attention to God. In order to keep the imagination quiet, Chapman suggests using what writers on contemplative prayer today would call a "prayer word."

17. Ibid., 53.
18. Peterson, *Eat This Book*, 111.
19. Weil, *Waiting for God*, 105.
20. Chapman, *Spiritual Letters*, 294.
21. Ibid., 58.

This is not a word one focuses attention on (another valid way of Christian contemplation, most notably espoused in the twentieth century by John Main[22]), but gentle acts in the mind that give the imagination something to do, thus quieting it.

> So, to keep the imagination quiet, the best thing is *to keep it in tune with the will* and higher intellect, by very simple "acts." The mere *imagined words* give the imagination food; by sticking to them (the same act or many, as you like) the imagination may even get lazy, or almost mesmerized (for a short time usually). But, generally, one has to go on keeping it quiet, running after it, and bringing it back. But there is the curious feeling that *these imaginations are not you*—they are mechanical, like those in a dream. You leave them as nearly uncontrolled as possible, in order to have the will fixed on nothing in particular—which is God, of course.[23]

There could be lot to unpack in this paragraph but I simply want to point out that Chapman is giving advice on how to engage in the activity of contemplative prayer by repeating words or phrases in the imagination, not as a point of focus, but as merely something to keep the imagination busy.

It's important to point out that this kind of prayer, for Chapman, a Benedictine, finds its context in a life saturated with Scripture and the regular praying of the Psalms. One of the challenges in the way this kind of prayer is packaged and delivered today, or at least practiced is that it becomes disconnected from life (one thinks of the popularity of Thomas Keating's method of centering prayer in this regard[24]), and can be practiced apart from the regular prayerful attention to Scripture that would have been the *sine qua non* of prayer for Chapman and Peterson (and for Keating).

And for both Peterson and Chapman, the life of prayer must be judged by the living. "The one thing that prayer can be judged by is its *fruit*."[25] This is where the two come together in perfect agreement. The point, in the end, is the contemplative *life*. It is the discovery of "Christ-living-in-me."

> The one thing you should gain by quiet prayer (just remaining with God, and making a number of aspirations to keep your

---

22. See Main, *Essential Writings*.

23. Chapman, *Spiritual Letters*, 58.

24. See Keating, *Open Mind, Open Heart*.

25. Chapman, *Spiritual Letters*, 67.

imagination from wandering) is to feel the rest of the day that you want God's Will and nothing else.[26]

John Chapman knows that for many, an essential part of this kind of life will be a kind of prayer in which God prays in us, the kind of prayer that is "one long act of love—not of my love to God, but of His to me. It is always going on—but in prayer you put yourself into it by an act of faith."[27]

Conclusion

I suppose the reason I want to hang John Chapman's picture along with the rest is that I'm one of the folks who would have written to him. I find myself drawn to the kind of prayer he describes, and I suspect others do as well. What else explains the phenomenon of centering prayer? Or the diffusion of Buddhist meditation and practices of mindfulness? Though Chapman was sometimes accused of sounding too Buddhist, he is really democratizing the kind of prayer familiar to John of the Cross and Theresa of Avila. And it is necessary today for two reasons.

One reason is the growing popularity of anything that has the word "mystical" in it. Much literature today that tries to reintroduce the "mystical" aspect of Christianity to the wider public is suggesting that Christians are missing a certain kind of *experience*. And it's the quest for a new, deeper, richer, felt experience of God that I believe is driving much of the interest in mysticism and contemplative practice. But Chapman shows us a way of prayer that rejects experiential gluttony. For Chapman, contemplation does not promise a kind of experience. It is a way of prayer, of being with God, that may deliver no experience at all. Peterson would appreciate this, because the only thing worse than strategizing a successful life or church is strategizing successful prayer, and engaging in prayer as a means to an end, rather than an end in itself. For Chapman, however it *feels*, this prayer is an end in itself.

Exploring this way prayer is also important (if one feels drawn to it) as a way of cultivating life as an un-busy pastor. Much prayer involves a kind of imaginative or intellectual "busyness" that parallels the busyness of the pastoral life Peterson decries. Even his account of *lectio divina*, by lopping off *contemplation* as a distinct aspect of the prayer and landing it

26. Ibid., 36.

27. Ibid., 46.

in "everyday life," tends toward prayer as a kind of mental busyness insofar as for Peterson prayer maintains a kind of wordiness (even if its biblical wordiness). But Chapman's account of contemplation truly leaves busyness behind and attacks functional atheism head on. As he says, "Do not worry yourself about vocal prayer. It is good to say some. But simply to stay with God is best."[28] Surely a contemplative pastor could benefit from learning simply "to stay with God."

My own functional atheism manifests itself in my imagination's relentless strategizing to see to it that what I think is right—and what I think *God* thinks is right—works out. I have discovered that cultivating *in*attention to my imagination (and all other created things) in order to make what Chapman calls an act of attention to God—though this kind of prayer is technically purposeless, in the sense that it has no end beyond itself—has fostered in my pastoral ministry an ability to let go predetermined outcomes (which makes me less anxious—functional atheists can't help but be anxious). When I can let go of the presumption that "if anything good is going to happen here, I'm going to have to do it" I find that I am not only more capable of staying "with God" during set times of prayer, but I'm better at staying with the people whose pastor I am; I'm better able to slow down and pay attention to them and to God's work in our midst. I'm better able to be the kind of contemplative pastor Peterson learned to be and I am still learning to be.

28. Ibid., 109.

PART FOUR

LİFE

Reflections on Twenty-Five Years of "Working the Angles"

Tim Conder

IN 1987, I WAS just completing my Master of Divinity at Gordon-Conwell Theological Seminary. I was also in process in securing my first ministry position, a staff position in a regional megachurch, a job that was well beyond my experience if not my skill set. This was a season of constant discovery. A sampling of these discoveries included the driving social critique of post-punk alternative music, that the Dukakis "Massachusetts Miracle" meant that you had to pay twice the value of any home, that the Red Sox would never win a World Series, and that too many cannolis would kill you (though there was hardly a better way to go). Newly married, I would have also said at that point that combination of ministry and marriage was near lethal. Now I would reframe this equation by explaining that ambition, ego, piety, and insecurity do not combine well with marriage regardless of what one does professionally. Nonetheless, living and working within the confines of the church were proving to be frighteningly difficult and intoxicatingly rewarding. In both failure and success, there were so many times when I felt like I had fallen into a rapidly flowing river where I lacked the strength to make the shores and had little sense of the origin or destination of the flow. All I could do was keep my head above water and see where the current took me.

During this same season, I discovered Eugene Peterson's *Working the Angles: The Shape of Pastoral Integrity*. Sometimes you just know. A text not only immediately commends itself as essential at the moment of its reception, but you also sense that this text will be formative for a lifetime. Adler and Van Doren in their classic primer, *How to Read a Book,* recommend that reading is not a race whose outcome is determined by volume. Instead, they challenge the reader to find a few great books and read them many times. Peterson, warning about the perils of Gutenberg's invention, echoed that very sentiment:

> When we read more books, look at more pictures, listen to more music, than we can possibly absorb the result of such gluttony is not a cultured mind but a consuming one; what it reads, looks at, listens to, is immediately forgotten, leaving no more traces behind it than yesterday's newspaper.[1]

When I read this, I was four years away from owning my first computer, eight years from my first email address, twelve from blogging, eighteen years from Facebook, and nineteen years from my first tweet. No one had *any* idea what the possibilities of such gluttony would be. But I did know that I had found one of those texts that I would read again and again, argue with, and be repetitively formed by its ideas.

Ugaritic Lexicons and Speedwalking to Photocopiers

To get some sense of the immediate value that I derived from *Working the Angles* (*WtA*), one needs only a picture of the discontinuity that I felt from my primary ministry models. I will quickly add that my discernment of the ministry imperatives from these models was incomplete. No one would have accused me of being a great listener at that point. Nevertheless, I was listening as best I could to two radically divergent stories.

In an Old Testament exegesis course, a professor paused his lecture and reached for his Ugaritic lexicon and said—with a straight face, no less—you'll certainly need to buy this text or one like it before departing to serve a parish. Most of my classmates drove what we called "seminary cars," vehicles so in need of repair that only prayer could get you through the next state inspection. The regular fasting on the weekends, when the school's cafeteria was closed hence making the meal plan ineffectual, was *not* some form of spiritual discipline. In light of these economics, it may have been difficult to justify the purchase of an $80 text on an obscure Ancient Near

---

1. Peterson, *Working the Angles*, 64.

Eastern language even if it included the hidden words of Jesus. You can't eat textbooks, despite Peterson's assertion to the contrary!

Economics notwithstanding, some of the clearly coded messages of the seminary experience included the privileging of the mind, a deeply rationalist reading of the biblical texts, scholarly exegesis, and the academic journey. In postmodernity, we have long been "Foucault'ed" and tried to wash the stains of the Enlightenment from our garments, but this directive on the primacy of academics and cognitive exegesis still remains strong. We always felt that we let the institution and our instructors down a bit if there wasn't a PhD in our future (of course, the schools had the last laugh with the creation of the highly profitable DMin degree, a doctorate that you *get* to pay for!). In this model, the purchase of an expensive Ugaritic lexicon made all the sense in the world. We left for our parishes and mission agencies armed with our Hebrew Old Testaments and Greek New Testaments determined to keep our language skills up. The sacred axiom was an hour in the study for every minute in the pulpit. Those well-crafted sermons would always begin with a significant immersion in the original languages.

For me, this strong lesson from the academy crashed on the hard seawall of the program-driven megachurch. The megachurch was beginning its halcyon years. This edifice was the true center of God's best work on earth. Our mantra was *excellence*. Located on Boston's thriving 128 technology belt, our church was filled with engineers, military officers, MBAs, corporate executives, and the children or youth who grew up in communities where you started on your resume at birth. Our pastoral staff probably all owned that Ugaritic lexicon, but they were placed on the highest shelf in the office, the one you could not reach without a stool, right beside that awkward gift of an overly churchy plaque. We did not carry lexicons in our briefcases. Peter Drucker claimed that space. As interns in this system, we learned several new axioms. Our boss and mentor explained, "As long as there is a full program, you'll be fine." We figured out that with a glossy and well-organized brochure, you were well more than halfway to success. If you didn't work in this era, it is difficult to imagine the immensity of the program church's assault on the academy. Against the perceived irrelevance of the academy, larger churches were starting their own seminaries and training organizations. An axis had shifted.

And there was a pace to this work—relentless and urgent—that of important persons proceeding on essential errands. As interns auditioning for prized staff positions, we learned to walk rapidly with clear purpose from our shared offices to the workroom where the photocopier held court. At twenty-six years old, I didn't know much. But you still had to call the receptionist, who would buzz my secretary, who would decide whether to buzz me or walk down the hall to my closed office door and slide a pink message note under my door—if you wanted to talk to me in a hurry! We were busy, important, well-organized, leaders in the middle of critical tasks.

Stop Making Sense

It is an understatement to say that we were also confused. As seminarians and young pastors, we were caught in a surreal no fly zone between two radically divergent models and their leading voices. I was just as desperate for the approval of Gordon Fee (the legendary New Testament scholar at Gordon-Conwell, also a passionately gifted pastor) as I was for that of Gordon MacDonald (the equally prominent and insightful founder of our church). I do not believe these historical reminisces apply to just the young professional dukes and duchesses of the '80s megachurch. Everybody seemed to be buying what we were selling. Our church graciously encouraged the staff to spend up to a day each week teaching, leading seminars, and consulting with other churches in the region. My calendar was filled with speaking engagements to share the innovations and glories of the large church with those eager to follow in this path.

Then I read *Working the Angles*:

> I don't know of any other profession in which it is quite as easy to fake it as ours. By adopting a reverential demeanor, cultivating a stained-glass voice, slipping occasional words like "eschatology" into conversation and *heilsgeschichte* into our discourse—not often enough actually to confuse people but enough to keep them aware that our habitual train of thought is a cut above pew level —we are trusted, without any questions asked, as stewards of the mysteries.[2]

That caught my attention. Peterson continued on this rant by declaring his belief that he could produce a suitable pastor for almost every congregation in America out of a person with a high school diploma and six months in a pastor-making trade school. His trade school would have four courses: Creative Plagiarism, Voice Control for Prayer and Counseling, Efficient

2. Ibid., 6.

Office Management, and Image Projection.[3] I knew that I had found a voice that needed to be heard. It was impossible to overlook Peterson's exquisite education and scholarly training combined with the wit that could only come from an experienced parish leader and an astute cultural observer. I had found a guide who could deconstruct both the pretensions and excesses of both the academy and highly marketed and consumer-driven church without entirely dismissing either.

Learning the Angles

As a young pastor I was surprised by how visible the job was. An absence at certain church-wide events was noted. It was not only essential to attend certain gatherings and worship services, but it was also important that my wife did so. Where we lived was a matter of public discourse. The church's leadership and those involved in the youth ministry expressed a desire that we live near the church, despite the fact that it was located in one of the most expensive communities in the Boston suburbs. Overextending the set amount of time for a corporate prayer in the worship service or delaying on an administrative report yielded a gentle correction in one's box on Monday morning. When a sermon, retreat, or program went well, there were many compliments. Administrative failures, errors in judgment, struggles in public speaking, or controversial opinions yielded a stack of phone messages and memos. And then there were the students. These students had been well trained in writing genuine notes of affirmation and support. I received scores and scores of these encouragements. These kids noticed almost everything. Even as one staff pastor on a large staff, the job was exceedingly visible.

I was admittedly drawn to this visible nature of the job. I trained in seminary with outstanding scholars, received supervision from excellent mentors, and listened to peers and volunteers to improve continually. But it was obvious that one could succeed in the visible and yet still utterly fail. Talent, giftedness, or quality support in the areas of one's weaknesses were not enough. Even at a tender professional age, the strong sense emerged that the interior aspects of ministry might be equally as significant. Peterson explained that the "visible lines of pastoral work are preaching, teaching, and administration."[4] But then he offered a simple geometry, "What

3. Ibid., 5.
4. Ibid., 3.

determines the proportions and the shape of the whole are the angles."[5] The angles are the quiet, often invisible acts of attentiveness: praying, reading Scripture, and spiritual direction.

Except for the surprise (in 1987) inclusion of spiritual direction, this portrait was not earth shatteringly unexpected. Even if we were ignorant of how prayer and Scripture fully integrated with the visible functions of ministry, we understood their importance. As anyone knows who has read Peterson's dynamic translation of Bible, *The Message* (2002), his genius is encoding new life into the familiar, expected, and even the obvious. As a deeply perceptive practitioner of these angles, he presented new insights in descriptive language that literally begged for my replication and experimentation.

I bought this book many, many times. I maintained a stack of five to ten extras in my office. I gave it to youth ministry volunteers, colleagues, and students. Some of his language became the primary language in the ministries that I led. *WtA* quickly became a first responder in my ministry for a variety of questions and concerns on the nature of prayer, the relationship of the narrative of Scripture to the spiritual life, and what I perceived my job to be.

As a young pastor, I realized that I had indeed been called to be "a steward of the mysteries" regardless of my bewilderment regarding those same mysteries.[6] When volunteers, parents, or students made appointments to discuss theodicy, the relationship of an ancient text to contemporary sexuality, the complexities of prayer, or how to manage family conflict, I always had that alarming mental subtext of "why are you asking me?" I found *WtA* to be a gentle invitation to explore those same mysteries and a wonderful resource to invite others into this same exploration. That enthusiasm has not waned in twenty-five years.

Twenty-Five Years of Working These Angles

Much has changed for me in twenty-five years. I've mastered the art of being downwardly mobile. My megachurch days led to a medium-sized church in a college town (Chapel Hill, North Carolina) and finally to the founding of an intentionally small, organic, emergent church and community in Durham, North Carolina. This journey feels like a lived epitaph

5. Ibid.
6. Ibid., 4.

to a Dr. Suess book or a Grateful Dead song. Along the way, I have had the privilege to being instrumental in helping start and lead the emerging church movement (EmergentVillage), written a couple of books including a text on reading the Bible through community hermeneutics (*Free for All*), served on the board of a seminary for a decade (the Seattle School of Theology and Psychology), wandered back into the PhD program that I almost started twenty years ago ("Culture, Curriculum, and Change" in UNC-Chapel Hill's School of Education), planted a church that still gives me hope for what Christian communities can be, traded youth ministry for parenting two amazing teenagers, and stayed married while finding this to be the most blessed angle in the many lines of my life. I'm still shocked most of the time to be considered a "steward of the mysteries," and still working the same angles in hopes of becoming a more attentive person in a life with too many lines. I now reflect on Peterson's angles from many more lenses than that newly married, neophyte pastor who felt caught between the massive inertia of the growing church and the academy.

Being much longer of tooth, my appreciation for Eugene Peterson's angles has only deepened. Three concepts in the book have radically changed the trajectory of the professional journey for me. The first is Sabbath and Sabbath-keeping.[7] He reads the first creation story in Genesis as a rhythm of evening then morning, seeing an invited dance of rest that proceeds collaboration in creative work of God. He inverts the binary of work/grace to grace/work, offering the most gracious "get out jail free card" to anyone caught in a nightmare of personal meaning through productivity (that is, everyone in our market-driven, consumption-oriented, individualistic culture). Peterson continues with two powerful definitions of Sabbath-keeping: *prayer* from the Exodus narrative and *play* from the Deuteronomy narrative. These acts radically differentiate the keeping of Sabbath from the "bastard Sabbath" of a day off.[8]

Rarely does worship go by in our community of Emmaus Way or at the Seattle School of Theology and Psychology where the concepts of prayer and play are not lifted up as intermingled spiritual practices. These two trajectories of worship relate in a dynamic fashion that is liberating and emancipatory to the core of one's created being. Peterson writes elsewhere, "Praying and playing share this quality: they develop and mature with age, they don't go into decline. Prayerfulness and playfulness reverse

7. Ibid., 44–58.

8. Ibid., 46.

the deadening effects of sin-determined lives."[9] Peterson's gift to me was that I have been exploring these two practices in a generative relationship rather than an adversarial tension. This thought has redefined how I grew to understand the postures of prayer and worship. I can't count the times of delight. When I have been in the joyful part of a long run (that moment when your aching muscles have relaxed, you have too much inertia from the distance traveled to consider stopping, and your mind is freed from the labor of moving your body). Or when I am in the midst of our community's weekly pub group where we are wildly bantering about theology, politics, art, or life. Or when I am in the midst of a worship gathering where I am so fully engaged by the art and craft of our musicians to the point that I forget that I have a sermon dialogue to lead. In each place I often suddenly realize that I am working an angle of utter enjoyment rather than an angle of labor.

The second concept that has changed my professional story is Peterson's description of "contemplative exegesis."[10] I came from the tradition where exegesis was the art of finding *the* word: using the critical tools of historiography, genre, grammar, language, and literary structure to discern a specific historical and timeless word in the biblical text. Prayerful contemplation was a welcome guest at the feast, but as an appetizer to the serious meal of interpretation. Imagination was nowhere on the invitation list. Now the church commonly uses terms like *wonder* and *imagination* as integral elements of listening to the text. The late Reynolds Price recently referred to our comingling with the Gospels as "a serious way of wondering."[11]

After Peterson, it is more common now to pursue a living narrative rather than a static word in the biblical text. To put this in the much larger context of the history of thought, Charles Taylor in *The Sources of the Self* advocates persuasively for a break from a rationalistic tradition that had created the notion of the atomized, individualized, disconnected self or individual person. His correction includes the assertion of the absolute necessity for social narratives as the source of collective meaning. To put it bluntly, isolated human beings without a story are overwhelmingly lost. There were also other voices before Peterson that were pushing against the notion of isolated persons and disconnected words, before postmodernity became popular or cool.

---

9. Peterson, *Eat This Book*, 54.

10. Peterson, *Working the Angles*, 74–86.

11. Price, *A Serious Way of Wondering*.

Peterson's was one of the voices that unearthed the narrative structure of the Bible and gave us permission to interact with a living text in
a contemplative, imaginative, and even playful manner. *WtA* describes a
contemplative exegesis and the narrative perspective of self in this manner:

> If the recovery of contemplative exegesis begins with a realization
> that words are basically sounds that reveal, it matures with the
> recognition that when words are put together they form stories
> that shape. Whenever we open our mouths to speak, it isn't long
> before we are telling a story. Whenever we open our ears to listen,
> it isn't long before we are hearing a story. The most common and
> natural way to assemble words together is in story form. Words do
> not occur in isolation; they connect. And when they connect they
> make a narrative.[12]

In this return to the primacy of story, *incarnation* was breathing once more
into the very text that bore the name of the Incarnate One. Peterson would
later show us how beautiful this could be in his writing of *The Message.*
Peterson often comments that this is what he really does in ministry: connect the narrative of the text to the narrative of peoples' lives through the
use of a common idiom.

This idea of lives connected through narratives changed the way I did
almost everything. Retreats with highly planned activities and polished
speakers yielded to storytelling weekends that engage a much more diverse
population of students with astonishing results. I began to include corporate story reading as a regular and primary practice in regular meetings.
Today I serve in a context where the traditional sermon has been replaced
by a dialogue and intersection of community stories. I have worked this
angle now for most of my life.

A third profession-changing concept to me was the matter of *naming.* Peterson writes, "Naming is important. What is unnamed is often
unnoticed. Naming focuses attention. The precise name confers dignity."[13]
In 1987, the church in North America was just learning the term *spiritual
direction* through the life-changing writings of Henri Nouwen—Peterson
pushed this relearning further. For Peterson, spiritual direction is a commitment to noticing the small, the obscure, and the mundane. Spiritual
direction takes seriously the interruptions that barge into our intentionality. This practice is framed by assertions that God is graciously active and

12. Ibid., 80–81.
13. Ibid., 107.

speaking, and that "responding to God is not sheer guesswork."[14] Persons and moments are unique—which requires the active work of discernment rather the application of generalized formulas or platitudes in these moments. Peterson *names* the encompassing practice of spiritual direction as one of the key angles of pastoral work—the persistent active work to discern the voice and work of God. He writes,

> Ironically this is the work that many people assume that pastors do all the time: teaching people to pray, helping parishioners discern the presence of grace in events and feelings, affirming the presence of God at the very heart of life, sharing a search for light through a dark passage in the pilgrimage, guiding the formation of a self-understanding that is biblically spiritual instead of merely psychological or sociological. But pastors don't do it all the time or nearly enough of the time.[15]

This naming was both emancipatory and revolutionary. Emancipatory in that, for pastors, it is easy to be frustrated at interruptions or simply to ignore opportunities for conversation on the spiritual life. Naming this as an essential angle of ministry redeemed so many of the simple moments of ministry and motivated far greater intentionality in these moments. It was also revolutionary in that it demanded that the angles take precedence over the visual lines. The visual aspects of ministry were the locations for praise and critique. This angle challenged my obsession with the visual acts of ministry. It reframed them by demanding that they be evaluated by their ability to support the collective processes of spiritual formation. I have failed often at this renaming. Writing, speaking, preaching, affirmation, critique, grand plans, and simple schemes often form an impenetrable fog on my perceptive radar. But this renaming has always served a generous anchor that reconstitutes my attention and intentionality.

An (Imagined) Single Malt with Eugene

I hope that it is abundantly clear how significantly I have been formed by Peterson's angles. I have never had the privilege of meeting Eugene Peterson. But I have often imagined a personal conversation around a couple of single malt scotches. The scotch seems appropriate (apologies to

14. Ibid., 104.
15. Ibid.

Methodist quadrilateral

teetotalers) because it is a drink that is often enjoyed slowly and also matures wonderfully with age. In my dilettante understanding of scotch and budget-minimized experiences of it, there seems to be only two types: good and better, with "better" often dictated significantly by age. I'm curious to ask about how what I've learned over a lifetime of ministry and forays in the academy might challenge or refine his ideas.

Peterson's succinct triangular geometry might be enhanced by another angle. Perhaps ministry is polygon. I have spent a good portion of the last decade gaining experience in local, non-partisan, faith-based political organizing. I wonder if missional activism is missing.

Postmodern epistemology makes us sensitive to an individualism in our constructs. Critical theory reminds us that the gospel is entirely concerned with the work of justice, collaboration with God in constructing the jubilee economics and society announced by Jesus in his first public declaration in Luke 4. In the last couple of decades, the Christian community has learned that we are spiritually formed in missional activism. Gospel-driven action not only follows contemplation, but also can precede and inspire the attentiveness of Peterson's angles. The pastor is spiritually formed and also guides the formation of the people of God by serving the needs of God's created world. Sometimes the most needed expression of pastoral integrity is to be at ground zero of a natural disaster, in the front of the march, at the microphone of dissent and dialogue, in a cot at the shelter, and even under the yoke of governmental punishment. Though all of Peterson's angles can be expressed in social and non-solitary manners, missional activism overwhelmingly challenges any notion of pastoral integrity being locked in a personal or individual dimension.

If this visible line were added, what would be the commiserate angle of attentiveness? My suggestion would be *the physical body*. We are now aware that the body can be a location of personal and cultural enslavement as well a location of received grace and liberation. Any liberation of mind and soul that does not include the body is no true emancipation. The promise of God includes not only the salvation of the soul, but also the resurrection of the physical body and a restoration of the created world (see Ezekiel 37:1–14). In his chapter on Sabbath, Peterson makes a profound point (while exhibiting a prejudice of that time). He laments that the pastor's *study* has now become an *office*. His critique exhibits the tendency to privilege the mind and the soul over and against the body. I have friends in the pastorate and academy who like to refer to this same space as their *studio,* which is as likely to be filled with an art project in progress or a yoga mat as a wall of books. This naming can remind us that creative expression and physical expression are angles of pastoral integrity.

Before the scotch expired, I would tell Eugene (since we are now familiar) that even twenty-five years earlier, I had transgressed the boundaries of his title. Even in my first reading, I recognized that this was not just a book for pastors. After two decades of intimate and dynamic association with various free churches, organic churches, house churches, neo-monastic communities, and post-church Christian communities, I would strongly suggest the Peterson's life-giving vision of integrity extends far beyond the boundaries of a professional clergy and a highly institutional church. Without engaging a long discussion on ecclesiology, I think we would both agree to limit this text would be a disservice to all who struggle, create, conspire, and most certainly pray and play, in order to join the active grace of a God who continually reverses our overly ambitious, often wounded, and occasionally numbed lives.

I hope the bartender sent over the whole bottle because my toasts of gratitude are voluminous.

The Vow of Stability

EUGENE PETERSON AND THE LONG PASTORATE

Martin B. Copenhaver

ACCORDING TO EUGENE PETERSON, I have just gotten started.

For eighteen years I have served as Senior Pastor of Wellesley Congregational Church, United Church of Christ. That is longer than any pastor in the last hundred years of the church's history, longer than my father served any church in his forty-year ministry. It feels to me, and probably to my congregation, that I have been here a long time. To Peterson, however, it is more like a good start: "The *norm* for pastoral work is stability. Twenty-, thirty-, and forty-year-long pastorates should be typical among us (as they once were) and not exceptional."[1]

Drawing on *The Rule of Saint Benedict*, Peterson advocates, and for many years lived out, a "vow of stability," which he summarizes in four words: "stay where you are."

Peterson makes the case for long pastorates in several of his books, but the most in-depth reflection is in *Under the Unpredictable Plant*. Ironically, that book was published just as Peterson was leaving the church he had served for twenty-nine years, Christ Our King Presbyterian Church near Baltimore, to teach at Regent College in Vancouver. In that book he never explicitly states that he is writing about his own vocational discernment at a critical juncture, but the reader hardly needs to be told. The book has the

---

1. Peterson, *Under the Unpredictable Plant*, 29.

immediacy and urgency of dispatches from the front lines of a battle that is still actively waged.

Peterson's advocacy of long pastorates derives from his approach to pastoral ministry, which is always contextual and relational. It is rooted in the particularities of a place and a people. It requires knowing individuals as individuals—each with unique stories, gifts and burdens—in ways that are possible only over an extended period of time. Peterson borrows a phrase from Nietzsche to make his point, saying that pastoral ministry requires "long obedience in the same direction" (a phrase Peterson also used as the title for one of his books). One might also add a variation on that theme: pastoral ministry requires "deep obedience in the same place."

If pastoral ministry were about building an institution, that could be done in a shorter period of time. Peterson recalls one pastoral colleague who explained why he was moving on after serving his congregation for only five years: "'I have accomplished what I came to do,' he said. 'I have my program in place and working. There is nothing left here for me to do.'" Peterson then comments derisively, "Program? What has program got to do with spirituality?"[2]

Peterson grants that ministry in one setting over a long period of time is confining, but he contends that confinement is necessary for a pastoral ministry to flourish: "It is the spiritual equivalent to the old artistic idea that talent grows by its very confinement, that the genie's strength comes from his confinement in the bottle. . . . Without confinement, without intensification resulting from compression, there is no energy worth speaking of."[3]

According to Peterson, it is this very confinement in a particular congregation that "provides the rhythms, the associations, the tasks, the limitations, the temptations—the *conditions*" for a pastor to grow up and grow into what he calls "vocational holiness."[4]

Peterson generalizes that most pastors leave their congregations either from personal ambition or boredom, and he readily admits that he was susceptible to both.

In an interview, Peterson delineates different kinds of ambition: "In the best sense, ambition is wanting to do your best. But sometimes ambition

2. Ibid., 166–67.
3. Ibid., 74–75.
4. Ibid., 22.

can be simply the need to be noticed. And I think, in me, there was that kind of ambition in my restlessness."[5]

So three times during his pastorate at Christ Our King he sought to break his "vow of stability" and move to another congregation. He likens those congregations to Tarshish, the temptingly glamorous setting where Jonah sought to go after God told him that he was supposed to head out for gritty and difficult Nineveh. Each time Peterson was turned down by the glittering Tarshish churches (by the way, what congregation would not want Eugene Peterson as their pastor?) and ended up back at Ninevah—spit up, as Jonah was, onto the shores of a familiar land he had tried to leave.

Boredom is a particular temptation in pastoral ministry because, for the most part, it is not glamorous work. Peterson likens it to farm work: "Most pastoral work involves routines similar to cleaning out the barn, *technical maintenance* mucking out the stalls, spreading manure, pulling weeds."[6]

Peterson's ambition may have been thwarted by a God who refused to play along, but he had to alleviate the boredom himself. In that same interview, Peterson confided that the key to getting over his boredom was the eventual realization that the boredom was his fault: "I wasn't paying attention to things. It was like I was walking through a field of wildflowers and not seeing any of them because I'd seen them 500 times before. So I learned to start looking."[7]

Writing helped him alleviate the boredom because it prompted him to look more closely at what was going on around him, particularly in the lives of the members of his congregation. In this attempt to pay attention, he was helped by two authors in particular: Fyodor Dostoevsky and James Joyce.

Dostoevsky reminded Peterson of the grandness of the human drama, which can be camouflaged so easily by the mundane surface of lives. "Dostoevsky made [the people in my congregation] appear large again, vast in their aspirations, their sins, their glories. . . . Now when I came across dull people, I inserted them into one of the novels to see what Dostoevsky would make of them."[8]

In *Ulysses*, James Joyce tells the story of a single day in the life an ordinary man, Leopold Bloom, living in an ordinary city, Dublin. Not much to write about, one might think, particularly for 600 pages. But a close reading

5. Wood, "The Best Life."

6. *Under the Unpredictable Plant*, 16.

7. Wood, "The Best Life."

8. *Under the Unpredictable Plant*, 62–63.

reveals that, within twenty-four hours in this most ordinary life, something like an epic odyssey is unfolding. Peterson found this realization transformative: "Now I knew my work: *this* is the pastor's work. I wanted to be able to look at each person in my parish with the same imagination and insight and comprehensiveness with which Joyce looked at Leopold Bloom."[9]

Peterson would contend that, the longer one stays in a particular congregation, the more this kind of pastoral vision becomes possible.

Eighteen years ago I stood in the pulpit of Wellesley Congregational Church for the first time. I was leaving a church in Phoenix, where I had served for three years. This is how I started my first sermon to the congregation in Wellesley:

> So many faces! For me, it's almost like looking out on the ocean. It's a beautiful sight. The experience inspires awe. And it's a bit overwhelming. When I look out at my own congregation in Phoenix the faces are so familiar. After all, in my years there I have encountered with many of them the twin mysteries of birth and death. I know many of their hopes and triumphs and have shared many of their hurts and disappointments. Although I have had a chance to meet many of you already, it takes a long time before someone can look out on a gathering such as this and see individuals, which of course is the way God sees us. It takes time. There is a lot of life to live together before that happens.

I had only served the church in Phoenix for three years, but three years was enough to provide a contrast with standing before a congregation of people I did not know.

Now that I have been in Wellesley for eighteen years, however, the contrast is enormous. When I first looked out at my congregation eighteen years ago I was overwhelmed by the sight of a largely anonymous sea of faces. Now, after so many years, there is hardly a trace of anonymity to be found. As I look out at that same congregation, I am still overwhelmed, but for an entirely different reason—now I see so much. I am overwhelmed by the familiar.

After all, now I see not just the faces, but faces over time. I see a face traced with grief, and I also see that same face from an earlier time when laugh lines spread like beams of light from the corners of his eyes. I see the young mother trying to keep her son still in the pew, and I also see her when she was a restless teenager herself. I see the pot-bellied man, and I

9. Ibid., 125.

also see him at an earlier stage when he was fit enough to run a marathon. These days, more often than not, I am confirming teenagers whom I baptized as infants or young children, which feels a bit like picking up a corner of time, peering inside, and seeing it in all its dimensions.

I can even see people who are no longer there. When I stand in the pulpit and look out at my congregation, I can see the deceased husband of the woman who now comes to worship alone. I can see the man who somehow ended up with the church in the break-up with his partner, but I can see the now absent partner, as well. And there is a pew that may be full today, but still seems somehow empty because the family that used to fill it has moved across the country. It is like what interpreters of art call *pentimento*—the reappearance in a painting of an underlying image that had been painted over. In a *pentimento* one can see both the old and the new somehow together and at the same time.

A pastor who is new to a congregation will not be able to see a *pentimento*. A new pastor is not able to see the older layers or the people who are no longer there. That kind of pastoral vision comes only over time.

The layering of time adds thick texture to both individual narratives and the narrative of the congregation. After eighteen years I not only know the back stories, I also know the back stories of the back stories. I know who has a difficult time getting along with whom. I can sense when a particular person is out of sorts, because I have seen her in enough contexts to be able to sort out the range of emotions reflected on her face. I do not take it personally when one man falls asleep during the sermon, because I know he does that most Sundays and, besides, he is working a lot of nights these days. When one person says he is overwhelmed I know not to take it too seriously because he is often overwhelmed. When another person says she is overwhelmed I take notice because this is something unusual for her.

So, yes, a congregation does become more interesting over time, much as a good novel becomes more interesting as each chapter nuances character development and plot in ways that are not possible in shorter literary forms.

I am convinced the best preaching is done by pastors in their own congregations. That is because preaching is highly contextual. It benefits from deep and nuanced readings of three complex entities: the biblical text, the wider world, and the congregation. The best preaching, in my experience, stands at the intersection of all three. A visiting preacher may be able to exegete the text and analyze what is going on in the world with brilliance, but an extra dimension is added when the preacher knows the congregation, particularly over a period of years. Harry Emerson Fosdick was fond of saying, "Preaching is sometimes like trying to put drops into someone's eyes out of a ten-story window." Preaching to one's own congregation over time may not change Fosdick's image, but it shrinks the distance. When you know a congregation well, you feel like you are preaching at much closer range. The drops are more likely to find their target.

And after all of these years the congregation knows me well, too. They know my gifts and how those gifts can be put to optimal use. They also know what gifts I lack and have learned over time how others can help shore up my ministry where it is weakest. They can follow my train of thought, often arriving ahead of me, and they are tuned into my sense of humor. They know a good deal about my passionate commitments and they know all too much about my pet peeves.

Most important of all, they know they can trust me: I will listen without being judgmental; I will keep confidences; I won't bear grudges or play favorites; my judgment is largely sound; for the most part, I will not say or do something that is harmful to the congregation. We might like to think all pastors are trustworthy in these basic ways, but in congregations like the ones I have served, that kind of trust is earned over time, sometimes over many years, one pastoral engagement at a time.

When I first started at my church, I asked the Moderator when the Nominating Committee was going to meet. He cleared his throat and said, "It is not our practice to have the pastors attend meetings of the Nominating Committee." He was gentle, but firm. I was shocked. At other congregations I had served I not only attended the meetings of the Nominating Committee, I considered it one of my most important duties.

Fast forward fifteen years: The chair of the Nominating Committee tells me about some of the challenges he faces in filling various positions. I respond, "How about if I come to one of your meetings? Perhaps I can help." He jumps on the offer, obviously thrilled that I would deign to attend such a meeting: "Oh, would you? That would be wonderful." I now have an open invitation.

When that kind of mutual understanding and trust exists between a pastor and congregation so much becomes possible. Like partners who have been dancing together for decades, they can anticipate each other's moves, which means that whoever is leading can use a lighter touch, more gentle and more graceful. In such instances, grace arises out of familiarity.

Peterson's advocacy of long pastorates is a bracing reminder to those who approach their ministry as a career to be managed: pastoral ministry is not a career, but a vocation. This is another instance in which the rules and assumptions by which most lives are governed do not apply to ministry. Workers in most settings are wise to chart out a career plan. In ministry, such planning for "advancement" qualifies as unfaithfulness. The very notion of vocation requires a recognition that we are not in charge, but rather responding to the prompting of another. Add this reminder to the list of reasons why we are in Peterson's debt.

Nevertheless, I wonder if Peterson's depiction and evaluation of long pastorates tells the whole story and, particularly, whether he is guilty of generalizing from his own experience. We can grant that Peterson found a twenty-nine year pastorate generative and fruitful, both for himself and for the congregation he served. Not all long pastorates could be described that way, however, so I wonder if Peterson's almost unqualified advocacy for long pastorates is wise.

I have known pastors, even faithful and effective ones, who simply stayed too long in their churches. What began as generative and fruitful, faded through the wear of time, not through ambition or even boredom, but through something like an excess of comfort. Such pastorates can be like the home a family has lived in for twenty-five years. Over the years it may have become more comfortable, but after a certain point, it is less likely that the ragged carpet will be replaced or the paint will be freshened up. In fact, the need for such improvements might not even be seen by the family who lives there—ironically, because they have lived there so long, they may see less than a visitor will. The heart and mind have a way of making accommodations for the familiar.

What is more chastening, I have known pastors, even savvy ones, who do not see when it is time to leave. They could spot such a time in another pastor's life from a hundred paces, but not in their own. Knowing when it is a good and appropriate time to leave is more art than science, of course, but that may be just another way of saying that it is difficult to know. (In my own setting, I have toyed with the idea of giving one or two trusted members a poison pill, so they could slip it to me when they sense I have stayed too long.)

So I am left largely to my own perceptions, as well as the counsel of friends and family. I have learned a few things by observing other pastors. Clearly, a severe loss of energy is a sign one should leave, but noting where a pastor's energies are deployed can be telling, as well. Most of us lose energy for routine eventually, but if there is a lack of energy for anything new, that is a sign that one has stayed too long. Some pastors devote more and more energy to commitments outside their congregations—to church-related organizations and social service organizations, for example—and that can be a sign, as well.

I have noticed some pastors, the longer they stay, make more references to the past than to the future of their congregations, and that seems telling.

I would also add that a telltale sign a pastor has been in a congregation too long is when she makes frequent reference to how long she has there. I would add that, but I don't think I will because, increasingly, that describes me.

Before we can fully assess the benefits of a long-term pastorate, it is necessary to consider what happens after a long-term pastor leaves. Often successors of long-term pastors struggle, many only remaining for a few years. We could speculate about the reasons why this is so often the case—and certainly the factors vary in each instance—but whatever the reasons, the experience of so many who follow long-term pastorates should give us pause. It may not be possible to know if a pastor has stayed too long until a number of years after he or she has left. It may be only then that anyone can know if the long-term pastorate equipped the congregation to thrive after the long-term pastor leaves. That means the only way to assess fully the impact of Peterson's decision to serve Christ Our King for twenty-nine years would be to see how the congregation fared five or even ten years after he left.

Peterson's reflections on his own parting from Christ Our King are brief and startlingly matter-of-fact: "We anticipated it would be extremely difficult—uprooting ourselves from all the emotional attachments and well-developed intimacies that gave such a rich texture to our lives. Leaving this place of worship and witness where God had faithfully revealed himself and God's Spirit had created so much resurrection life. But as it turned out, leaving our congregation was surprising easy. Effortless almost."[10]

Throughout his work, Peterson describes the work of the pastor as deeply relational, his own life interwoven with the life of his congregation, its members, and the gospel story. In his rendering, the work of the pastor

10. Peterson, *The Pastor*, 299.

is rich, life-giving work. So I wonder how leaving after twenty-nine years of such a pastorate could be "Effortless almost."

I do not believe that Peterson, whose work benefits from such a clear-eyed approach to pastoral ministry, has suddenly taken a Pollyannaish turn here. Rather, it seems like a witness, however unintentional, to the complexity of long-term pastorates, a complexity that is found in even more concentrated form in parting. The kind of pastorate Peterson and his congregation enjoyed was infused with such life-giving richness that one would expect the parting to be not only complex, but painful. If such a parting after such a pastorate seemed anything close to effortless, I can only imagine that being possible through the authoritative intervention of grace.

In the meantime, a mother tells me I cannot possibly retire because ever since her three daughters were little they envisioned me officiating at their weddings. Another parishioner hands me plans for her memorial service. Although she is in good health, she assumes I will be there to carry out these plans. Those kinds of encounters are happening more frequently these days.

So I remind myself that Paul planted, Apollos watered, and the rest of us are just passing through. In the church, none of us pastors is indispensable. That is a good thing because, in the larger scheme of things, none of us will remain for long. Only Jesus is indispensable.

Take and Read

James Howell

MY INTRODUCTION TO EUGENE Peterson was not through his books, but during a pastoral call I made to a woman who had visited our church. I was a bit surprised she had begun worshiping with us. Small churches struggling for survival in less than desirable neighborhoods don't get many visitors—and she wasn't like us. The socio-economic status of our handful of folks ranged from poor to lower-middle class, few had attended any college, and virtually all were lifelong southerners. This woman was from up north, had nearly completed her doctorate, and was single, in her mid-thirties. With her arrival, our singles group grew from zero to one.

She explained she was uninterested in the obvious, cool, trendy churches. Her preference was a church where the pastor would be able to do what I was doing, namely, sitting in her living room, talking about God and life in the world. She spoke deftly of the body of Christ as just plain people, who need no snazzy programming or dazzling music. She had come from a church that wasn't busy so much as calm, worshipful, and loving.

Her pastor? One Eugene Peterson.

After my visit, I didn't put a big check mark on my to-do list, and I resisted the urge to stamp "solid prospect" next to her name. She was already a friend, and in the sense of finding ourselves surprised by the gift of immediate presence in the body of Christ.

Now I am pastor of a church so large it seems impossible to sit in a visitor's living room and chat. In fact, for all the glory, high pay, and comforts that accrue to the pastor of a large congregation, I find I need that woman who would never come to my large church, and I need her pastor whom I access not through her now but through his writing. And I find I don't need to read more and more of his writing, but I need simply to reread a handful of prescient passages each week, or perhaps daily. I'm haunted by the possibility that this assessment from *Under the Unpredictable Plant* might just be about the ministry of which I've been a part: "The pastoral vocation in America is embarrassingly banal. It is banal because it is pursued under the canons of job efficiency and career management."[1] Or, in *The Jesus Way*: "More often than not I find my Christian brothers and sisters uncritically embracing the ways and means practiced by the high-profile men and women who lead large corporations . . . who show us how to make money, manage people, sell products, manipulate emotions."[2] When these words make me wobbly in the knees, I feel sure we need to haul in a wrecking ball and demolish our institutions as we experience them now and start all over. But the harder truth is that I need to start over with me. It is a personal disposition within the pastor, a new kind of life for those of us who attempt to serve as such, that is required. Peterson may be our generation's most able guide.

Last year, our clergy were talking informally about goals for the coming year. Typically, we ratchet up a host of worthy objectives and well-crafted strategies, and we get busy. That's the one thing I know we're good at: getting busy. But the stars aligned in such a way that three of us happened at about that time to be reading Peterson's autobiographical *The Pastor*. A few selections jumped out at us. The following is a bit long, but what is striking is that when he speaks of worship and community, he isn't merely suggesting that he came up with a better idea. Instead, he exposes what we have baptized and admired in church life as "taking the Lord's name in vain," and an outright "sin against the Holy Spirit."

> By the time I arrived on the scene as a pastor, the American church had reinterpreted the worship of God as an activity for religious consumers. Entertainment, cheerleading, and manipulation were conspicuous in high places. American worship was conceived as a public-relations campaign for Jesus and the angels. Worship had been cheapened into a commodity marketed by using tried-and-true advertising techniques. If so-called worshippers didn't "get anything out of it," there had been no worship worth coming

1. Peterson, *Under the Unpredictable Plant*, 5.
2. Peterson, *The Jesus Way*, 8.

back for. Instead of calling people to worship God, pastors all over the country were inviting people to "have a worship experience." Worship was evaluated on the "consumer satisfaction scale" of one to ten. It struck me as a violation of the holy, a secularization of the sacred. Taking the Lord's name in vain. I determined to reintroduce the rubric "Let us worship God" for my congregation, and then really do it. I knew this wasn't going to be easy. The entertainment model for worship in America was pervasive. And community. The church as a community of faith formed by the Holy Spirit. Church in America was mostly understood by Christians and their pastors in terms of its function—what it did: build buildings, become "successful," change the neighborhood, launch mission projects, and create programs that would organize and motivate people to do these things. Programs, mostly programs. Programs had developed into the dominant methodology of "doing church." Far more attention was given to organizing and giving leadership to programs than anything else. But there is a problem here: a program is an abstraction and inherently nonpersonal. A program defines people in terms of what they do, not who they are. The more program, the less person. Church was understood not in terms of personal relationships and a personal God but in terms of "getting things done." This struck me as violation of the inherent personal dignity of souls. The abstraction of a programmatic approach to men and women, however well-meaning, atrophied the relational and replaced it with the pragmatic. Treating souls for whom Christ died as numbers or projects or resources seemed to me something like a sin against the Holy Spirit. I wanted to develop a congregation in which relationships were primary, a household of hospitality. A community in which men and women would be known primarily by name, not by function. I knew this wouldn't be easy, and it wasn't.[3]

To comment on these searing insights and brutal truth-telling would only detract from their power. Our pastors began to ask, "*Why* are we a beehive of activity more than a worshipful community? We are noteworthy for our program menu and intense mission functions; but might we be called by God to become a different sort of community that simply is, where names matter more than function, where efficiency and success might frighten us enough to slow down and invite our people into a worship that is not the well-rehearsed, brilliant enacted hour on Sunday, but something people actually breathe when they aren't in our building?" To help people become

3. Peterson, *The Pastor*, 254.

worshipful, we must become worshipful. There are some schedule complications if we're serious about this. Peterson speaks of "interruptibility," which isn't a flexible calendar so much as a sacrificial disposition, "a readiness to interrupt whatever we are doing and build an altar"[4]—a lovely image, this altar-building here and then there, throughout the day.

A second passage pummeled us, as Peterson typed a mere seven sentences that have become the legendary "paradigm shift" for what we are about:

> I realized that I was gradually becoming more interested in dealing with my congregation as problems to be fixed than as members of the household of God to be led in the worship and service of God. In dealing with my parishioners as problems, I more or less knew what I was doing. In dealing with them as a pastor, I was involved in mysteries, mostly having to do with God, that were far beyond my understanding and control. I had been shifting from being a pastor dealing with God in people's lives to treating them as persons dealing with problems in their lives. I was not being their pastor. I could have helped and still been their pastor. But by reducing them to problems to be fixed, I omitted the biggest thing of all in their lives, God and their souls, and the biggest thing in my life, my vocation as pastor.[5]

Unfixed people can worship. Unfixed people can love. The body of Christ is not composed of fixed or about-to-be-fixed people. I'm not a repairman. And there's an all-enveloping grace in that realization. I am not ordained to fix others. How much ego is in this addictive kind of ministry anyway? Peterson's diagnosis: "What started out as managing people's gifts for the work of the kingdom of God becomes the manipulation of people's lives for the building up of my pastoral ego."[6]

And I don't need to fix myself either. I can't fix what is out of sorts in my life, or what is awry in me. That's the grace, the mercy, the mystery. The pressure is off. That is why we worship, and even walk around in a worshipful, broken, unfixed but unforsaken way. That is why we need Christ and need not vaunt ourselves or strive for "heroic" ministry in which "my messianic work takes center stage and Messiah is pushed to the sidelines."[7] I'm

4. Peterson, *The Jesus Way*, 49.
5. Peterson, *The Pastor*, 139.
6. Peterson, *Under the Unpredictable Plant*, 181.
7. Ibid., 179.

ready to return to the sidelines, where I started, and let the Messiah be the one I once loved before I thought of replacing him.

I like it that Peterson doesn't stick with how we do pastoral ministry, but names what is biggest in his own life—which compels me to ask about what is the biggest thing in my life. Why did I go into ministry? To organize a dazzling round of activities? To raise funds? To fix people? Somewhere in the distant recesses of memory, I recall a murky but alluring request from Jesus to stick close to him, to be near him, to do whatever I could for him. I applied to seminary because (and this wasn't actually asked of me on the forms I filled out) I simply loved Jesus. We lose our way—and that's not a professional issue, but a most pointedly personal issue.

Peterson's great gift to me (and I might need the rest of my ministry and possible retirement years to live into this) is to remind me about the biggest thing, which is not my work and certainly not my success. Peterson helps me confess my ugliest sin to the Lord: the plaudits, the ladder I've climbed, the metrics of which I pretend to be too humble to boast about, the heady grand work my congregations have accomplished—all of which may be a pale substitute for the real thing to which God initially called me. Perhaps at my best I unwittingly let this life with God become balkanized—or synonymously, Americanized. Peterson seems like a kind person, but his onslaught against the enculturation of the church and ministry is all but unbearable, and therefore life-giving. Consider the sarcasm in *The Jesus Way*: "Why didn't Jesus learn from Herod? Why didn't Jesus take Herod as his mentor in getting on in the world? All Jesus had to do was adopt and then adapt Herod's political style, his skills, his tested principles, and put them to work under the rule of God."[8] Or this reminiscence from *The Pastor*:

> The ink on my ordination papers wasn't even dry before I was being told by experts, so-called, in the field of church that my main task was to run a church after the manner of my brother and sister Christians who run service stations, grocery stores, corporations, banks, hospitals, and financial services. This is the Americanization of congregation. It means turning each congregation into a market for religious consumers, an ecclesiastical business run along the lines of advertising techniques, organizational flow charts, and energized by impressive motivational rhetoric. But this was worse. This pragmatic vocational embrace of American technology and consumerism that promised to rescue congregations

8. Peterson, *The Jesus Way*, 203.

from ineffective obscurity violated everything—scriptural, theological, experiential—that had formed my identity as a follower of Jesus and as a pastor. It was a blasphemous desecration of the way of life to which the church had ordained me—something on the order of a vocational abomination of desolation.[9]

Peterson's words perform their surgery on me because of . . . his choice of words. "Abomination of desolation"? "Sin against the Holy Spirit"? Herod? Clergy talk is usually more banal ("metrics," "strategies," "accountability," Jim Collins, Peter Drucker); Peterson's language bears larger truth because his words fly right off the pages of the Bible. We need not be surprised. The one who translated *The Message* has spent a lot of time in Scripture, knowing the Bible intimately, figuring out how to put the Word into words that are plain and direct. This is what pastors do, and this is a secondary reason most of us went into ministry—not for clerical gatherings, filling out forms, conducting business and devising programs. We loved Scripture, delighted in its nuances, and wanted to tell somebody else about it. Again, this is not a professional agenda item; this is simply what Christians do, their way of being in the world. We think about God, reflect upon holy things, and share what we know and who we're becoming while listening to others.

Scanning the Peterson section on my shelf, I have picked out my two favorites. The one I rank as my #2 is not one of his bestsellers. It is *Reversed Thunder: The Revelation of John and the Praying Imagination*.

I stumbled upon this when preparing a class on the Apocalypse, and I kept shoving it to the side of my book pile. Finally and reluctantly, I started thumbing through, only to discover that while I was devising ways to thump the Hal Lindseys and Tim LaHayes of the world, unscrambling biblical symbolism and the dastardly deeds of pseudo-divine Roman emperors, Peterson was *praying* the same book I was dissecting. He treated what I was seizing upon as a means to correct bogus spirituality (and to buttress my image as a rather brilliant person) as God's Word to the people of God. John, after all, was a pastor—and a poet too, and his book is one we use to listen to God, and to talk with God. In *Reversed Thunder*, Peterson (fully cognizant of the socio-political "facts" I was trumpeting in my class) cites real people, thoughtful sages, like Saul Bellow, Emily Dickinson, Marshall McLuhan, Flannery O'Connor, Wendell Berry, Annie Dillard, W. B. Yeats, Teilhard de Chardin, George Herbert, Czeslaw Milosz, Erik Erikson, Walker Percy, and Martin Luther King, Jr. Peterson isn't just flitting about,

9. Peterson, *The Pastor*, 112.

in flight from a text to what he might really wish to talk about. He is entirely responsible exegetically, but bows before the text as Scripture, interlacing his reading with not just literature but the real life of which literature is the most eloquent voice.

My favorite, #1 Peterson book is similarly obscure. *Take and Read: Spiritual Reading, An Annotated List* is a thin, hundred-page book that could keep you profitably busy for a few decades. I always wonder what others are reading, especially what the wise are reading, and Peterson favors us with a list, clumped into categories like Prayer, Fiction, Spiritual Direction, History, Commentaries, Poets, North American Spirituality, and Jesus. Because of *Take and Read*, I have a more crowded, richer, and more satisfying list of favorites, including Charles Williams's *The Descent of the Dove*, Hans Urs von Balthasar's *Prayer*, George Eliot's *Middlemarch*, and Frederick von Hügel's *The Life of Prayer*, and quite a few others I would otherwise have missed.

Take and Read does not list a single how-to book, not a one of those big sellers that tell you how to be entrepreneurial in ministry, how to attract singles, how to build your stewardship campaign. Peterson suggests that ministry (and not just ministry, but also the Christian life of being) is about reveling in the company of Bernard of Clairvaux, Norman Maclean, Luci Shaw, Gregory of Nyssa, Søren Kierkegaard, P. T. Forsyth, Aelred of Rievaulx, Henry Adams, Luther, Calvin, Teresa, Augustine, Day, and yes, Peterson himself. The point of the reading life is not to become more effective, or to enlarge one's problem-solving tool kit, or to file away snappy sermon quotations. Reading is *being*, a shared conversation about life with God, or life when God isn't obvious but is nonetheless present.

I can acknowledge with only a little embarrassment that I thought if I just mange to read what Peterson has read, I might be a wise pastor too! Of course, I can't be Eugene Peterson. I have to be James Howell. In fact, granted the immense blessing Peterson has and hopefully will continue to be for me, I have a few reservations about his project. Some of it is I just can't be him, but don't always know how to imbibe his way without pretending to be somebody else. Silly as this may sound, I see photos and admire his garrulous eyes, broad smile, with his white sage-like beard. He looks his own part. I could try the gray beard, but I look more corporate, not as earthy; my soul may be so riddled with issues that I can never convey his immense calm and warmth.

The extraordinary hospitality in the life of his congregation hinged upon his personality, or at least I believe this is so. Some of us just can never exude such an all-enveloping embrace, and thus for right or wrong we can't be the lovely contagion we might wish to be. Perhaps this is good; we rely on the subtle, hidden reality of Christ's embrace—but I find myself paling in comparison to Peterson's sheer physical manner.

The kind of pastoral life he describes is inseparable from community, and I am intrigued by the way he speak of his wife's total immersion in the life of the congregation, her own ministry to the people, their virtual oneness as paired beings whose unity itself must have had a happily viral impact on others. Many clergy I know have spouses who are more shy, or are reluctant to be a paired entity—or who have been wounded by the shenanigans of church folk and therefore keep a distance. This whole adventure of "being" instead of "doing" may be more dependent on realities in the home of the pastor than we often are willing to realize or talk about.

I find my anxious self worrying that Peterson's portrayal of church-as-being, church-as-worshipful-community, is more laid back than even the Scriptures might allow us. Our earliest Gospel seems hell-bent on the repetitive use of *euthus*, "immediately." In Mark, Jesus is a bit frenetic, rushing about, not cranking out programs but unmistakably active. Isn't there an urgency to work as hard as we can, albeit in a worshipful, non-anxious mode? Programming can usurp the place prayer and worship ought to occupy in the Christian life; but programming might still be the best last hope of getting people to give God a little bit of time, to learn the ways of God, to adapt to an altered way of being, to find good company with others.

When I read Peterson, I wonder what he would say if he walked into my megachurch; I feel an undercurrent that might be cynicism, or tenderly intended judgment. We are big; so are we doomed? If our culture, even for misguided reasons, forms people who are drawn to large full-service institutions, then can we find ways to be big and faithful? Jesus fed—how many? Five thousand: precisely the membership of my church. At Pentecost, the church grew by the explosive number of three thousand in a single day. To affirm the value and beauty of the small congregation is theologically helpful, and encouraging. Can we find ways to be worshipful, and prayerful, and even insist upon the knowing of names, in the outsized congregations that, at this point, can't help being big?

I think we can, but that would be another article on another day. Peterson teaches us to embrace inefficiencies, to have some levity about ministry and life, and to fix our gaze on the theological virtues implied in following Jesus, not the proficient craft and impressive success of Herod who, after all, was the one who was murderously scared of Jesus. Let us mention two, humility and holiness—which may be identical, or at least twin sisters. I think the category I'm drawn to when thinking about ministry, or just my life, is holiness. Elaine Heath wrote a marvelous book that I think should be read by institutional leaders and every working pastor: *The Mystic Way of Evangelism: A Contemplative Vision for Christian Outreach*. In the face of structural tinkering and aggressive plotting for how to be a better run machine of a church, Heath suggests that the church finds itself in a "dark night of the soul," and that the church is in "the kind of trouble that requires leadership from those who are holy."[10] Institutions will be timid about embracing such a risky angle; but holiness has stood the test of time, and it is, after all, what Jesus came to create in us and among us.

Holiness is not a stalwart, heroic spirituality, but simple humility that lets God be God. My favorite Peterson sermon, "My Eyes Are Not Raised Too High,"[11] is a sermon that clergy should read quite regularly to quell the unruly, Faustian ambition pervading the church that Peterson diagnoses and laments. He cites one of his favored authors in *Take and Read*, Charles Haddon Spurgeon, who shrewdly suggested that Psalm 131 is "one of the shortest Psalms to read, but one of the longest to learn."

I am a slow learner. But slowness is a virtue. I hope to find more men and women like the one who introduced me to Eugene Peterson. I hope to become worshipful, and prayerful. I pledge to start today, but the swirl of tasks might force a postponement. Perhaps as I ease toward retirement, or if I'm graced with a few years afterward, I will live into this notion of prayerful being. I read recently that St. Augustine, as he lay on his deathbed, thinking his life's work was being obliterated, asked that the penitential Psalms be copied out on large sheets of paper and hung where he could see them. To avoid distraction, he insisted on no visitors so he would have time to pray.[12] I hope to pray sooner, not because prayer *works* or will make me preach better or be more effective, but because that is the truest hankering in my being, my lone vocation, the rehearsal for eternity where all names will be known, and nothing will happen except worship, which will be more than enough.

10. Heath, *The Mystic Way of Evangelism*, 12.
11. Peterson, *A Long Obedience in the Same Direction*, 145–54.
12. Miles, *Augustine and the Fundamentalist's Daughter*, 212.

How Baptism Makes My
"Job Description" Different

Jenny Williams

I SUPPOSE I OUGHT to explain my point of view. I am United Methodist—a mainline Protestant denomination (and declining), a Gen X, female, first-career pastor (a numerical minority). I was raised in a suburb of Los Angeles and lived there until I was twenty-three years old (West Coast metropolitan), went to seminary at Duke (southern) and have spent the last ten years serving churches in small towns in West Virginia (Appalachian). This chapter is colored by the places I've lived and the people who have been in them.

Which is fairly Petersonian.

Most church folk want to know their pastor (and whoever else might be living in the parsonage). They want us to like their town. They want us to like *them*. They want to think of us as a friend. If the kind of friendship they have in mind is rooted in being siblings in Christ, then our work among the congregation is fairly easy. If the kind of friendship they have in mind is rooted in being pleasant with one another, then our work is really difficult.

How can you be prophetic amidst people who want you to be nice?

The Pastor as Chaplain: Bad for the Pastor

In my context, the word "pastor" connotes chaplaincy as the primary task of an ordained person serving a congregation. Some parishioners expect the same things from us as they would a hospital chaplain: to visit frequently when they are sick or having a medical procedure, to pray with them at those times, and then to follow up with them. The pastor also needs to be a prison chaplain of sorts: providing "spiritual" care to those who are homebound or live in nursing homes.

I mean no disrespect to *actual* chaplains. Their role is important. However, a congregational pastor is charged with many other responsibilities: preaching, teaching, administering the sacraments, overseeing administration, and serving the poor, to name a few. The expectation that the pastor perform as a chaplain ignores those other tasks and places us dangerously close to being mistaken for the Good Shepherd.

Eugene Peterson has often critiqued a psychotherapeutic understanding of pastoral care. As Stanley Hauerwas says, the pastor should not be a "quivering mass of availability" to all. If a pastor is expected to be constantly available, how can she pray? Study? Serve at the soup kitchen? Prepare a sermon? Stop for a cup of coffee with someone who doesn't go to church but has just asked about VBS?

In my own denomination, short tenures have contributed to the expectation that the pastor primarily function as a chaplain. "Old-timers" in West Virginia Methodism tell of how they were moved to a new appointment every two years or so. Two years is just enough time for the congregation to grieve the loss of their previous pastor, welcome their new one, get to know him (they were all male back then), and then send him on his way. If a pastor has two years with those folks, how could he be expected to do anything *but* preach and visit? A pastor could never start a year-long study of Revelation, or hold a confirmation class longer than six weeks, or help the church think long term about how God is calling that congregation to ministry in that place.

My denomination is declining numerically and failing to retain the small number of young people among us. Thirty-four percent of U.S. United Methodists are sixty-five and older, compared to 17 percent of the U.S. population.[1] Approximately 11 percent of Methodists are ages eighteen to twenty-nine.[2] This makes the sixty-five and older population in an average congregation three times as large as the adult population under twenty-nine years old in that same congregation.

1. Statistics from the Institute on Religion and Democracy.

2. Statistics released on February 25, 2008 by the Pew Forum on Religion and Public Life.

Which group makes more trips to the hospital and the doctor?

The answer to that question means a lot of trips for the pastor to the hospital, a lot of phone calls to see how that consultation with the specialist went, and, to put it bluntly, a lot of funerals. Should the pastor be the *only* one to provide that care? Few who hold that expectation are looking at the bigger picture.

In my first four years of ministry, I served as an associate pastor at a large suburban church, where my primary responsibility was youth. I was part of a wonderful Clergy Covenant Discipleship Group. One of the books we read together was Peterson's *Under the Unpredictable Plant*, his exploration of vocational holiness. He notes, "Working as a pastor, with surprising frequency, seemed to put me at odds with living as a Christian. . . . The volume of business in religion far outruns the spiritual capital of its leaders."[3] I began to wonder, "Do my youth need me to pursue busyness? Or holiness?"[4] A version of that question has been a touchstone for me in ministry since.

The congregation I now serve averages about one hundred people in worship. The percentage of worshipers over sixty-five in this congregation stands at almost 65 percent of our worshipping body—almost double the national average. One week during the writing of this chapter, I had nineteen pastoral contacts that needed to be made. Ten were members of the church in the midst of medical situations, six were church members who have been "missing in action" recently, and three were people in the community whom I am trying to invite to worship. When a parishioner approaches me to talk about a divisive issue in his marriage, does he want me to be internally frenetic from such a pace, or does he want me to be ready to listen and offer counsel? Busyness competes with holiness, and holiness often loses.

I also serve as a mentor for Stella, a twenty-something pastor who has entered the three-year provisional period between commissioning for pastoral ministry and ordination. She is brilliant, reflective, mission-minded, very intentional about her work, and compassionate. She wants to help her two churches be faithful now and in the future. She's the best kind of pastor a denomination can hope for. Her recent pastoral evaluation was good in every area but one: *she doesn't visit enough.*

3. Peterson, *Under the Unpredictable Plant*, 2–3

4. My realization that busyness is the enemy of holiness is in part due to Dean and Foster's *The Godbearing Life*.

As far as I can tell, she visits quite a bit! Having heard criticism about visitation early on, she spent time asking her congregations about pastoral visitation. It turned out that all they really wanted was a Christian to be with them in the hospital. So she worked with them to develop Visitation Teams of church members who would pray and sit with families during their loved one's minor medical procedures.

Another pastor, Joan, heard similar concerns in her congregation. Joan welcomed a nearby retired pastor's offer to help visit the homebound of her church.

Neither option was enough for people in these congregations. They say, "It's nice to have these visits, but we think The Pastor should come." Let us call this the doctrine of *sola Pastora*: the belief of church members that only The Pastor's visit "counts." For these congregations, *sola Pastora* means that if The Pastor doesn't visit frequently, she doesn't care about them.[5] In both Stella and Joan's churches, this belief drew down the cache of informal authority granted to the pastor by their congregations. Some members have left these churches—at least until the next pastor comes.

These women are not unfeeling, uncaring, or lazy. They want their parishioners to receive contact from their church in their times of need. Both also saw significant opportunities for their congregations to share God's love in their communities through various ministries of missional service and hospitality, but their members' expectations about visitation has prevented them from attending to forward-looking areas of congregational life.

I am not advocating abandoning the title "Pastor" for "Preacher." That latter reduces the ordained person's responsibilities to preaching or only working on Sundays. "Pastor" rightly speaks to the many kinds of care we provide, including equipping the congregation for ministry and leading the church into mission. But *sola Pastora* narrows pastoral care and places a disproportionate value on those types of pastoral tasks.

Stella gets discouraged, of course. She can see a faithful future for her churches, and yet they will not trust her leadership if she does not adhere

---

5. This criticism is further evidence that congregations want their pastors to be "nice" people. Long-time Christians generally don't believe that if the pastor doesn't visit, God doesn't like them. A person who is not a Christian, however, might believe that if a pastor who has developed a relationship with him or her is not present at a time of crisis, God does not care for him or her. Which group of people should the pastor be with, for the sake of the gospel?

to their doctrine of visitation. What if her next church acts the same way? Will she lose heart?

Friendship Formed by the Font

I'm involved with the Ekklesia Project—an ecumenical association of lay folk, pastors, and scholars. It describes one of its purposes as "helping us to discover friends we didn't know we had."[6] When a person attends an EP Gathering, she or he is welcomed as if he had been part of that group all along. People are so happy she or he has come. They ask questions about his or her life and how they learned about the group and what his or her church is like. She or he is swept up into eating and worshiping together with the gathered community. Every year we meet other interesting and committed Christians of all stripes and are buoyed by the companionship and support we find.

It's kind of like Acts chapter 2.

The liturgy of the Baptismal Covenant of the United Methodist Church[7] begins with the following introduction:

> Brothers and sisters in Christ: Through the Sacrament of Baptism
> we are initiated into Christ's holy church. We are incorporated into
> God's mighty acts of salvation and given new birth through water
> and the Spirit. All this is God's gift, offered to us without price.

Baptism marks a person's entry into a people who existed long before her and will continue to exist long after her. God brings this person in. Members of a church are not bound together by our own choice. We do not vote to accept a new member of a club. God's gracious invitation and calling and through the work of Jesus Christ makes the church.

After the baptismal candidate (or her parents, in the case of an infant) renounces sin and makes a profession of faith, the congregation is asked about their willingness to make a commitment to the newly baptized: "Will you nurture *one another* in the Christian faith and life and include this person now before you in your care?"

The congregation responds,

> With God's help, we will proclaim the good news and live accord-
> ing to the example of Christ. We will surround this person with a

6. For more on the Ekklesia Project, see www.ekklesiaproject.org.

7. *The United Methodist Hymnal.*

community of love and forgiveness, that s/he may grow in his/her trust of God, and be found faithful in his/her service to others. We will pray for [this person] that s/he may be a true disciple who walks in the way that leads to life.

"Belonging to a church" sometimes sounds as if one belongs to a group that is separate from oneself. But since the church is the called-out people of God (ek-klesia) the organization is not distinct from ourselves. We are that organization, that Body. We belong to one another. We are siblings in Christ, called "brothers and sisters" by the One who gave his mother and the beloved disciple to one another, who grafts us into the people of God. Siblings rejoice with one who rejoices, weep with one who weeps, and have counted the cost and understand the sacrificial nature of being a follower of Jesus. God gives our body a new limb, and we promise to care for that new member.

Baptism authorizes us for ministry. The "us" is not only ordained people, but every baptized person. The liturgy when a person joins the UMC through profession of faith or transfer from another denomination asks whether she will participate in our church through her "prayers, presence, gifts, service and witness." In joining a local congregation, a person commits to *ministry*, not just membership. Baptism, membership, and ministry are inseparable. A person who is baptized and a member pledges to care for others in her church.

The sacrament of baptism will not let us leave the ministry of visitation to someone who is ordained. It is a job for each of us.[8] Jesus did not say in Matthew 25:32, "I was sick and you paid the pastor to visit me."[9] John Wesley preached a sermon called "On Visiting the Sick" that bluntly states that visitation with the sick should be performed by all who desire to "inherit the kingdom" and "escape everlasting fire." He further stated that a Christian needed to visit the sick in person and not try to relieve the needs of the sick from a distance.[10] Wesley counted visiting the sick as a means of grace. The congregation should ask why they are giving their pastor all the

8. During a conversation with an acquaintance who is a pastor of a non-denominational church, I mentioned how much hospital visitation my current appointment requires of me. He said, "Oh, I'm never in the hospital. The small groups do that for each other. I only go when a baby is born or someone is dying."

9. I am riffing here off a comment of Shane Claiborne's.

10. Sermon 98, "On Visiting the Sick." Wesley defines "the sick" as "all such as are in a state of affliction, whether of mind or of body . . . whether they are good or bad, whether they fear God or not."

opportunities to receive grace. Pastors should ask if we want to lead our parishioners into "everlasting fire" by doing all the visitation.

The Clergy Covenant Discipleship Group in which I have been involved for the past two years has existed for thirteen years, exhibiting care for one another in concrete ways, receiving each other's confessions and exhorting one another in love. These clergy have attended the funerals of each others' parents. They've even moved their monthly meeting to hospital rooms when members became gravely ill. They've taken care of the family of a member who died. Since I've come to be a part of them, I've heard stories and seen concrete forms of support that all say, "This is how we care for one another as Christ's family."

This clergy group has eight members. Peterson often says that he never wants to serve a church that has more members than the number of names he can remember. This is a welcome contrast to the siren songs of the church growth movement. Perhaps Peterson makes this comment in the context of knowing his parishioners well, but it also makes sense for Christians who want to care deeply for one another. If the baptized commit to caring for one another, we cannot possibly do that well or deeply for a large group of people.

A group of Mennonite friends from seminary were the first ones to show me what a commitment to mutual care looks like. The nearby Mennonite church had gotten too big, so a few people from that church began to meet in another town. As soon as it was numerically feasible, this new congregation divided into two dinner groups. The groups were small enough to meet in each other's homes weekly. They shared a meal and discussed their lives while their kids played with each other. They knew each other well, so it was quite natural to care for one another in material ways. Long before buying locally grown food became hip, one dinner group pooled their funds to buy a whole pig from a local farmer, which provided each family in the group with meat. When a need arose, they would be present with a listening ear or child care. They didn't need a formal, organized ministry of care. When new folks would become part of the congregation they would join up with an existing dinner group. And when that dinner group got too big to care for each other well, it split into smaller groups. They didn't want to get large. They wanted to stay small enough to live out their commitment to one another.

A handful of young adults and families with school-aged children belong to my church. When I first came, the only time those young adults and families were in the same place at the same time was during the one week of Vacation Bible School each summer. People in this age group sometimes travel on weekends; their kids are involved in band or soccer; they accidentally sleep through the alarm on Sundays. I wanted to bring these younger people together so we began meeting on the second Sunday of each month for a low-pressure potluck dinner and discussion of something we'd read together. I knew that their involvement with the church would largely depend on whether they were in relationship with one another. Who wants to be part of a church where no one notices when you are absent? "You want to be where everybody knows your name."[11]

Meeting together just once a month for the last twenty months has accomplished more than I had hoped for. These folks know and enjoy one another. Two of the guys have become running buddies. We lend each other power tools. We watch each other's kids when there's a gap in child care arrangements. What's even better is that these young adults and families have become committed to Sunday school for both themselves and their kids, and being in worship more regularly has become a higher priority for them—because someone they know is there. We began with two families and three couples, and since then have added one more family and four more single people. Had we not had something to invite those new people to, they would have disappeared.

For all that has been accomplished, it's hard to remember that these folks still aren't very practiced at caring for one another. About fourteen months into the life of this group one of the couples announced that they were expecting their first child. I waited for someone in the group to suggest throwing them a baby shower or to develop a schedule of bringing meals to them. I waited a couple of months. Then *I* floated the baby shower idea. They were totally game for it. They planned the shower, which was lovely, and we pooled our money to get the couple a group gift: a jogging stroller for the new daddy, who is one of the runners.

There were several reasons that no one else thought to throw the shower. In small-town West Virginia, families take care of one another. Family throws the shower, brings the meals, and babysits the child. The culture of care here originates in biological rather than baptismal relationships. The church is not thought of as the first family.

But lives are shaped much differently than they used to be. In the first half of the twentieth century, Christian women learned to care for one

11. Thanks, *Cheers*.

another in Christian women's societies such as United Methodist Women. A local unit of the UMW was composed of several small groups, called circles, which met often, usually on a weekday morning. Circles reached out in mission, read books on a variety of topics, raised money for mission and education, and incidentally supported one another. Their circle was like my Mennonite friends' dinner groups.

This model worked when women stayed home, men went off to work, and children went off to school. Few Christian women's groups have been able to alter their model so that working women can be equally involved. If working women are part of a church that holds onto the old model, and does not have any type of small group ministry, how can they be expected to learn to care for one another?

The problem does not only affect women. The United Methodist *men's* group of my church meets on Sunday mornings at seven. The average age of the group is around seventy-five. They have repeatedly invited the younger men in the congregation. A few have attended a time or two. The younger men, mostly fathers, don't commit to the group, because they share with their spouses the responsibility of helping the family get ready for Sunday morning at church. Despite knowing this, the older men continue to meet at seven.

Today, the household—not the church—is the center of social activity. In slightly wealthier families, the kids might play in the same sport league, but on separate teams, which means a multitude of games and practices. One has Scouts, the other is in the science club. Both adults in a two-parent household often work full-time outside the home. Parents are scrambling for time for themselves as well as time together as a family. Single parents bear all the pressure of balancing the needs of their children and themselves. For households in the lower socioeconomic demographic, the household's income earner(s) may be working shifts, multiple jobs, or at minimum wage, finding their schedules inconsistent and packed. Regardless of what makes this generation's families busy, they are largely not people who sit on the porch with their neighbors. People who succumb to overcommitment or whose schedules are not in their own control have little time to care for their brothers and sisters in Christ. Relationships take time. And no one seems to have any time.

There is a blessing to be found in this context. Younger folks don't need their pastor to visit. They don't have many medical procedures. And they don't have the time. I've found younger adults *do* want their pastor to help them overcome their biblical illiteracy. They also want their pastor's advice on faith and family matters. The pastor has a delightful opportunity here: to reclaim the position of resident theologian within the congregation, as Peterson desires. And we can teach and equip younger adults to care for one another as part of their baptismal responsibility.

The Pastor as Drug Dealer: Bad for the Church

A church member sought me out to discuss my role as pastor. She was saddened by a criticism that she'd heard: I do not visit enough. She had been in church meetings where we had discussed my vision for the congregation. She knew that my goals involved working to develop a youth ministry and helping the church strengthen its ministries of reaching out in service to our community, particularly to folks in poverty. I told her that the congregation would have to make a choice: I could either be a chaplain to everyone *or* I could help the church be faithful in study, mission, service, and ministry. The majority of the congregation wants the former, though that would nearly guarantee that the congregation would close its doors in thirty years. Choosing the latter would create the opportunity for our congregation to grow in their love of God and neighbor and to be the church for the world.

In an "aha" moment, she said, "Visitation by the pastor is like heroin! It makes us feel really good at the time, but it's bad for us! Your job is not to give us this drug. Your job is to tell us that it's killing us!"

Helping a congregation understand that they are addicted to pastoral care is a very difficult job. It can create tensions. When a pastor talks about baptism as having implications for relationships among the baptized (and not just between them and Jesus), aspersions may be cast for "not understanding the way we do it" or "teaching something we've never heard of before." The pastor may be seen as not liking the congregation, which means that the congregants' expectation of relationship with the pastor (that the pastor is nice to them) will not have been met, and therefore that the pastor has failed.[12] So much for the pastor. Transitioning from *sola Pastora* to one of congregational care will make some people mad and even leave.

12. A UM pastor I know began an appointment in a small town and saw a large percentage of children in the community who weren't part of any church. She worked to try to help her congregation reach out to these kids. That wasn't what they wanted. In one of her annual pastoral evaluations, they set as a goal for her "to make us feel like you love *us*."

But we pastors cannot let the possible tensions prevent us from helping the church change its views and practices of being in relationship with one another. If we avoid these possible negative repercussions in favor of an absence of conflict, then a congregation's addiction to the drug of pastoral care will hurt us as much as it does them.[13] With the Boomers' growth into old age, the chaplaincy work is only going to increase. The pastor who primarily functions as chaplain in a local congregation is a drug dealer. Do you want to be a drug dealer or someone who showed tough love?

What's a Pastor to Do?

If the pastor is going to suggest that baptism requires church members to visit one another, the pastor must work to equip the congregation. In larger churches, Stephen Ministry[14] can be helpful in reshaping the congregation's expectations about pastoral visitation. In a congregation of any size, visitation teams can be trained to go out two-by-two to visit a homebound or ill person and pray with them. The pastor can bring confirmands with him when visiting the sick and homebound,[15] "training them in the way they should go" (Prov 22:6). The pastor should regularly voice the expectation that being part of any small group means that a person will tend to the needs of another group member. New Christians will learn from the start that visiting their siblings in Christ is part of how Christians act within a community of faith. Over time, others will take up this practice (which makes it more difficult to be irritated with the pastor).

In some churches, an additional pastor could assist with pastoral visitation. A retired clergy whose gifts lie in the area of visitation could both visit and train the congregation to make such visits—working him or herself out of a job. This option helps fill the gap between *sola Pastora* and the baptismal belief that church members ought to care for one another. It also frees up the lead pastor to direct her energies toward leading the church into serving the wider community, into Bible study, into disciple formation. Pastors who are able to envision this kind of arrangement could propose

13. In this setting of addiction, the Clergy Covenant Discipleship group functions as Al-Anon: a place of support for people who are living with addicts and suffer the consequences of their loved ones' addiction.

14. See http://www.stephenministries.org/.

15. Thanks to Reverend Kyle Childress for this suggestion.

such an idea to the pastor's superior or to the decision-making body for the congregation, depending on your polity.

Peterson is right to lift up the value of relationships in pastoral ministry, particularly relationships between a pastor and his congregants. Now, we pastors have the wonderful joy of helping church members experience the blessing of being in deeper relationship with one another.

On the other side of this culture change is a church full of people who, having been cared for by God, and trusting that someone will care for them, can go out and care for others.

One + One + One = Five
(Or, Building Community and Curing Souls)

Prince Raney Rivers

The Accidental Pastor

EUGENE PETERSON'S ACCOUNT OF his unanticipated entry into the vocation of pastor resonated with me. My father was a chemist who spent his professional life as a teacher or administrator mostly in university settings. The work he did and the life he lived seemed to be a good fit for me, too. When I enrolled in college, I charted a course for graduate school with the aspiration of ascending the ivory tower of university administration. Of course, these things do not always work out like we plan.

During the summer after my college graduation, I began to sense something awkward about my life. It felt as though I was walking around in someone else's clothes. I had on a shirt that used to fit me well, but now it pulled and pinched in places I had not noticed before. I was being called to go in a new direction, but could not easily let go of the old vision. Nevertheless, I declined a fellowship to do graduate studies at my father's alma mater (I will not bore you with the sordid details of the dinner table conversation when I announced this decision).

As haphazard as this choice seemed at the time, it was a pivotal moment in my vocation as pastor. It was during this season of life that I met a wise pastor who remains a key mentor to me today. His prayerful spirit and intellectual curiosity deeply impressed me. In retrospect, his ministry was the vision God used to call me into the pastoral vocation. I was like Samuel who needed Eli to help him recognize God's voice.

Ministry was not the vocation I had envisioned, so even when I enrolled in seminary my intent was to double back and pick up my original aim of teaching and university administration, albeit in a seminary. It turns out that God had something else in mind.

I am a pastor and have been one for thirteen years. Over the years I have discovered that "pastor" means different things to different people. The first time I stopped by the church office wearing shorts, I was stunned by a member's utter astonishment that I did not always wear a dark wool suit, polished black shoes, and necktie. I later learned that she was not opposed to people or even Christians wearing shorts. She just did not imagine that her *pastor* did such things. Maybe she was just being biblical, since Psalm 147:10 says that the Lord takes no delight in the legs of a man.

Many people are quite curious about what pastors do every day. One morning I dropped off my daughter at her day care and crossed paths with a church member as she arrived to drop off her son. This young mother, pregnant with her second child, was clearly expecting to deliver any day. I slowed my pace to match hers so we could chat on our way out of the building. When we were about to go our separate ways, she lobbed an interesting question in my direction, "So, what do you have planned for the day?"

Perhaps the confusion on my face gave away my uncertainty. Was she simply trying to be polite, or did she really want me to pull up the calendar on my smart phone and tick off my itinerary? She quickly explained that as a social worker she was fascinated by people and their work environments. She had been in church all her life, but the work of a pastor was something she knew little about. We were around the same age so I guess she thought she could quench her professional and personal curiosity without offending me.

This points to a critical question with which Eugene Peterson and others have wrestled: *What do pastors do?* The work of pastoral ministry is a mystery to many people—to the congregants we serve and even to some pastors. After a Sunday service a precocious seven-year-old girl standing beside her mother asked me what I did the other six days of the week. I laughed heartily, but the little girl's mother was not amused.

This innocent mind only expressed what many people are too respectful to say. The most visible part of pastoral work occurs on Sunday mornings when we lead worship, baptize, offer public prayers, and preach sermons. Only a fraction of the congregation is involved in governance. We typically prepare sermons and Bible studies in hermit-like seclusion. We do not travel with an entourage to do visitation in the hospital or in members' homes. Few people ever truly see what constitutes the daily rhythm of a pastor's life.

Part of the genius of Eugene Peterson's writing is that he disentangles the beauty of the pastoral vocation from other noble, but not identical, activities, such as therapist, CEO, educator, activist, and director of operations. Peterson plumbs the depths of Scripture and Christian tradition to recover authentic wisdom for the practice of pastoral ministry. He celebrates the unique calling of a pastor and spreads a garment of dignity on who we are and the work we are called to do.

Six months out of seminary I was serving as a pastor for the first time. I quickly came to a conclusion about what pastors do: We lead. The church that had called me as pastor was in need of leadership. These members expected their pastor to lead, not dominate or dictate, but lead. The main problem for me was that I had not actually taken a seminary course in leadership. I knew the fundamentals of teaching Scripture and how to sniff out bad theology. I knew how to write good exegesis papers and to prepare thoughtful sermons. I did have formative internship experiences, but I knew I needed something more if I was going to be effective as a congregational leader.

In the absence of a course on pastoral leadership, I picked up some of the popular leadership books readily available at the time. These resources helped insofar as they described what happens when effective leadership is present. That is, they named the results of leadership. However, I found little that deepened my understanding of the source and soul of Christian leadership in a congregational setting.

Eugene Peterson skillfully articulates the practice of pastoral leadership through narratives that are poignant and profound. He paints a portrait of living with and engaging God, the congregation, and himself, in a way that cannot be reduced to a few alliterated leadership principles. All too often leadership is boiled down to a set of tactics that enable the leader to make the organization do what he or she wants it to do. Peterson exposes such a model of leadership as having little to do with God.

On a recent white water kayaking trip, I quickly discovered (the hard way!) that my first responsibility is to understand what the river is doing and follow. Ignoring the flow of the current can have painful consequences.

The pastor's life is a call to be on the lookout for what God is already doing. Good pastors keep their ears tuned to the frequency of the Holy Spirit.

Peterson does not write explicitly about strategies and models of leadership. He describes a rhythm of life that is punctuated by Sabbath, Scripture, holiness, and discipleship. His way of life shaped his leadership. His vision of leadership shaped his way of life. I want to turn now to explore some of the individual parts of Peterson's pastoral life, keeping in mind that the whole of ministry is much greater than the sum of its parts.

A Gestalt Perspective

Around the beginning of twentieth century in Austria and Germany a new branch of psychology was conceived. A philosopher named Max Wertheimer was on a train from Vienna to the Rhineland when he looked out of the window and noticed that the telephone poles appeared to be in motion. This phenomenon intrigued Wertheimer so much that he got off the train in Frankfurt and with the help of colleagues at the University of Frankfurt began thinking about what has become known as Gestalt psychology.

Gestalt is a German concept that describes the way we perceive phenomena. Specifically, it has to do with the way we perceive a whole rather than a collection of parts. A chair has four legs, a seat, a back and arms, but we see a "chair" rather than separate pieces of furniture. Gestalt theorists say that the whole is both greater than and different from the sum of its parts. Think about the difference between a fully assembled car and a pile of the car's component parts. The car is both greater than and different from its component parts. When we listen to John Coltrane's *A Love Supreme*, we hear much more than a series of half notes and whole notes. We hear emotional, intellectual, and spiritual genius coursing through the veins of captivating melodies and mesmerizing solos in one of the most important records ever made.

So much of what is marketed as leadership development tends to focus on the parts without attention to the whole. One pastoral leadership conference promised to teach me strategies to help me break the next growth barrier in my church. Another leadership event offered workshops on how to maximize the use of social media and build momentum in youth ministry. Social media and youth ministry are critical factors in the contemporary church, but these are parts of a much greater whole. It is true that budgets must be prepared. Programs have to be planned. Reports must be completed. But pastoral leadership is at its best when these functional habits take place within a life consecrated by prayer, holiness, Sabbath, and discipleship. Sadly, leadership conferences for pastors rarely address these subjects. It is much easier to deal with questions around ministry management and technology.

Peterson writes at length about various pieces of the pastoral ministry puzzle. In this chapter, I want especially to examine community building and the cure of souls. These practices are enormously important, especially within our contemporary environment of isolation and fragmentation. Community building addresses the necessity of forming individual persons into one body. For the church to be the church, people must do more than occupy the same space on Sunday morning. They must learn, remember and live into the meaning of being one in Christ. Curing souls is Peterson's brilliant way of calling pastors back to the core of pastoral work. Pastors easily lose their way in the fog of good intentions or become casualties on a minefield of competing obligations. These are not the only parts in Peterson's construct of pastoral leadership; however, each part plays a significant role in how we must understand pastoral leadership in our time.

The Quest for Community

I grew up in a suburban Presbyterian church in Decatur, Georgia. The congregation was distinct in at least one way that I can recall. The pastor was African American and, by my recollection, about half its members were African American and half were white.

In the early 1980s, the neighborhood around the church was "changing," the polite southern term for transitioning from nearly-all-white to not-all-white. Hillside Presbyterian Church resisted the cultural undertow that swept other congregations into more racially homogeneous areas of the city. It remained and continues to remain in the same location, offering a dynamic witness to God's reconciliation in a changing community.

One of my most vivid memories of life together at Hillside is the potluck suppers. We did not have a well-appointed banquet room in which we hosted elaborate meals. We had a gymnasium and we made the best of it. The gym floor was made from light brown and putty-colored square tiles. The cinder block walls were painted white. Wire screens covered the windows to prevent rambunctious youth from breaking glass with a carelessly thrown basketball.

On the days when we had potluck suppers, something wonderful happened. It was as if the vision of Isaiah 25:6 came to life: "On this mountain the Lord Almighty will prepare a feast of rich food for all peoples, a banquet of aged wine—the best of meats and the finest of wines." I do not remember any aged wine at these meals, but the array of foods, the aroma of joy along with the high calorie, deep fried love made an unusual impression on me. As families sat down together at the rectangular folding tables arranged in diagonal rows across the gym floor, we formed one body in Christ. Anyone driving past the L-shaped church edifice would not have known that anything spectacular was happening inside, but indeed a miracle was taking place. Through acts of ritual celebration, like our monthly suppers and our annual spiritual formation retreat (we did not call it spiritual formation, but that is precisely what it was) we were being and becoming a community of faith. Building community is never sufficient, but it is an essential part to the pastoral vocation.

When Peterson served as a pastor in Baltimore, he belonged to a clergy group called "The Company," which met every Tuesday. As The Company struggled to discern a clear model of the pastoral vocation in the scriptures, a rabbi in the group named Paul chimed in with insights from the Jewish faith. In *The Pastor,* Peterson writes that Paul told the group that at some point in Israel's history five annual acts of public worship were mandated in order to perpetuate Israel's self-understanding as the people of God. The five annual celebrations are Passover, Pentecost, the Ninth of Ab, Tabernacles, and Purim. Each act of worship highlighted one dimension of what it meant to be God's people. Purim, which was rooted in the story of Esther, was instituted to commemorate the deliverance of the Jews from genocide in Persia. This annual feast centered around the notion of community in that it affirmed the truth that "salvation is not only individual, but corporate as well."[1]

Peterson unpacks his view of community, which relies heavily on the biblical text of Esther, in *Five Smooth Stones for Pastoral Work.* The appeal of Esther is that "it presents the issue of the nature and function of God's people in stark and simple terms: survival versus annihilation."[2]

Pastoral leadership is severely limited without a vision of how God is forming unrelated individuals into fellow members of God's household. "The pastor is never a private chaplain to individuals; the pastor is never an

1. Peterson, *The Pastor,* 154.
2. Peterson, *Five Smooth Stones for Pastoral Work,* 157.

impersonal speaker to crowds; the pastor is set in community and given the task of building that community."[3]

The contemporary voices in pastoral leadership can tell us a lot about convening a crowd and little about building a community. Peterson wisely advises all of us to be wary of crowds. He knows that the crowd mentality is a distraction to faithfulness. In his classic text on Jeremiah, *Run with the Horses,* Peterson devotes a chapter to the prophet's encounter with the Recabites. The Recabites were nomadic metalworkers who lived a disciplined life. Following the command of their ancestor, Jonadab ben Recab, they drank no wine at all. They built no houses and planted no vineyards or fields. When the Recabites sought safety from the Babylonians inside the walls of Jerusalem, God commanded Jeremiah to invite these teetotalers over for a glass of wine. The Recabites accepted Jeremiah's invitation, but refused to go along with the crowd when the wine was served. Going along with the crowd would have undermined the integrity of their community.[4] What a vivid reminder: pastors build community, not crowds! Peterson makes sure we know that there is a difference.

I do wonder how Peterson views large congregations in light of his suspicion of crowds. Some worshipers at the largest churches today arrive early for worship by the thousands and stand in line to fill stadium-style seats in "centers" hewn from of the quarries of urban industrial landscapes. So what must pastors do to carry out critical leadership task at a time when the term "community" has become a catch-all term for any group of people who share similar interests or backgrounds? Society is increasingly fragmented, and yet community is a word we hear all of the time—the business community, the online community, the Hispanic community, the nonprofit community.

Instead of a mass of individuals, true community is one body in which each member is both distinct and interconnected to others. A simple suggestion for pastors of larger congregations who want to build community is to make sure that our sermon titles are not written in the first person. Employing the third person plural might be one concrete act of using language to shape the narrative of community in an increasingly disconnected culture.

The heightened emphasis on radical individualism has deepened this dilemma for those among the most economically and socially vulnerable

3. Ibid., 151.

4. Peterson, *Run with the Horses.*

segments of society where annihilation is a real threat. The siren song of the gospel of prosperity has lulled many congregations into a narcissistic sleep. The envious clamoring for the materialistic trappings of upward mobility has many churchgoers caught up in a frenzy of social indifference. One cannot hope to build a community of salvation following this path. To have salvation be truly communal, especially when what is at stake is survival or annihilation, as it was for Esther and her fellow Jews, pastors will need to lead congregations to imagine salvation in every aspect of the human condition. Community building cannot ever be limited to those who are already a part of the community. Community building takes place within the context of a broken world. The community must be a living, vibrant, and transformative witness in that world.

Among African American Christians, community that does not engage the world runs the risk of contributing to the double-marginalization of a people. The first ring of marginalization is historically rooted in systems of injustice. The second is self-imposed by a failure to engage, challenge, and collaborate with the wider society to minimize the risk of annihilation. Disenfranchised people who hope to survive do not have the luxury of retreat from the dominant culture.

Peterson writes in *The Pastor* that a "minority people working from the margins has the best chance of being a community capable of penetrating the noncommunity, the mob, the depersonalized, function-defined crowd that is the sociological norm of America."[5] In America, mainline Protestants have seldom been relegated to the margins. Pastoral leaders like Bishop Richard Allen (1760–1831), Reverend Adam Clayton Powell (1908–1972), Jr. and Reverend Dr. Martin Luther King, Jr. (1929–1968) took a different approach. They offered pastoral leadership that refused to accept a position on the margins and in so doing made the church a community of salvation for the poor and disenfranchised. These pastors represent the spirit of the New Testament church that Peterson describes as being focused on more than individual salvation.

The Pastor is a brilliantly written memoir on the Petersons' ministry in Baltimore. I would have loved to hear more in it about how pastoral leadership took on flesh in the Baltimore community. How did Christ Our King Presbyterian Church live into their vision of a God-formed community within the neighborhood around the church? How did the church's leaders

---

5. Peterson, *The Pastor*, 16.

enable the Christian community to invite others into their Christ-centered fellowship?

The faithful presence of a church or community building demands that a pastor be particularly sensitive to the joy and pain in her own specific locale. She may lead the congregation, or find someone who can, to take seriously the long-term objectives of the local health department if the infant mortality is high. Authentic pastoral leadership encourages a pastor to lead a congregation to mentor elementary students if the evidence shows that without it, many of these students will drop out of school and possibly end up in prison (or worse).

At the same time, the boundaries of the community of faith and the responsibility of pastoral leadership must be clearly defined to avoid losing focus. I recently received a call from a university board member who wanted me to assist her with the school's recruitment and retention strategy. Why she thought I could help her was a mystery to me. What struck me as odd was the woman's huffiness when I informed her that I was neither qualified nor available to assist her with such a project.

Peterson affirms the fact that wise pastors do not seek to be validated by their perceived value to the larger society. We may be called to seek the welfare of the city (Jer 29:4–7), but we do not exist for the sake of the city. We exist for God's purposes alone. Pastors that fail to make this distinction lose their focus and diminish the power of the good they seek.

Curing Souls

A second practice at the core of pastoral leadership is the work of curing souls. Community building and curing souls are part of a much greater pastoral life in which the minister seeks integrity in her or his calling. Curing souls is not an online course we can offer. Curing souls is the fruit of Christ-centered and embodied ministry.

We do not talk about curing souls anymore. It even sounds a bit pompous when I read the words on the page. Curing souls is hard to define, but it certainly sounds a lot different than running programs. We can say that this ancient art calls "attention to how remote present-day pastoral routines have become."[6]

Curing souls is the "Scripture-directed, prayer-shaped care that is devoted to persons singly or in groups, in settings sacred and profane. It

6. Peterson, *The Contemplative Pastor*, 66.

is a determination to work at the center, to concentrate on the essential."[7] If you are a pastor, you know that a vision of ministry grounded in soul work is a radical reformation of current trends and expectations of church leadership. There are numerous committee meetings to attend. Community groups often like to have a "representative of the faith community" on their boards of directors. If the congregation averages more than 400 in attendance in worship, then there will likely be staff to supervise, evaluations to oversee, programs to delegate, volunteers to recruit, and a building to maintain. Nothing is inherently wrong about pastors being involved in any of these duties. Yet, none of these activities constitute the heart of pastoral work. When these duties come to define a pastor's work, spiritual gangrene works its way throughout the pastor's life and ministry. The spirit is amputated and little strength is left to conceive of a larger vision of building a community of faithful servants of God.

The importance of curing souls is difficult to keep at the forefront of pastoral consciousness when dealing with the demands of budgets and buildings. No person in any church I served has ever asked me if I was praying or reading the Bible as often as I should. I am routinely asked about the status of maintenance projects or administrative concerns.

A couple of years ago during Lent I decided to do something about this. I did not have in mind the language of curing souls, but in retrospect that is exactly the phrase I would use. I changed my daily rhythm and focus and allowed the Spirit to pull me back toward the center of pastoral ministry. I removed myself from non-essential tasks and meetings and focused on leading the church through a preaching and teaching series in the four Gospels called "Four by Forty." I prepared daily reflections and questions and wrote a weekly Bible study on the six assigned passages for that week. The Sunday sermons drew from the Scripture readings for the week. Developing these materials required an enormous amount of time and energy, which I reclaimed from so many important but nonessential tasks that normally demanded my attention. The effect of this six-week engagement with Scripture was palpable.

Members crammed into the weekly Bible study. They commented on intertextual connections they had not noticed before. Some participants who had been studying the Bible for years remarked that the Gospels finally made sense to them. This change in focus impacted me, too. My own personal and pastoral study took priority over other responsibilities. Saying no

7. Ibid.

to important but not essential requests felt liberating. Something else that happened as I changed my focus and cultivated deeper engagement with Scripture is this: the church did not fall apart. Members expressed a genuine appreciation for the fruit of my labor. Each year I try to do a church-wide Bible study as a way of calling myself back to God's life-giving Word and inviting the congregation to remember that we are people of the Book.

The church is not like any other organization. Therefore, its leaders embrace the truth that their work is unlike any other practice of leadership. Often the individual parts of pastoral leadership may not be altogether different from leadership in other organizations. Pastors must offer community clearly to diverse audiences. CEOs must communicate clearly to diverse audiences. Pastors lead staff and set goals. Non-profit leaders also lead staff and set organizational goals. What is apparent from reading the beautiful language and compelling memories of Eugene Peterson is the that sum total of the parts of pastoral leadership amounts to something that cannot be accounted for by addition alone. One and one and one do not equal three. They equal five.[8] Pastors represent the eternal word and will of God and do so among the particularities of certain communities and unique people.[9] This work is eternally significant, culturally subversive, and Spirit-filled when it is offered in faithful service to God. As I view the landscape of ministry today, the temptation to choose the path of celebrity over faithfulness is as strong as ever. Eugene Peterson writes in such a way that offers the hope of God's word and counsel from ancient practitioners.

After drinking from the well of his wit and experience, I know that I will not get weary in well doing.

---

8. Peterson, *The Pastor*, 19.

9. Peterson, *Five Smooth Stones*, 14

Bibliography

Adler, Morimer J., and Charles Van Doren. *How to Read a Book*. New York: Touchstone, 1972.

Austen, Ben. "The Story of Steve Jobs: An Inspiration or a Cautionary Tale?" *Wired Magazine*, July 23, 2012. Online: http://www.wired.com/business/2012/07/ff_stevejobs/all/

Barth, Karl. "Biblische Fragen, Einsichten und Ausblicke." In *Das Wort Gottes und die Theologie*. Munich: Chr. Kaiser, 1929.

———. *Church Dogmatics*. Vol. IV, No. 1. Translated by G. W. Bromiley. Edinburgh: T. & T. Clark, 1956.

———. *Church Dogmatics*. Vol. IV, No. 2. Translated by T. F. Torrance and G. W. Bromiley. Edinburgh: T. & T. Clark, 1958.

———. *Church Dogmatics*. Vol. IV, No. 3. Translated by T. F. Torrance and G. W. Bromiley. Edinburgh: T. & T. Clark, 1962.

———. *Dogmatics in Outline*. San Francisco: Harper, 1959.

———. *The Word of God and the Word of Man*. San Francisco: Harper & Row, 1957.

Berry, Wendell. *Standing by Words*. San Francisco: North Point, 1983.

Braaten, Carl, and Robert Jenson, editors. *In One Body Through the Cross: The Princeton Proposal for Christian Unity*. Grand Rapids: Eerdmans, 2003.

Burrows, Ruth. *Before the Living God*. Mahwah, NJ: HiddenSpring, 2008.

Byassee, Jason. *Praise Seeking Understanding: Reading the Psalms with Augustine*. Grand Rapids: Eerdmans, 2007.

Campbell, Charles. *The Word Before the Powers: An Ethic of Preaching*. Louisville: Westminster John Knox, 2002.

Chapman, John. *Spiritual Letters*. London: Burnes and Oates, 1935.

Chaucer, Geoffrey. *The Canterbury Tales*. Translated by Burton Raffel. New York: Modern Library, 2008.

Coakley, Sarah. *Powers and Submissions: Spirituality, Philosophy, and Gender*. Oxford: Blackwell, 2002.

Conder, Tim, and Dan Rhodes. *Free For All: Rediscovering the Bible in Community*. Grand Rapids: Baker Books, 2009.

Copeland, M. S. *Enfleshing Freedom: Body, Race, and Being*. Minneapolis: Fortress, 2010.

Dawn, Marva J., and Eugene Peterson. *The Unnecessary Pastor: Rediscovering the Call*. Grand Rapids: Eerdmans, 2000.

Dean, Kenda Creasy, and Ron Foster. *The Godbearing Life: The Art of Soul Tending for Youth Ministry*. Nashville: Upper Room, 2005.

Emerson, Ralph Waldo. *The Divinity School Address: Delivered Before the Senior Class in Divinity College, Cambridge, Sunday Evening, July 15, 1838*. http://www.emersoncentral.com/divaddr.htm.

Flex, Walter. *Der Wanderer zwischen beiden Welten. Ein Kriegserlebnis*. 27th ed. Munich: H. Beck, 1918.

Galli, Mark. "Spirituality for all the Wrong Reasons: Eugene Peterson Talks about Lies and Illusions that Destroy the Church." *Christianity Today*, March 4, 2005. Online: http://www.christianitytoday.com/ct/2005/march/26.42.html?start=2.

Gregory the Great. *Pastoral Care*. Translated by Henry Davis. New York: Newman, 1950.

Hauerwas, Stanley, and Romand Coles. *Christianity, Democracy, and the Radical Ordinary: Conversations Between a Radical Democrat and a Christian*. Eugene, OR: Cascade, 2008.

Heath, Elaine. *The Mystic Way of Evangelism: A Contemplative Vision for Christian Outreach*. Grand Rapids: Baker Academic, 2008

Heifetz, Ronald. *Leadership Without Easy Answers*. Cambridge, MA: Harvard University Press, 1998.

Hertig, P. "The Jubilee Mission of Jesus in the Gospel of Luke: The Reversal of Fortunes," in *Missiology: An International Review* 26:2 (1998) 167–79.

Hunter, James Davison. *To Change the World: The Irony, Tragedy, and Possibility of Christianity in the Late Modern World*. New York: Oxford University Press, 2010.

The Institute on Religion and Democracy. Online: http://www.theird.org/page.aspx?pid=1560.

The Investigative Staff of the *Boston Globe*. *Betrayal: The Crisis in the Catholic Church* Boston: Little, Brown, 2002.

Jenson, Robert. *Systematic Theology, Volume I: The Triune God*. New York: Oxford University Press, 1997.

Johnson, Kristen Deede. "Patience, Trust, and Vision," *Comment*. Online: http://www.cardus.ca/comment/article/3283/patience-trust-and-vision.

Kamenetz, Anya. "The Four-Year Career: Lessons from the New World of Quicksilver Work where 'Career' Planning is an Oxymoron." *Fast Company*, January 12, 2012. Online: http://www.fastcompany.com/1802731/four-year-career.

Keating, Thomas. *Open Mind, Open Heart: The Contemplative Dimension of the Gospel*. New York: Continuum, 2006.

Kotter, John. *John Kotter on What Leaders Really Do*. Cambridge, MA: Harvard Business Leaders, 1999.

Levertov, Denise. *Selected Poems*. New York: New Directions, 2002.

Little, Jonathan. "An Interview with Charles Johnson." In *Passing the Three Gates*, edited by Jim McWilliams, 97–122. Seattle: University of Washington Press, 2004.

McCormack, Bruce L. *Karl Barth's Critically Realistic Dialectical Theology: Its Genesis and Development, 1909–1936*. Oxford: Oxford University Press, 1997.

Main, John. *John Main: Essential Writings*. Edited by Laurence Freeman. Maryknoll, NY: Orbis, 2002.

Marsh, Charles. *The Beloved Community: How Faith Shapes Social Justice, from the Civil Rights Movement to Today*. New York: Basic, 2005.

Marty, Martin E. *The Mystery of the Child*. Grand Rapids: Eerdmans, 2007.

Mead, Loren. *The Once and Future Church: Reinventing the Congregation for a New Mission Frontier.* Herndon, VA: Alban, 1991.

Miles, Margaret. *Augustine and the Fundamentalist's Daughter.* Eugene, OR: Cascade, 2011.

Newbigin, Lesslie. *The Household of God: Lectures on the Nature of the Church.* London: SCM, 1952.

Niebuhr, Reinhold. *Moral Man and Immoral Society.* New York: Scribner, 1932.

Palmer, Parker. *A Hidden Wholeness: A Journey Toward an Undivided Life.* San Francisco: Jossey-Bass, 2009.

Payne, Charles. *I've Got the Light of Freedom: The Organizing Tradition and the Mississippi Freedom Struggle.* Berkeley, CA: University of California Press, 1997.

Peterson, Eugene. *Answering God: The Psalms as Tools for Prayer.* New York: HarperOne, 1991.

———. *Christ Plays in Ten Thousand Places: A Conversation in Spiritual Theology.* Grand Rapids: Eerdmans, 2005.

———. *The Contemplative Pastor.* Carol Stream, IL: Christianity Today, 1989.

———. *Eat This Book: A Conversation in the Art of Spiritual Reading.* Grand Rapids: Eerdmans, 2009.

———. *Five Smooth Stones for Pastoral Work.* Grand Rapids: Eerdmans, 1980.

———. *The Jesus Way: A Conversation on the Ways That Jesus Is the Way.* Grand Rapids: Eerdmans, 2007.

———. *A Long Obedience in the Same Direction: Discipleship in an Instant Society.* Downers Grove, IL: InterVarsity, 1980.

———. *The Message: The Bible in Contemporary Language.* Colorado Springs: NavPress, 2002.

———. *The Pastor: A Memoir.* New York: HarperOne, 2011.

———. *Reversed Thunder: The Revelation of John and the Praying Imagination.* San Francisco: Harper, 1991.

———. *Run with the Horses: The Quest for Life at its Best.* Downers Grove, IL: InterVarsity, 1996.

———. *Subversive Spirituality.* Grand Rapids: Eerdmans, 1994.

———. *Take and Read: Spiritual Reading: An Annotated List.* Grand Rapids: Eerdmans, 1995.

———. *Under the Unpredictable Plant: An Exploration in Vocational Holiness.* Grand Rapids: Eerdmans, 1992.

———. *The Wisdom of Each Other.* Grand Rapids: Zondervan, 1998.

——— *Working the Angles: The Shape of Pastoral Integrity.* Grand Rapids: Eerdmans, 1987.

The Pew Forum on Public Life. Online: http://religionblog.dallasnews.com/archives/2008/03/pew-study-underscores-trouble.html.

Price, Reynolds. *A Serious Way of Wondering: The Ethics of Jesus Reimagined.* New York: Scribner, 2003.

Raz, Guy. "Eugene Peterson Chronicles Memories in 'Pastor.'" National Public Radio, March 6, 2011. Online: http://www.npr.org/templates/transcript/transcript.php?storyId=134233358.

Reno, Russell. *In the Ruins of the Church: Sustaining Faith in an Age of Diminished Christianity.* Grand Rapids: Brazos, 2002.

Robinson, Tony. *Transforming Congregational Culture.* Grand Rapids: Eerdmans, 2003.

Scholder, Klaus. *The Churches and the Third Reich: Volume 1, Preliminary History and the Time of Illusions, 1918–1934*. Philadelphia: Fortress, 1988.

Stringfellow, William. *An Ethic for Christians and Other Aliens in a Strange Land*. Waco, TX: Word, 1973.

Taylor, Charles. *Sources of the Self: The Making of Modern Identity*. Cambridge: Cambridge University Press, 1989.

The United Methodist Hymnal. Nashville: Abingdon, 1989.

Weil, Simone. *Waiting for God*. Translated by Emma Crauford. New York: Harper and Row, 1951.

Wesley, John. "On Visiting the Sick." http://www.umcmission.org/Find-Resources/John-Wesley-Sermons/Sermon-98-On-Visiting-the-Sick.

Wink, Walter. *The Powers That Be: Theology for a New Millennium*. New York: Doubleday, 1998.

Wilson, John E. *Introduction to Modern Theology: Trajectories in the German Tradition*. Louisville: Westminster John Knox, 2007.

Wood, David. "'The Best Life': Eugene Peterson on Pastoral Ministry." *The Christian Century*. http://www.christiancentury.org/article/2002-03/best-life.

Wuthnow, Robert. *God and Mammon in America*. New York: Free Press, 1998.

Contributors

Jason Byassee is the senior pastor of Boone United Methodist Church in Boone, North Carolina. He is also a contributing editor to *The Christian Century* magazine, a Fellow in Theology and Leadership at Leadership Education at Duke Divinity School, and a Research Fellow in the New Media Project at Union Theological Seminary in New York. He is the author of five books, most recently *Discerning the Body* (Cascade). His work has also appeared in *Theology Today, Books and Culture, Sojourners*, and *First Things*.

Kyle Childress has served as the pastor of the Austin Heights Baptist Church, Nacogdoches, Texas since 1989. He is a frequent contributor to *The Christian Century, Christian Reflection*, and other journals, and a speaker at conferences and retreats. In 2008 he was invited to preach and lecture by Andover Newton Theological School as they honored him in their "The Future of Great Preaching" series. In 2011 he was the annual Hoover Lecturer at the Bapist Seminary of Richmond, Virginia.

Tim Conder is the founding pastor of Emmaus Way in Durham, North Carolina and a PhD candidate in "Culture, Curriculum, and Change" at the University of North Carolina in Chapel Hill. He serves on the Board of Trustees at The Seattle School of Theology and Psychology, participates in grassroots community organizing with Durham CAN and IAF International, and experiences the emergent church community as a space of generative prayer, play, hope, and friendship. He is married to Meredith Conder and has two inspiring teenagers, Keenan and Kendall.

Martin B. Copenhaver is President of Andover Newton Theological School in Newton Centre, Massachusetts. He is the author, or co-author, of five books, most recently, *This Odd and Wondrous Calling: The Public and Private Lives of Two Ministers* (with Lillian Daniel). He once made a television commercial with Larry Bird.

Lillian Daniel has served as the Senior Minister of the First Congregational Church, United Church of Christ, Glen Ellyn, Illinois since 2004. She is the author of the book *Tell It Like It Is: Reclaiming the Practice of Testimony*, which is the story of one church's attempt to get mainline Protestants to talk to each other about God. Her newest book is *This Odd and Wondrous Calling: The Public and Private Lives of Two Ministers*, co-authored by Martin B. Copenhaver. An editor at large for *The Christian Century*, and a contributing editor at *Leadership*, her work has also appeared in *The Huffington Post*, *Christianity Today, Leadership Journal, Books and Culture*, and *The Journal for Preachers*.

Tee Gatewood has been the pastor at Arbor Dale Presbyterian Church in Banner Elk, North Carolina since 2008. A graduate of Regent College and University of St. Andrews, Tee is married to Kathryn and has two children, Thomas and Sarah.

James C. Howell is senior pastor of Myers Park United Methodist Church in Charlotte, North Carolina and adjunct professor of preaching at Duke Divinity School. He earned a PhD in Old Testament from Duke. His publications include fourteen books, including *Yours are the Hands of Christ, Introducing Christianity, Conversations with St. Francis, The Will of God*, and *The Beauty of the Word*.

Kristen Deede Johnson is Associate Professor of Theology and Christian Formation at Western Theological Seminary in Holland, Michigan. Her research lies in the areas of political thought, theology, and culture, and her publications include *Theology, Political Theory, and Pluralism: Beyond Tolerance and Difference* (Cambridge).

Trygve David Johnson is Hinga-Boersma Dean of the Chapel at Hope College in Holland, Michigan. His doctoral degree is in systematic theology from the University of St. Andrews, and he has written regularly for *The Christian Century, Faith and Leadership*, and a variety of other publications.

Carol Howard Merritt is a Presbyterian (USA) pastor in Chattanooga, Tennessee. She wrote *Tribal Church* and *Reframing Hope*, and has contributed to several other books. She is a columnist at the *Christian Century*, and she facilitates Unco, an organization which supports and incubates creative ministries.

L. Roger Owens is Associate Professor of Leadership and Ministry at Pittsburgh Theological Seminary, and has pastored United Methodist congregations in North Carolina. He is the author of *The Shape of Participation: A Theology of Church Practices* (Cascade). He is also co-editor of *Wendell Berry and Religion: Heaven's Earthly Life* (University of Kentucky Press). His writing has appeared in *The Christian Century, Currents in Theology and Mission*, and *The Journal of Religious Ethics*. His most recent book is *Abba, Give Me a Word* (Paraclete).

Stephanie Paulsell is Houghton Professor of the Practice of Ministry Studies at Harvard Divinity School. She is the author of *Honoring the Body: Meditations on a Christian Practice*, co-editor of *The Scope of Our Art: The Vocation of the Theological Educator*, and author, with Harvey Cox, of *Lamentations and the Song of Songs*.

Mark Ralls holds a PhD in systematic theology from Princeton Theological Seminary. He also studied theology at Duke Divinity School and the University of Bonn, Germany. Mark is Senior Minister of Centenary United Methodist Church in Winston-Salem, North Carolina. Before coming to Centenary, Mark was the Senior Pastor of Asbury First United Methodist Church, Rochester, New York. Mark is co-author of a best-selling series of courses that introduce basic Christian beliefs and practices. He is also the author of one book and more than thirty published articles.

Prince Raney Rivers is the senior pastor of United Metropolitan Missionary Baptist Church in Winston-Salem, North Carolina. He blogs regularly about his experiences in pastoral leadership at *FaithandLeadership.org*. Prince is a graduate of Morehouse College. He earned a Master of Divinity from Duke Divinity School and completed the Harvard Divinity School Summer Leadership Institute.

Anthony B. (Tony) Robinson is a United Church of Christ pastor and a speaker, writer, consultant, and coach for pastors based in Seattle. He is the author of twelve books, including *Transforming Congregational Culture* (Pilgrim). His most recent book is *Called to Lead* (Eerdmans). He is also a frequent contributor to various magazines and journals, including *The Christian Century, Congregations,* and *Journal for Preachers.*

Jenny Williams is the pastor of Wesley United Methodist Church in Kingwood, West Virginia. She was born into a large urban congregation in southern California. In North Carolina she was an intern at rural small-membership churches and an associate pastor at a large suburban church, and in West Virginia she was the pastor of a two point charge in small towns and later a station church in a small town. Her work has been published in *The Christian Century* and *Homily Service.*

William H. Willimon has been a Bishop of The United Methodist Church since 2004. He led the 157,000 Methodists and 792 pastors in North Alabama from 2004–2012. For twenty years he was Dean of the Chapel and Professor of Christian Ministry at Duke University. He has been awarded honorary degrees from a dozen colleges and universities including Wofford College, Lehigh University, Colgate University, Birmingham-Southern College, and Moravian Theological Seminary. He is the author of sixty books, over a million copies of which have been sold. In 1996, an international survey conducted by Baylor University named him one of the Twelve Most Effective Preachers in the English-speaking world. He is currently Professor of the Practice of Christian Ministry at Duke Divinity School.